LUKE
for
EVERYONE

20TH ANNIVERSARY EDITION WITH STUDY GUIDE

NEW TESTAMENT FOR EVERYONE
20TH ANNIVERSARY EDITION WITH STUDY GUIDE
N. T. Wright

Matthew for Everyone, Part 1

Matthew for Everyone, Part 2

Mark for Everyone

Luke for Everyone

John for Everyone, Part 1

John for Everyone, Part 2

Acts for Everyone, Part 1

Acts for Everyone, Part 2

Romans for Everyone, Part 1

Romans for Everyone, Part 2

1 Corinthians for Everyone

2 Corinthians for Everyone

Galatians and Thessalonians for Everyone

Ephesians, Philippians, Colossians and Philemon for Everyone

1 and 2 Timothy and Titus for Everyone

Hebrews for Everyone

James, Peter, John and Judah for Everyone

Revelation for Everyone

LUKE

for

EVERYONE

20TH ANNIVERSARY EDITION WITH STUDY GUIDE

N. T.
WRIGHT

STUDY GUIDE BY MICHAEL L. KIRKINDOLL

WESTMINSTER
JOHN KNOX PRESS
LOUISVILLE • KENTUCKY

First published in Great Britain in 2001 by the
Society for Promoting Christian Knowledge
36 Causton Street
London SW1P 4ST
www.spckpublishing.co.uk

Copublished in 2004 by the Society for Promoting
Christian Knowledge, London, and Westminster John Knox Press,
100 Witherspoon Street, Louisville, KY 40202.

20th Anniversary Edition with Study Guide
Published in 2023
by Westminster John Knox Press
Louisville, Kentucky

23 24 25 26 27 28 29 30 31 32—10 9 8 7 6 5 4 3 2 1

Cover design by Allison Taylor

Library of Congress Cataloging-in-Publication Data

Names: Wright, N. T. (Nicholas Thomas) author. | Kirkindoll, Michael L., 1953-
Title: Luke for everyone / N. T. Wright ; study guide by Michael L. Kirkindoll.
Description: 20th anniversary edition with study guide. | Louisville : Westminster John Knox Press, 2023. | Series: New testament for everyone | Summary: "This expanded edition contains Wright's updated translation of the biblical text, a new introduction, and a study guide designed for use in Bible study classes and individual reflection. Helpful summaries and insightful questions assist group leaders, study participants, and solo learners to encounter the gospel of Luke in exciting and enriching new ways"-- Provided by publisher.
Identifiers: LCCN 2023031434 (print) | LCCN 2023031435 (ebook) | ISBN 9780664266394 (paperback) | ISBN 9781646983520 (ebook)
Subjects: LCSH: Bible. Luke--Commentaries.
Classification: LCC BS2595.53 .W75 2023 (print) | LCC BS2595.53 (ebook) | DDC 226.4/07--dc23/eng/20230720
LC record available at https://lccn.loc.gov/2023031434
LC ebook record available at https://lccn.loc.gov/2023031435

For
Margaret Eleanor Forman
(herself a historian)
with gratitude for the love, support and prayers
of over fifty years

CONTENTS

CONTENTS

CONTENTS

CONTENTS

INTRODUCTION TO THE
ANNIVERSARY EDITION

It took me ten years, but I'm glad I did it. Writing a guide to the books of the New Testament felt at times like trying to climb all the Scottish mountains in quick succession. But the views from the tops were amazing, and discovering new pathways up and down was very rewarding as well. The real reward, though, has come in the messages I've received from around the world, telling me that the books have been helpful and encouraging, opening up new and unexpected vistas.

Perhaps I should say that this series wasn't designed to help with sermon preparation, though many preachers have confessed to me that they've used it that way. The books were meant, as their title suggests, for everyone, particularly for people who would never dream of picking up an academic commentary but who nevertheless want to dig a little deeper.

The New Testament seems intended to provoke all readers, at whatever stage, to fresh thought, understanding and practice. For that, we all need explanation, advice and encouragement. I'm glad these books seem to have had that effect, and I'm delighted that they are now available with study guides in these new editions.

N. T. Wright
2022

INTRODUCTION

On the very first occasion when someone stood up in public to tell people about Jesus, he made it very clear: this message is for *everyone*.

It was a great day – sometimes called the birthday of the church. The great wind of God's spirit had swept through Jesus' followers and filled them with a new joy and a sense of God's presence and power. Their leader, Peter, who only a few weeks before had been crying like a baby because he'd lied and cursed and denied even knowing Jesus, found himself on his feet explaining to a huge crowd that something had happened which had changed the world for ever. What God had done for him, Peter, he was beginning to do for the whole world: new life, forgiveness, new hope and power were opening up like spring flowers after a long winter. A new age had begun in which the living God was going to do new things in the world – beginning then and there with the individuals who were listening to him. 'This promise is for *you*,' he said, 'and for your children, and for everyone who is far away' (Acts 2.39). It wasn't just for the person standing next to you. It was for everyone.

Within a remarkably short time this came true to such an extent that the young movement spread throughout much of the known world. And one way in which the *everyone* promise worked out was through the writings of the early Christian leaders. These short works – mostly letters and stories about Jesus – were widely circulated and eagerly read. They were never intended for either a religious or intellectual elite. From the very beginning they were meant for everyone.

That is as true today as it was then. Of course, it matters that some people give time and care to the historical evidence, the meaning of the original words (the early Christians wrote in Greek), and the exact and particular force of what different writers were saying about God, Jesus, the world and themselves. This series is based quite closely on that sort of work. But the point of it all is that the message can get out to everyone, especially to people who wouldn't normally read a book with footnotes and Greek words in it. That's the sort of person for whom these books are written. And that's why there's a glossary, in the back, of the key words that you can't really get along without, with a simple description of what they mean. Whenever you see a word in **bold type** in the text, you can go to the back and remind yourself what's going on.

There are of course many translations of the New Testament available today. The one I offer here is designed for the same kind of reader: one who mightn't necessarily understand the more formal, sometimes even ponderous, tones of some of the standard ones. I have of course tried to keep as close to the original as I can. But my main aim has been to be sure that the words can speak not just to some people, but to everyone.

Let me add a note about the translation the reader will find here of the Greek word *Christos*. Most translations simply say 'Christ', but most modern English speakers assume that that word is simply a proper name (as though 'Jesus' were Jesus 'Christian' name and 'Christ' were his 'surname'). For all sorts of reasons, I disagree; so I have experimented not only with 'Messiah' (which is what the word literally means) but sometimes, too, with 'King'.

This particular volume opens up one of the most brilliant writings in early Christianity. Luke tells us that he had had a chance to stand back from the extraordinary events that had been going on, to talk to the people involved, to read some earlier writings, and to make his own quite full version so that readers could know the truth about the things to do with Jesus. He was an educated and cultured man, the first real historian to write about Jesus. His book places Jesus not only at the heart of the Jewish world of the first century, but at the heart of the Roman world into which the Christian gospel exploded and which it was destined to change so radically. So here it is: Luke for everyone!

Tom Wright

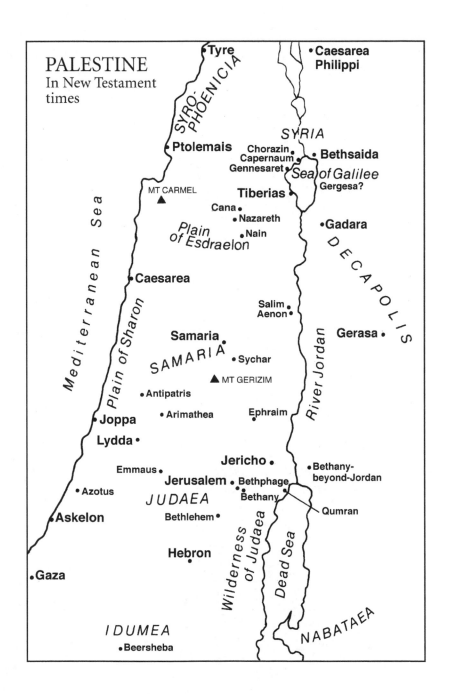

PALESTINE
In New Testament times

Tyre

Caesarea Philippi

SYRO-PHOENICIA

SYRIA

Ptolemais

Chorazin
Capernaum
Gennesaret

Bethsaida

Sea of Galilee

Gergesa?

MT CARMEL

Tiberias

Cana
Nazareth
Nain

Gadara

Plain of Esdraelon

DECAPOLIS

Mediterranean Sea

Caesarea

Salim
Aenon

Gerasa

Samaria

SAMARIA

Sychar

River Jordan

Plain of Sharon

MT GERIZIM

Antipatris

Arimathea

Ephraim

Joppa

Lydda

Jericho

Emmaus

Bethany-beyond-Jordan

Jerusalem

Bethphage

Azotus

JUDAEA

Bethany

Qumran

Askelon

Bethlehem

Wilderness of Judaea

Dead Sea

Hebron

Gaza

IDUMEA

NABATAEA

Beersheba

LUKE 1.1–4

Prologue

1Many people have undertaken to draw up an orderly account of the events that have been fulfilled in our midst. 2It has been handed down to us by the original eyewitnesses and stewards of the word. 3So, most excellent Theophilus, since I had traced the course of the whole thing scrupulously from the start, I thought it a good idea to write an orderly account for you, 4so that you may have secure knowledge about the matters in which you have been instructed.

'SPACE ALIENS TOOK MY BABY', screams the headline. Or perhaps 'GRANDMOTHER SWIMS ATLANTIC'. And what do people say? 'It must be true; it was in the newspapers.' 'I saw it on television.' 'The person who told me was told by someone who was there at the time.'

We have learnt to laugh at all of these. News is 'packaged' to tell us what we want to hear. Television cameras often deceive. And stories which come from 'a friend of a friend' might as well be fiction. How do we know what to believe?

Luke opens his **gospel** with a long, formal sentence, like a huge stone entrance welcoming you impressively to a large building. Here, he is saying, is something solid, something you can trust. Writers in the first-century Mediterranean world quite often wrote opening sentences like this; readers would know they were beginning a serious, well-researched piece of work. This wasn't a fly-by-night or casual account. It would hold its head up in the world at large.

'Of course,' we think, with our suspicious modern minds, 'he would say that, wouldn't he?' But look at the claims he makes. Luke isn't asking us simply to take it on trust; he is appealing to a wide base of evidence. Several others have written about these events; he has these writings, some of which we may be able to trace, as sources. He has been in touch with eyewitnesses who have told him what they saw and heard. And, perhaps most important, he has listened to accredited teachers within local communities. We need to say a further word about these people.

Imagine a village in ancient Palestine. They didn't have printed books or newspapers, television or radio. They had official storytellers. Some great event would happen: an earthquake, a battle, or the visit of an emperor. Within a day or two the story would be told all round the village, and would settle into a regular form. Everyone would know the story, but some of the better storytellers in the village would be recognized by the others as the right people to tell it.

And that's what they'd do. They wouldn't change the story or modify it; if they did, people would notice and set them straight. Perhaps the

1

closest we get to this in the modern Western world is when a family tells a story or anecdote, often with everybody knowing what's coming. In the same way, you don't change the words of your national anthem, or of the songs that you sang as a child. So when Luke went round the villages of Palestine and Syria in the second half of the first century, listening to the stories told by the accredited storytellers – 'the stewards of the word', as he calls them – he would know he was in touch with solid, reliable evidence that went right back to the early events. Plato had said, five hundred years earlier, that there was a danger in writing things down; human memories, he thought, were the best way to get things right and pass them on. In the century after Luke, one of the great Christian teachers declared that he preferred living testimony to writings. You can't tell where a book has come from, but you can look witnesses in the eye, and use your judgment about whether to trust them.

So why is Luke writing it all down now? Isn't he shooting himself in the foot? Who was he, anyway, and when was he writing?

I wish we knew for sure who the author of this book was, but actually we don't. We call him 'Luke' because that's who the church, from very early on, said had written this gospel and the Acts of the Apostles (as you'll see from Acts 1.1, Acts appears to be written by the same person, and there are signs throughout both books that this is in fact the case). He may well have been the Luke whom Paul mentions as his companion (Colossians 4.14; Philemon 24; 2 Timothy 4.11). He could have been writing any time between AD 50 and 90; there must have been time for the 'many others' he refers to to have written and circulated their works, but equally there is no particular reason to insist that he must have been writing as late as 90, or even 80. A fair guess is probably that he was indeed Luke, one of Paul's companions, and that he was writing in the 60s and 70s.

The main reason he's writing is that the **message** about Jesus has spread far and wide, way beyond the original communities in the regions Jesus himself visited. Peter, Paul and other missionaries had carried the message in all directions, and doubtless there were garbled, muddled and misleading reports circulating about who exactly Jesus was, what he did and said, and what had happened to him. Luke knows of other writings that have begun the task of putting it down on paper, but he has a wider audience in mind, an educated, intelligent, enquiring public. 'Most excellent Theophilus' may be a real person, perhaps a Roman governor or local official, whom Luke has come to know; or this may be a literary device, a way of addressing anyone who has heard about Christianity, and who is perhaps 'a lover of God' (that's what 'Theophilus' means in Greek). He does imply that 'Theophilus' has already been officially taught something about Jesus and what it means to follow him, so perhaps he also intends it for recent converts who are eager to learn more.

In any case, if he is writing in the late 60s or early 70s, a further reason would be the horrendous war that was raging in Palestine at the time. The Jews rebelled against the occupying Roman forces in 66, until finally, after a long siege, Jerusalem was destroyed in 70. The result was that many towns and villages where Jesus had been seen and known were decimated. Not only was the older generation dying out, but communities that had witnessed Jesus' activities were being dispersed or destroyed. The stories, which depended for transmission on a peaceful, stable society, were in danger of dying out. Unless steps were taken to write them down, the message would not be passed on to the next generation. And since Luke, like all the early Christians, believed that the things that had actually happened – what we would call the historical facts – had changed the course of the world, it was vital that they be presented as clearly and unambiguously as possible.

Luke thus constructs a grand doorway into his gospel. He invites us to come in and make ourselves at home. Here we will find security, a solid basis for lasting **faith**.

LUKE 1.5–25

Gabriel Visits Zechariah

⁵In the time when Herod was king of Judaea, there was a priest called Zechariah, of the priestly division of Abijah. His wife, who came from the Aaron family, was called Elisabeth. ⁶Both of them were righteous in God's sight; they followed all the Lord's commandments and ordinances without fault. ⁷They had no children. Elisabeth was barren, and both of them were of an advanced age.

⁸It so happened, when Zechariah was performing his priestly service before God, according to the order of his division, ⁹that the lot fell to him, according to the priestly custom, to go in to the Lord's sanctuary to offer incense. ¹⁰The people were praying outside in a large crowd, at the time of the incense-offering. ¹¹An angel of the Lord appeared to him, standing on the right-hand side of the incense-altar. ¹²Zechariah was troubled and terror-struck when he saw the angel.

¹³But the angel said to him:

'Don't be afraid, Zechariah: your prayer has been heard. Your wife Elisabeth will bear you a son, and you shall call his name John. ¹⁴This will bring you joy and celebration, and many will rejoice at his birth. ¹⁵He will be a great man in God's sight; he will drink no wine or strong drink. He will be filled with the holy spirit from his mother's womb, ¹⁶and will turn many of the children of Israel to the Lord their God.

3

[17]He will go before him in the spirit and power of Elijah, and he will turn the hearts of fathers to children, and of unbelievers to the wisdom of the righteous. He will get ready for the Lord a prepared people.'

[18]'How can I be sure of this?' said Zechariah to the angel. 'I'm an old man! My wife's not as young as she used to be, either!'

[19]'Look here,' replied the angel, 'I'm Gabriel. I stand in God's presence. I was sent to speak to you and give you this splendid news. [20]Now, listen: you will be silent – you won't be able to speak – until the day when it all happens, because you didn't believe my words. But they will come true at the proper time.'

[21]Meanwhile, the people were waiting for Zechariah, and were surprised that he was taking such a long time in the sanctuary. [22]But when he came out he couldn't speak to them, and they understood that he had seen a vision in the sanctuary. He made gestures to them, but remained speechless.

[23]So, when the days of his priestly service were complete, he went back home. [24]After that time, Elisabeth his wife conceived. She stayed in hiding for five months.

[25]'This is the Lord's doing,' she said; 'at last he has looked on me, and taken away my public shame.'

The capital of Ireland is the wonderful old city of Dublin. It is famous for many reasons. People go there from all over the world to stroll around its streets, to drink in its pubs, to visit its historic buildings, and to see the places made world-famous by writers such as James Joyce.

Perhaps surprisingly, the attraction that draws most visitors in Dublin is the zoo. And, perhaps equally surprisingly, the second most popular site for visitors is the Book of Kells, displayed at the centre of a special exhibition in Trinity College. This wonderfully ornamented manuscript of the gospels dates to around AD 800 – considerably closer in time to the New Testament itself than to us today.

The people who arranged the exhibition don't let the public see the gospels themselves straight away. Wisely, they lead you first past several other very old books, which prepare you step by step for the great treasure itself. By the time you reach the heart of the exhibition you have already thought your way back to the world of early Celtic Christianity, to the monks who spent years of their life painstakingly copying out parts of the Bible and lavishly decorating it. You are now ready to appreciate it properly.

Luke has done something very similar in the opening of his **gospel**. His story is, of course, principally about Jesus, but the name 'Jesus' doesn't occur for the first 30 verses, and Jesus himself is not born until well into the story. Luke is going to tell us about Mary's extraordinary pregnancy and Jesus' extraordinary birth, but he knows we will need to prepare our minds and hearts for this story. So he begins with the story of Zechariah and Elisabeth, a devout couple going about their everyday life.

First he grips us with their human drama. This couple, well past childbearing age, are going to have a son at last, in a culture where childless women were mocked. This drama is heightened by the comic encounter between Zechariah and the angel (don't be frightened of finding the Bible funny when it really is!). Luke indicates that through this all-too-human story of puzzlement, half-faith, and dogged devotion to duty, God's saving purposes are going to be dramatically advanced. The son to be born will fulfil the biblical promises that had spoken of God sending someone to prepare Israel for the coming divine visitation. The scriptures had foretold that the prophet Elijah would return one day to get the people ready for God's arrival. Gabriel tells Zechariah that this will be John's task.

The story would remind any Bible reader of much older stories: Abraham and Sarah having a child in their old age (Genesis 21), Rachel bearing Jacob two sons after years of childlessness (Genesis 30; 35), and particularly the births of Samson (Judges 13) and Samuel (1 Samuel 1). This story, Luke hints, is not a strange new thing, but takes its place within a long-standing sequence of God's purposes. The child to be born, who will be called **John**, will play a key role in God's fulfilment of his promises. The story thus prepares us, like tourists getting into the mood for the central exhibit, for the still more remarkable events that will follow swiftly.

Zechariah and Elisabeth weren't expecting any of this. They were simply devout people going about their regular business. They were 'righteous in God's sight', observant Jews, keeping the law as a sign of grateful devotion to God. They lived outside Jerusalem, in the Judaean hill country. Like all **priests** except the chief priests, who lived in Jerusalem itself, Zechariah would come in to the city when it was the turn of his division to perform the regular Temple liturgy; he would stay in lodgings within the **Temple** precincts, and then return home to continue his normal work as a teacher and leader in the local community. On this occasion Zechariah was appointed by lot to go into the inner court, out of sight of the lay people, to offer incense. Sometimes regular duty provides the context for extraordinary visions.

Luke is careful not to dress up the story by making Zechariah a great hero of **faith**. Like some of the Old Testament leaders, his first reaction to the news is to clutch at straws: he needs a sign, something that will help him to believe. He is given one, but it comes as a punishment; we can almost see the angel putting his hands on his hips and telling Zechariah off for presuming to doubt his word. Zechariah is struck speechless, and the dark comedy continues with the old priest coming out to the people and making signs and gestures to indicate what had happened (how would you describe seeing an angel, just using your hands and arms?). The account concludes, of course, with Elisabeth's joy at her unexpected pregnancy.

This story, preparing us for the even more remarkable conception and birth of Jesus himself, reminds us of something important. God regularly works through ordinary people, doing what they normally do, who with a mixture of half-faith and devotion are holding themselves ready for whatever God has in mind. The story is about much more than Zechariah's joy at having a son at last, or Elisabeth's exultation in being freed from the scorn of the mothers in the village. It is about the great fulfilment of God's promises and purposes. But the needs, hopes and fears of ordinary people are not forgotten in this larger story, precisely because of who Israel's God is – the God of lavish, self-giving love, as Luke will tell us in so many ways throughout his gospel. When this God acts on the large scale, he takes care of smaller human concerns as well. The drama which now takes centre stage is truly the story of God, the world, and every ordinary human being who has ever lived in it. That's how Luke intends it to be.

LUKE 1.26–38

The Annunciation of the Birth of Jesus

²⁶In the sixth month, Gabriel the angel was sent from God to a town in Galilee called Nazareth, ²⁷to a virgin engaged to a man called Joseph, from the family of David. The virgin was called Mary.

²⁸'Greetings, favoured one!' said the angel when he arrived. 'May the Lord be with you!'

²⁹She was disturbed at this, and wondered what such a greeting might mean.

³⁰'Don't be afraid, Mary', said the angel to her. 'You're in favour with God. ³¹Listen: you will conceive in your womb and will have a son; and you shall call his name Jesus. ³²He will be a great man, and he'll be called the son of the Most High. The Lord God will give him the throne of David his father, ³³and he shall reign over the house of Jacob for ever. His kingdom will never come to an end.'

³⁴'How will this happen?' said Mary to the angel. 'I'm still a virgin!'

³⁵'The holy spirit will come upon you,' replied the angel, 'and the power of the Most High will overshadow you. For that reason the holy one who is born from you will be called God's Son.

³⁶'Let me tell you this, too: your cousin Elisabeth, in her old age, has also conceived a son. This is the sixth month for her, a woman

who people used to say was barren. [37]With God, you see, nothing is impossible.'

[38]'Here I am,' said Mary; 'I'm the Lord's servant-girl. Let it happen to me as you've said.'

Then the angel left her.

Ask a newspaper editor what sort of stories will sell the most copies, and three categories come swiftly to mind: sex, royalty and religion. If they can be combined, so much the better. 'POP STAR'S LOVE CHILD' is good; 'PRINCESS HAS SECRET AFFAIR' is better; 'KING'S SECRET NIGHT WITH NUN' is better still. So when people read the story of Gabriel visiting Mary, with the child to be born being the future Lord of the world, their minds easily jump in the way the newspapers have conditioned them to do. People have read into the story all sorts of things that aren't there, and have failed to notice some of the really important things that are.

Let's begin with the obvious point. The story makes it clear that Jesus was conceived in Mary's womb before she had had any sexual relations. Many people today find this impossible to believe, but they often think that this difficulty has only arisen in modern times, because of all we now know about the precise mechanics of conception and birth. Not so. The ancient world didn't know about X chromosomes and Y chromosomes, but they knew as well as we do that babies were the result of sexual intercourse, and that people who claimed to be pregnant by other means might well be covering up a moral and social offence. Yet Mary's story is told by both Luke and Matthew, in versions so different that they can hardly be dependent on one another; in other words, the story seems to have been widely known in the very early church, rather than being a fantasy invented several generations after the fact. Why would these two writers, and devout Jewish Christian congregations that passed on such stories, have done so, giving hostages to fortune in this way, unless they had good reason to suppose they were true?

It's important to stress that the story says nothing about Mary remaining a virgin after Jesus' birth. That's a much later idea. Nor does it say anything about the goodness or badness of sexual identity or sexual relations. Whatever Luke (and Matthew) are trying to say with this story, they aren't saying that virginity is a morally better state than marriage. They are not denigrating sex, women, conception or birth. They are simply reporting that Jesus did not have a father in the ordinary way, and that this was because Mary had been given special grace to be the mother of God's incarnate self.

Luke has no thought that this might make Jesus somehow less than fully human. Scientists will say that virgin birth is in theory possible (it sometimes happens in small animals, e.g. lizards), and that a child thus produced would be a complete human being. The problem is that, always supposing such a thing were possible, the child would naturally be female. The truly remarkable thing from the scientific point of view is that Jesus was male.

The angel gives what looks like a double explanation for the whole event. The **holy spirit** will come upon Mary, enabling her (as the spirit always does) to do and be more than she could by herself. But at the same time 'the power of the Most High' will overshadow her. This is something different: God himself, the creator, will surround her completely with his sovereign power.

All this sounds extremely peculiar, but we should remember that in the Bible, and in Jewish and Christian thought at their best, the true God is the one in whose image humans were made in the first place. We aren't talking about a pagan god intervening roughly and inappropriately in the affairs of mortals, but about the one who, as St Augustine said, made us for himself. When he takes the initiative, it is always a matter of love, love which will care for us and take us up into his saving purposes. Mary is, to that extent, the supreme example of what always happens when God is at work by grace through human beings. God's power from outside, and the indwelling spirit within, together result in things being done which would have been unthinkable any other way.

Of course, no one is likely to be convinced of Luke's story who isn't already in some sense open to the possibility that Jesus, though certainly a fully human being, was also the one in whom Israel's God had made his personal appearance on the stage of history. And it's important to say that neither Luke nor Matthew (the two writers who speak about Jesus' conception directly) suggest that this is the most important thing about Jesus. In all of Paul's writings, he never mentions that there had been anything unusual about Jesus' conception or birth. Jesus' death and **resurrection** remain, for him, far more significant. But to those who have come to some kind of faith in the crucified and risen Jesus, whose minds are thus opened to God being uniquely present in him, there is a sense of appropriateness, hard to define, easy to recognize, about the story Luke and Matthew tell. It isn't what we would have expected, but it somehow rings true.

Far more important for the whole story, though, is the political or royal meaning Luke gives to the whole event. The child to be born will be the **Messiah**, the king of the house of David. God had promised David a descendant who would reign for ever – not over Israel only, but also the whole world. And this coming king would be, in some sense, 'God's son' (2 Samuel 7.14; Psalm 2.7; Psalm 89.27). As with a good deal of New Testament language about Jesus, this is both a huge theological claim (Jesus is somehow identified with God in a unique way which people then and now find it hard to grasp and believe) and a huge political claim (Jesus is the true ruler of the world in a way which leaves Caesar, and the powers of the world today, a long way behind).

Put all this together – the conception of a baby, the power of God, and the challenge to all human empires – and we can see why the story is so explosive. Perhaps that's one reason why it's so controversial. Perhaps some of the fuss and bother about whether Mary could have conceived Jesus without a human father is because, deep down, we don't want to think that there might be a king who could claim this sort of absolute allegiance?

Whatever answer we give to that, we shouldn't miss the contrast between muddled, puzzled Zechariah in the previous story and the obedient humility of Mary in this one. She too questions Gabriel, but this seems to be a request for information, not proof. Rather, faced with the chance to be the mother of the Messiah, though not yet aware of what this will involve, she says the words which have rung down the years as a model of the human response to God's unexpected vocation: 'Here I am, the Lord's servant-girl; let it be as you have said.'

LUKE 1.39–56

The Magnificat: Mary's Song of Praise

[39]Mary got up then and there, and went in excitement to the hill country of Judaea. [40]She went into Zechariah's house, and greeted Elisabeth. [41]When Elisabeth heard Mary's greeting, the baby gave a leap in her womb. Elisabeth was filled with the holy spirit, [42]and shouted at the top of her voice:

'Of all women, you're the blessed one! And the fruit of your womb – he's blessed, too! [43]Why should this happen to me, that the mother of my Lord should come to me? [44]Look – when the sound of your greeting came to my ears, the child in my womb gave a great leap for joy! [45]A blessing on you, for believing that what the Lord said to you would come true!'

[46]Mary said,
'My soul declares that the Lord is great,
[47]my spirit exults in my saviour, my God.
[48]He saw his servant-girl in her humility;
from now, I'll be blessed by all peoples to come.
[49]The Powerful One, whose name is Holy,
has done great things for me, for me.
[50]His mercy extends from father to son,
from mother to daughter for those who fear him.

> [51]Powerful things he has done with his arm:
> he routed the arrogant through their own cunning.
> [52]Down from their thrones he hurled the rulers,
> up from the earth he raised the humble.
> [53]The hungry he filled with the fat of the land,
> but the rich he sent off with nothing to eat.
> [54]He has rescued his servant, Israel his child,
> because he remembered his mercy of old,
> [55]just as he said to our long-ago ancestors –
> Abraham and his descendants for ever.'
>
> [56]Mary stayed with Elisabeth for three months, and then returned home.

What would make you celebrate wildly, without inhibition?

Perhaps it would be the news that someone close to you who'd been very sick was getting better and would soon be home.

Perhaps it would be the news that your country had escaped from tyranny and oppression, and could look forward to a new time of freedom and prosperity.

Perhaps it would be seeing that the floods which had threatened your home were going down again.

Perhaps it would be the message that all your money worries, or business worries, had been sorted out and you could relax.

Perhaps it would be the telephone call to say that you had been appointed to the job you'd always longed for.

Whatever it might be, you'd do things you normally wouldn't.

You might dance round and round with a friend.

You might shout and throw your hat in the air (I once did that without thinking, before I stopped to reflect what a cliché it was).

You might telephone everybody you could think of and invite them to a party.

You might sing a song. You might even make one up as you went along – probably out of snatches of poems and songs you already knew, or perhaps by adding your own new words to a great old hymn.

And if you lived in any kind of culture where rhythm and beat mattered, it would be the sort of song you could clap your hands to, or stamp on the ground.

Now read Mary's song like that. (It's often called *Magnificat*, because that is its first word in Latin.) It's one of the most famous songs in Christianity. It's been whispered in monasteries, chanted in cathedrals, recited in small remote churches by evening candlelight, and set to music with trumpets and kettledrums by Johann Sebastian Bach.

It's the **gospel** before the gospel, a fierce bright shout of triumph thirty weeks before Bethlehem, thirty years before Calvary and Easter. It goes with a swing and a clap and a stamp. It's all about God, and it's all about revolution. And it's all because of Jesus – Jesus who's only just been conceived, not yet born, but who has made Elisabeth's baby leap for joy in her womb and has made Mary giddy with excitement and hope and triumph. In many cultures today, it's the women who really know how to celebrate, to sing and dance, with their bodies and voices saying things far deeper than words. That's how Mary's song comes across here.

Yes, Mary will have to learn many other things as well. A sword will pierce her **soul**, she is told when Jesus is a baby. She will lose him for three days when he's twelve. She will think he's gone mad when he's thirty. She will despair completely for a further three days in Jerusalem, as the God she now wildly celebrates seems to have deceived her (that, too, is part of the same Jewish tradition she draws on in this song). All of us who sing her song should remember these things too. But the moment of triumph will return with Easter and Pentecost, and this time it won't be taken away.

Why did Mary launch into a song like this? What has the news of her son got to do with God's strong power overthrowing the power structures of the world, demolishing the mighty and exalting the humble?

Mary and Elisabeth shared a dream. It was the ancient dream of Israel: the dream that one day all that the prophets had said would come true. One day Israel's God would do what he had said to Israel's earliest ancestors: all nations would be blessed through Abraham's family. But for that to happen, the powers that kept the world in slavery had to be toppled. Nobody would normally thank God for blessing if they were poor, hungry, enslaved and miserable. God would have to win a victory over the bullies, the power brokers, the forces of evil which people like Mary and Elisabeth knew all too well, living as they did in the dark days of Herod the Great, whose casual brutality was backed up with the threat of Rome. Mary and Elisabeth, like so many Jews of their time, searched the scriptures, soaked themselves in the psalms and prophetic writings which spoke of mercy, hope, fulfilment, reversal, revolution, victory over evil and of God coming to the rescue at last.

All of that is poured into this song, like a rich, foaming drink that comes bubbling over the edge of the jug and spills out all round. Almost every word is a biblical quotation such as Mary would have known from childhood. Much of it echoes the song of Hannah in 1 Samuel 2, the song which celebrated the birth of Samuel and all

11

that God was going to do through him. Now these two mothers-to-be celebrate together what God is going to do through their sons, **John** and Jesus.

This is all part of Luke's scene-setting for what will follow, as the two boys grow up and really do become the agents of God's long-promised revolution, the victory over the powers of evil. Much of Mary's song is echoed by her son's preaching, as he warns the rich not to trust in their wealth, and promises God's **kingdom** to the poor.

But once again Luke hasn't just given us a big picture. Mary's visit to Elisabeth is a wonderful human portrait of the older woman, pregnant at last after hope had gone, and the younger one, pregnant far sooner than she had expected. That might have been a moment of tension: Mary might have felt proud, Elisabeth perhaps resentful. Nothing of that happens. Instead, the intimate details: John, three months before his birth, leaping in the womb at Mary's voice, and the holy spirit carrying Elisabeth into shouted praise and Mary into song.

Underneath it all is a celebration of God. God has taken the initiative – God the Lord, the saviour, the Powerful One, the Holy One, the Merciful One, the Faithful One. God is the ultimate reason to celebrate.

LUKE 1.57–80

Zechariah's Song of Praise

[57]The time arrived for Elisabeth's child to be born, and she gave birth to a son. [58]Her neighbours and relatives heard that the Lord had increased his mercy to her, and they came to celebrate with her.

[59]Now on the eighth day, when they came to circumcise the child, they were calling him by his father's name, Zechariah. [60]But his mother spoke up.

'No,' she said, 'he is to be called John.'

[61]'None of your relatives,' they objected, 'is called by that name.'

[62]They made signs to his father, to ask what he wanted him to be called. [63]He asked for a writing tablet, and wrote on it, 'His name is John.'

Everyone was astonished. [64]Immediately his mouth and his tongue were unfastened, and he spoke, praising God. [65]Fear came over all those who lived in the neighbourhood, and people spoke of all these things throughout all the hill country of Judaea. [66]Everyone who heard about it turned the matter over in their hearts.

'What then will this child become?' they said. And the Lord's hand was with him.

[67]John's father Zechariah was filled with the holy spirit, and spoke this prophecy:

12

⁶⁸'Blessed be the Lord, Israel's God!
He's come to his people and bought them their freedom.
⁶⁹He's raised up a horn of salvation for us
in David's house, the house of his servant,
⁷⁰just as he promised, through the mouths of the prophets,
the holy ones, speaking from ages of old:
⁷¹salvation from our enemies, rescue from hatred,
⁷²mercy to our ancestors, keeping his holy covenant.
⁷³He swore an oath to Abraham our father,
⁷⁴to give us deliverance from fear and foes,
so we might worship him, ⁷⁵holy and righteous
before his face to the end of our days.
⁷⁶You, child, will be called the prophet of the Highest One,
you'll go before the Lord, preparing his way,
⁷⁷letting his people know of salvation,
through the forgiveness of all their sins.
⁷⁸The heart of our God is full of mercy,
that's why his daylight has dawned from on high,
⁷⁹bringing light to the dark, as we sat in death's shadow,
guiding our feet in the path of peace.'

⁸⁰The child grew, and became powerful in the spirit. He lived in the wilderness until the day when he was revealed to Israel.

Many people today can't imagine what life would be like without a television. We are so used to it telling us what to think about all the time that, without it, some people become quite worried, lost in a world of their own unfamiliar thoughts like an explorer whose guide has just disappeared. Take away radio and newspapers as well, and ... what would *you* think about all day?

That was the situation, of course, of most people in the world until very recently. It was the situation for everybody in Jesus' time. If you were Zechariah, what would you think of all day?

Your family, certainly. Local village business, presumably. Your health, quite possibly. The state of the crops, the prospect for harvest.

But behind these obvious concerns, there are deeper questions. Something is wrong in the world. People are suffering. *Your* people are suffering. Wicked foreigners have come from far away, with hatred in their eyes and weapons in their hands. Darkness and death have stalked the land. Many people in many countries have had all this to think about over many centuries.

Behind that again, there may be a sense that, though much has gone wrong, somehow there is a larger hope. Things can be put right. Things *will* be put right. Let go of this and you're sunk. Often it's the old people, the ones who cherish old memories and imaginations, who keep alive the rumour of hope.

Zechariah comes across in this passage, especially in the prophetic poem, as someone who has pondered the agony and the hope for many years, and who now finds the two bubbling out of him as he looks in awe and delight at his baby son.

It's a poem about God acting at last, finally doing what he promised many centuries ago, and doing it at a time when his people had had their fill of hatred and oppression. One evil empire after another had trampled them underfoot; now at last God was going to give them deliverance. We can feel the long years of pain and sorrow, of darkness and death, overshadowing his mind. Nameless enemies are lurking round the corner in his imagination and experience. No doubt it was partly this that had made him question Gabriel's word in the first place.

But we can also feel the long years of quiet prayer and trust. God had made a **covenant** with Abraham. God had promised to send a new David. God had spoken of a prophet who would go ahead to prepare the way. All these things he had known, believed, prayed and longed for. Now they were all to come true.

Much of the poem could be read simply as the celebration of what we would call a 'political' salvation – though few ancient Jews, and not very many modern ones, would want to separate the secular from the sacred the way the modern West has done. But there are signs that Zechariah's vision goes beyond simply a realigning of political powers. God's mercy, the forgiveness of sins, the rescue from death itself; all of this points to a deeper and wider meaning of 'salvation'. Luke is preparing us to see that God, in fulfilling the great promises of the Old Testament, is going beyond a merely this-worldly salvation and opening the door to a whole new world in which sin and death themselves will be dealt with. This, of course, is the message that will occupy the rest of the book.

Zechariah's own story, of nine months' silence suddenly broken at the naming of the child, is a reflection on a smaller scale of what was going on in the Israel of his day. Prophecy, many believed, had been silent for a long time. Now it was going to burst out again, to lead many back to a true allegiance to their God. What had begun as a kind of punishment for Zechariah's lack of **faith** now turns into a new sort of sign, a sign that God is doing a new thing.

Luke's long first chapter holds together what we often find easier to keep separate. At point after point he has linked his story to the ancient biblical record of Israel, to the patriarchs, kings, prophets and psalms. He is writing of the moment when the centuries-old story was going to come round a corner at last, out of darkness into sudden light. He never forgets this larger perspective; everything that he will tell us about Jesus makes sense as the fulfilment of God's ancient promises, the hope of Israel come to fruition at last.

But Luke's story vibrates equally with the personal hopes and fears of ordinary people. Zechariah, Elisabeth and Mary stand out as real people, hesitating between faith and doubt, called to trust God at a new moment in history. It's a mark not only of Luke's skill as a writer but also of the nature of the God he is writing about that both the big picture and the smaller human stories matter totally. This is, after all, as Zechariah had glimpsed, the story of how the creator God came to rescue his people. It is the story, as Luke will now tell, of how God himself was born as a baby.

LUKE 2.1–20

The Birth of Jesus

[1]At that time a decree was issued by Augustus Caesar: a census was to be taken of the whole world. [2](This was the first census, before the one when Quirinius was governor of Syria.) [3]So everyone set off to be registered, each to their own town. [4]Joseph too, who belonged to the house and family of David, went from the city of Nazareth in Galilee to Bethlehem in Judaea, David's city, [5]to be registered with his fiancée Mary, who was pregnant.

[6]So that's where they were when the time came for her to have her baby; [7]and she gave birth to her firstborn, a son. She wrapped him up and put him to rest in a feeding-trough, because there was no room for them in the normal living quarters.

[8]There were shepherds in that region, out in the open, keeping a night watch around their flock. [9]An angel of the Lord stood in front of them. The glory of the Lord shone around them, and they were terrified.

[10]'Don't be afraid', the angel said to them. 'Look: I've got good news for you, news which will make everybody very happy. [11]Today a saviour has been born for you – the Messiah, the Lord! – in David's town. [12]This will be the sign for you: you'll find the baby wrapped up, and lying in a feeding-trough.'

[13]Suddenly, with the angel, there was a crowd of the heavenly armies. They were praising God, saying,

[14]'Glory to God in the highest,
and peace upon earth among those in his favour.'

[15]So when the angels had gone away again into heaven, the shepherds said to each other,

'Well then; let's go to Bethlehem and see what it's all about, all this that the Lord has told us.'

¹⁶So they hurried off, and found Mary and Joseph, and the child lying in the feeding-trough. ¹⁷When they saw it, they told them what had been said to them about this child. ¹⁸And all the people who heard it were amazed at the things the shepherds said to them. ¹⁹But Mary treasured all these things and mused over them in her heart.

²⁰The shepherds returned, glorifying and praising God for all they had heard and seen, as it had been told to them.

If you try to point out something to a dog, the dog will often look at your finger instead of at the object you're trying to point to. This is frustrating, but it illustrates a natural mistake we all make from time to time.

It's the mistake many people make when reading the Christmas story in Luke's **gospel**. What do people know about Jesus' birth? The manger – the Christmas crib. The most famous animal feeding-trough in all history. You see it on Christmas cards. Churches make elaborate 'cribs', and sometimes encourage people to say their prayers in front of them. We know about the animals, too, not that Luke even mentions any; the ox and the ass feature prominently in Christmas cards and carols, though there is no indication here either that the shepherds brought their own animals with them, or that there were any in the place where Mary and Joseph were staying.

Let's be clear about where they were lodging. Tradition has them knocking at an inn door, being told there was no room, and then being offered the stable along with the animals. But the word for 'inn' in the traditional translations has several meanings, and it's likely that they were, in fact, on the ground floor of a house where people normally stayed upstairs. The ground floor would often be used for animals – hence the manger or feeding-trough, which came in handy for the baby – but there is nothing to say that there were actually animals there at the time.

To concentrate on the manger and to forget why it was mentioned in the first place is like the dog looking at the finger rather than the object. Why has Luke mentioned it three times in this story?

The answer is: because it was the feeding-trough, appropriately enough, which was the sign to the shepherds. It told them which baby they were looking for. And it showed them that the angel knew what he was talking about. To be sure, it's another wonderful human touch in the story, to think of the young mother finding an animal's feeding-trough ready to hand as a cot for her newborn son. No doubt there are many sermons waiting to be preached here about God coming down into the mess and muddle of real life. But the reason Luke has mentioned it is because it's important in giving the shepherds their news and their instructions.

Why is that significant? Because it was the shepherds who were told *who this child was.* This child is the saviour, the **Messiah**, the Lord. The manger isn't important in itself. It's a signpost, a pointing finger, to the identity and task of the baby boy who's lying in it. The shepherds, summoned in from the fields (like David, the shepherd boy, brought in from the fields to be anointed as king), are made privy to the news, so that Mary and Joseph, hearing it from this unexpected source, will have extra confirmation of what up until now has been their own secret.

We have to assume that the shepherds, like other Palestinian Jews at the time, including old Zechariah in the previous chapter, would have known what a saviour, a Messiah, a Lord was to do. In case we need reminding, Luke has introduced the story by telling us about Augustus Caesar, way off in Rome, at the height of his power.

Augustus was the adopted son of Julius Caesar. He became sole ruler of the Roman world after a bloody civil war in which he overpowered all rival claimants. The last to be destroyed was the famous Mark Antony, who committed suicide not long after his defeat at the battle of Actium in 31 BC. Augustus turned the great Roman republic into an empire, with himself at the head; he proclaimed that he had brought justice and peace to the whole world; and, declaring his dead adoptive father to be divine, styled himself as 'son of god'. Poets wrote songs about the new era that had begun; historians told the long story of Rome's rise to greatness, reaching its climax (obviously) with Augustus himself. Augustus, people said, was the 'saviour' of the world. He was its king, its 'lord'. Increasingly, in the eastern part of his empire, people worshipped him, too, as a god.

Meanwhile, far away, on that same eastern frontier, a boy was born who would within a generation be hailed as '**son of God**'; whose followers would speak of him as 'saviour' and 'lord'; whose arrival, they thought, had brought true justice and peace to the world. Jesus never stood before a Roman emperor, but at the climax of Luke's gospel he stood before his representative, the governor Pontius Pilate. Luke certainly has that scene in mind as he tells his tale: how the emperor in Rome decides to take a census of his whole wide domain, and how this census brings Jesus to be born in the town which was linked to king David himself.

Historians have puzzled about the census. The one taken when Quirinius was governor of Syria was considerably later than Jesus' birth (and, interestingly, caused riots because the Jews resented being taxed by Rome). One way of translating the Greek here is to see this census as an earlier one, before the famous one under Quirinius. There are many puzzles the historians may never work out, and this may be one of them.

But the point Luke is making is clear. The birth of this little boy is the beginning of a confrontation between the **kingdom** of God – in all its apparent weakness, insignificance and vulnerability – and the kingdoms of the world. Augustus never heard of Jesus of Nazareth. But within a century or so his successors in Rome had not only heard of him; they were taking steps to obliterate his followers. Within just over three centuries the Emperor himself became a Christian. When you see the manger on a card, or in church, don't stop at the crib. See what it's pointing to. It is pointing to the explosive truth that the baby lying there is already being spoken of as the true king of the world. The rest of Luke's story, both in the gospel and, later on, in Acts, will tell how he comes into his kingdom.

LUKE 2.21–40

Simeon and Anna

[21]After eight days, the time came to circumcise the baby. He was called by the name Jesus, which the angel had given him before he had been conceived in the womb.

[22]When the time came for them to be purified according to the law of Moses, they took him up to Jerusalem to present him before the Lord. [23]That's what the law of the Lord says: 'Every firstborn male shall be called holy to the Lord.' [24]They also came to offer sacrifice, according to what it says in the law of the Lord: 'A pair of turtledoves or two young pigeons.'

[25]Now there was a man in Jerusalem named Simeon. He was righteous and devout, waiting for God to comfort Israel, and the holy spirit was upon him. [26]He had been told by the holy spirit that he would not die until he had seen the Lord's Messiah. [27]Led by the spirit, he came into the Temple. As Jesus' parents brought him in, to do for him what the law's regulations required, [28]he took the baby in his arms and blessed God with these words:

[29]'Now, master, you are dismissing your servant in peace,
just as you said.
[30]These eyes of mine have seen your salvation,
[31]which you made ready in the presence of all peoples:
[32]a light for revelation to the nations,
and glory for your people Israel.'

[33]His father and mother were astonished at the things that were said about him. [34]Simeon blessed them.

'Listen,' he said to Mary his mother, 'this child has been placed here to make many in Israel fall and rise again, and as a sign that will be spoken against [35](yes, a sword will go through your own soul as well), so that the thoughts of many hearts may be disclosed.'

[36]There was also a prophetess called Anna, the daughter of Phanuel, of the tribe of Asher. She was of a great age, having been widowed after a seven-year marriage, [37]and was now eighty-four. She never left the Temple, but worshipped with fasting and prayer night and day. [38]She came up at that moment and gave thanks to God, and spoke about Jesus to everyone who was waiting for the redemption of Jerusalem.

[39]So when they had finished everything according to the law of the Lord, they returned to Galilee, to their town of Nazareth. [40]The child grew and became strong, and was full of wisdom, and God's grace was upon him.

I watched as the craftsman went about his task. He carefully set the lead into the window to be the framework for the beautiful glass he had been staining. Now came the moment: where before was a plain window, now there was a riot of colour and shape, telling a story and making it sparkle at the same time.

Luke has now sketched the outline of a picture. He has placed the lead around the window. What coloured glass is he going to use to fill it in? What story will he tell, and what sparkle will he give it?

The picture is of Jesus as the true world ruler: the Lord, the **Messiah**, the saviour, the real king of the world instead of Caesar. How easy it would be to fill in this picture in glowing, royal colours, giving us a sense of future glory, world dominion, power and majesty.

Luke does the opposite. He chooses sombre colours; and the more he fills in the picture the more we realize that this is a different sort of kingdom to that of Caesar Augustus. It is indeed what God had promised; but, not for the last time, Luke is warning us that it doesn't look like what people had expected.

In particular, this is becoming a story about suffering. Simeon is waiting for God to comfort Israel. Anna is in touch with the people who are waiting for the redemption of Israel. They are both living in a world of patient hope, where suffering has become a way of life. It now appears that God's appointed redeemer will deal with this suffering by sharing it himself. Simeon speaks dark words about opposition, and about a sword that will pierce Mary's heart as well.

So this, Luke is saying, is what happens when the **kingdom** of God confronts the kingdom of the world. Luke invites us to watch, throughout the story, as the prophecies come true. Mary will look on in dismay as her son is rejected by the very city to which he offered the way of peace, by the very people he had come to rescue. Finally, the child who is, as Simeon says, 'placed here to make many in Israel fall and rise again', himself passes through death and into resurrection, taking with him the hopes and fears of the city, the nation and the world.

But if Luke is colouring in the picture with the dark notes of suffering, he is also showing that the kingdom brought by this baby is not for Israel only, but for the whole world. Simeon had grasped the truth at the heart of the Old Testament (which, Luke is careful to note, Jesus and his parents fulfilled): when Israel's history comes to its God-ordained goal, then at last light will dawn for the world. All the nations, not just the Jews, will see what God is unveiling – a plan of salvation for all people without distinction. This will be the true glory of Israel itself, to have been the bearer of promise, the nation in and from whom the true world ruler would arise: 'A light for revelation to the nations, and glory for your people Israel.' This is not the sort of revelation the world was expecting, and not the sort of glory Israel wanted, but true revelation and true glory nonetheless.

Luke adds yet another human dimension to the story. By the time the first two chapters are finished, almost all his readers will have found someone in the story with whom they can identify. We have met the older couple surprised to have a child at last. We have seen the young girl even more surprised to have a child so soon, and her husband coming with her to the **Temple**, offering the specified **sacrifice**. The next section will feature Jesus himself on the threshold of young adult life. Now, in this passage, we have the old man and woman, waiting their turn to die, worshipping God night and day and praying for the salvation of his people. Luke wants to draw readers of every age and stage of life into his picture. No matter who or where you are, the story of Jesus, from the feeding-trough in Bethlehem to the empty tomb and beyond, can become your story.

In becoming your story, it will become your vocation. Everybody has their own role in God's plan. For some, it will be active, obvious, working in the public eye, perhaps preaching the gospel or taking the love of God to meet the practical needs of the world. For others, it will be quiet, away from public view, praying faithfully for God to act in fulfilment of his promises. For many, it will be a mixture of the two, sometimes one, sometimes the other. Mary and Joseph needed Simeon and Anna at that moment; the old man and old woman needed them, had been waiting for them, and now thanked God for them. The births of **John the Baptist** and Jesus are already beginning their work, of drawing people of all sorts into new worship and fellowship.

LUKE 2.41–52

The Boy Jesus

[41]Jesus' parents used to go to Jerusalem every year for the Passover festival. [42]When he was twelve years old, they went up as usual for the festival. [43]When the feast days were over, they began the journey back, but the boy Jesus remained in Jerusalem. His parents didn't know; [44]they thought he was in the travelling party. They went a day's journey before looking for him among their relatives and friends.

[45]When they didn't find him, they went back to Jerusalem to look for him. [46]And so it happened that after three days they found him in the Temple, sitting among the teachers, listening to them and asking them questions. [47]Everyone who heard him was astonished at his understanding and his answers.

[48]When they saw him they were quite overwhelmed.

'Child,' said his mother, 'why did you do this to us? Look – your father and I have been in a terrible state looking for you!'

[49]'Why were you looking for me?' he replied. 'Didn't you know that I would have to be involved with my father's work?'

[50]They didn't understand what he had said to them. [51]He went down with them and came to Nazareth, and lived under their authority. And his mother kept all these things in her heart.

[52]So Jesus became wiser and taller, gaining favour both with God and with the people.

When I was a child, I walked a mile to the bus stop every morning, by myself or with my sister. At the other end of the trip, I walked by myself to school. In the evening, I came back the same way. I never felt unsafe, even in the dark winter days. Now, in many places, children are often taken to school by car. Parents are worried about all kinds of dangers that might be waiting for them.

Perhaps the first remarkable thing about this story is that Mary and Joseph were happy to set off with their large group from Galilee without checking that Jesus was with them. That tells us a lot about the kind of world they lived in, where extended families of kinsfolk and friends lived together in close-knit mutual trust. But, by the same token, once they had left Jerusalem, and when they returned to it by themselves, without the rest of the party, the city was a large and potentially dangerous place, full of dark alleys and strange people, soldiers and traders, not a place where one would be happy to leave one's son for a few days.

The agony of Mary and Joseph, searching for three days, contrasts sharply with the calm response of Jesus when they found him. Mary blurts out an accusation, perhaps tinged with that mixture of guilt and relief that most parents will recognize. Instead of saying, as she might have, 'How could *I* have done this to *you*, leaving you behind like that?', she says, 'How could *you* do this to *us*?' Jesus accepts no blame, and indeed issues a gentle rebuke that speaks volumes, in Luke's portrait, for his own developing self-awareness. 'Your father and I', says Mary, 'have been looking for you.' 'No,' replies Jesus, 'I have been busying myself in my father's work.' Some families today keep notebooks of the striking things their children come out with. Mary kept her notebook in her heart, and this remark in particular will have gone straight there with a stab.

The way Luke has told the story may strike a careful reader of his **gospel** as part of a large-scale framework around the main story, which is just about to begin. One of the best loved moments in his gospel is the story of the road to Emmaus (24.13–35), in which two **disciples** are sharing their anguish over the three days that have elapsed since Jesus' death. Jesus meets them, and explains how 'these things had to happen'. Here is another couple, coming back to Jerusalem, finding after three days the Jesus they thought they had lost, and having him explain 'that I would have to be involved with my father's work'. You might call the pair of stories something like, 'On Finding the Jesus You Thought You'd Lost'. And if that is the message of these two passages, maybe Luke is wanting to tell us something about his gospel as a whole: maybe he is writing, at one level at least, for people who may have some idea of Jesus but find he is more elusive than they had imagined.

Finding him, of course, will normally involve a surprise. Jesus doesn't do or say what Mary and Joseph, or the two on the road, were expecting. It will be like that with us, too. Every time we relax and think we've really understood him, he will be up ahead, or perhaps staying behind while we go on without thinking. Discipleship always involves the unexpected.

At the heart of the picture, though, is Jesus in the **Temple** – a theme full of meaning for Luke. We have, indeed, visited the Temple quite a bit in the gospel so far: Zechariah's vision, the meeting with Simeon and Anna, and now Jesus himself taking the initiative and entering into discussion with the teachers of the law. The gospel will end, too, with the disciples in the Temple praising God. But, in between this beginning and this end, the Temple, and the holy city which surrounds it, are the subject of some of Jesus' sternest warnings. From now on Jesus will be challenging his contemporaries to make real the promises that go with the Temple. If they don't, the Temple itself will be destroyed.

As we read this story prayerfully, then, we can probably identify quite easily with Mary and Joseph – and perhaps with Jesus, too, quietly asserting an independence of mind and vocation, while still returning home and living in obedience to Mary and Joseph. We may want to remember times when we thought we'd lost someone or something very precious. We may want to reflect on whether we have taken Jesus himself for granted; if Mary and Joseph could do it, there is every reason to suppose that we can too. We mustn't assume he is accompanying us as we go off on our own business. But if and when we sense the lack of his presence, we must be prepared to hunt for him, to search for him in prayer, in the scriptures, in the sacraments, and not to give up until we find him again.

We must expect, too, that when we do meet him again he will not say or do what we expect. He must be busy with his father's work. So must we.

LUKE 3.1–9

The Preaching of John the Baptist

¹In the fifteenth year of the reign of Tiberius Caesar, Pontius Pilate was governor of Judaea, Herod was tetrarch of Galilee; his brother Philip was tetrarch of Ituraea and Trachonitis, and Lysanias was tetrarch of Abilene. ²Annas and Caiaphas were the high priests.

At that time, the word of God came to John, the son of Zechariah, in the wilderness. ³He went through all the region of the Jordan, announcing a baptism of repentance for the forgiveness of sins. ⁴This is what is written in the book of the words of Isaiah the prophet:

'A voice shouting in the wilderness:
get ready a path for the Lord,
make the roads straight for him!
⁵Every valley shall be filled in,
and every mountain and hill shall be flattened,
the twisted paths will be straightened out,
and the rough roads smoothed off,
⁶and all that lives shall see God's rescue.'

⁷'You brood of vipers', John used to say to the crowds who came out to be baptized by him. 'Who told you to escape from the coming anger? ⁸You'd better prove your repentance by bearing the proper fruit! Don't start saying to yourselves, "We have Abraham as our father"; let me tell you, God can raise up children for Abraham from these stones! ⁹The axe is already standing by the roots of the tree – so every tree that doesn't produce good fruit will be cut down and thrown into the fire.'

Imagine massive floods sweeping through the countryside. Ancient cities suddenly find themselves under several feet of water. People aren't expecting it, and now can't quite believe it's happening.

If the authorities have enough warning, they do their best to get people out of their houses to stop them being trapped. They drive round parts of the city announcing that trouble is approaching and that people should leave at once. They make announcements on the local radio and television. Imminent danger needs urgent action.

That's the kind of work **John the Baptist** was doing. We don't usually think of preachers going around making that kind of announcement. Even politicians don't usually tell us things are getting very urgent – or, if they do, we usually take no notice. But people believed John, and came to him for a different sort of flooding: **baptism**, being plunged into the river Jordan.

What was the emergency, and how would being plunged in the Jordan help people to avoid danger?

Luke's introduction to the story of John the Baptist is designed to give us a fairly precise date when it all happened, but actually it gives us a lot more besides. Behind the list of names and places is a story of oppression and misery that was building up to explosion point.

Rome had ruled the area for about a hundred years, but only since AD 6 had there been a Roman governor resident in the area, living in Caesarea (on the Mediterranean coast) but also keeping a base in Jerusalem. Augustus Caesar, the first Emperor, had died in AD 14, and his place had been taken by the ruthless Tiberius, who was already being worshipped as a god in the eastern parts of the empire. Two of Herod the Great's sons, Herod Antipas and Philip, were ruling somewhat shakily, under Roman permission, in the north of the country, but Rome had taken direct control of the south, including Jerusalem itself. Most Jews didn't regard Herod's sons as real rulers; they were a self-made royal house, ruling, like Rome, by fear and oppression. The **high priests** weren't much better. Popular movements of resistance had come and gone, in some cases being brutally put down. Everybody knew they couldn't go on as they were. Something had to happen. But what?

Devout Jews had longed for a new word from God. Some believed that prophecy had died out but might one day be revived. Many expected that a movement would begin through which their God would renew the age-old **covenant**, bringing Israel out of slavery into a new freedom. The old prophets had spoken of a time of renewal, through which God himself would come back to them. They had only a sketchy idea of what this would all look like, but when a fiery young prophet appeared in the Judaean wilderness, going round the towns and villages telling people that the time had come, they were ready to listen.

Baptism, plunging into the river Jordan, was a powerful sign of this renewal. When the children of Israel had come out of Egypt – a story they all knew well because of their regular Passovers and other festivals – they were brought through the Red Sea, through the Sinai wilderness, then through the Jordan into the promised land. Now they were in slavery again – in their own land! – and wanted a new **Exodus** to bring them to freedom. Since the old prophets had declared that this slavery was the result of Israel's sin, worshipping idols rather than their one true God, the new Exodus, when it happened, would have to deal with this. The way to escape slavery, the prophets had said, was to 'return' to God with heart and **soul**; that is, to 'repent'. 'Return to me, and I will return to you', one of the last prophets had said (Malachi 3.7).

Hence John's agenda: 'a baptism of **repentance** for the forgiveness of sins'. John was doing what the prophet Isaiah had said: preparing a pathway for the Lord himself to return to his people. This was the time. Rescue was at hand.

But the people were not in good shape. Indeed, since baptism was part of the ritual Gentiles had to undergo if they wanted to convert to Judaism, John's summoning of Israel itself to baptism speaks for itself. Nor was it simply that the nation was in trouble politically; everybody in the crowds needed to face their own moral predicament. John wasn't going to be satisfied with a mere outward ritual, in which many could hide their real selves behind an outward conformity to this new movement. If God was coming back, he wasn't coming just to tell them that because they were Abraham's children everything would be all right. The reason God brings rescue and salvation is precisely because he is the holy and faithful God, keeping covenant with his people – but, if that is so, he is bound to bring judgment as well as mercy. He isn't a tame God.

John uses a picture which Jesus developed later. The tree is meant to bear fruit, but if it doesn't it will be cut down (see Luke 6.43–45). The fruit must show that repentance has been genuine. The warning echoes down the years, and must be taken to heart by all the baptized today. We cannot presume that because we have shared in the great Christian mystery, the new Exodus, coming through the water of baptism with all that it means, God will automatically be happy with us even if we show no signs of serious repentance. Of course, Christian living is far more than simply repentance, but it is not less. All spiritual advance begins with a turning away from what is hindering our obedience. If John were to come down your street with a megaphone, what would he be saying?

LUKE 3.10–20

John the Baptist Confronts the Crowds

¹⁰'What shall we do?' asked the crowds.

¹¹'Anyone who has two cloaks', replied John, 'should give one to someone who hasn't got one. The same applies to anyone who has plenty of food.'

¹²Some toll-collectors came to be baptized. 'Teacher', they said, 'what should we do?'

¹³'Don't collect more than what is laid down', he replied.

¹⁴Some soldiers, too, asked John, 'What about us? What should we do?'

'No extortion', replied John, 'and no blackmail. Be content with your wages.'

¹⁵The people were very excited, and everyone was questioning in their hearts whether John might not be the Messiah. ¹⁶To all of them John responded:

'I am baptizing you with water. But someone is coming who is stronger than I am. I don't deserve to untie his sandal-strap. He will baptize you with the holy spirit and with fire. ¹⁷He will have his winnowing-fork to hand, ready to sort out the mess on his threshing floor and gather the corn into his barn. Any rubbish he will burn with a fire that will never go out.'

¹⁸John urged his news on the people with many other words. ¹⁹But Herod the Tetrarch – whom John had accused in the matter of his brother's wife Herodias, and for all the evil things which Herod had done – ²⁰added this to his list of crimes, that he shut John up in prison.

A cartoon shows a sceptic shouting up to the heavens, 'God! If you're up there, tell us what we should do!'

Back comes a voice: 'Feed the hungry, house the homeless, establish justice.'

The sceptic looks alarmed. 'Just testing', he says.

'Me too', replies the voice.

John the Baptist doesn't seem to have wasted time and breath going into the details of ethical debate. Not for him the learned discussions of particular cases, the small details of law that take time and energy away from actually doing anything about the way the world is – and the way one's own life is. Of course, one might grumble that John hadn't said anything to the people who *didn't* have two cloaks or too much food, but that wasn't the point. If people were coming for **baptism**, they were committing themselves to be God's Israel, the light of the world, the people in whom God's justice would be seen by all. There was no time, and no need, for lengthy discussions such as we find in the writings of the **rabbis**. What they needed was rules of thumb. 'Two cloaks? Give one away. Too much food? Same applies.' Nobody could miss the point. Like the great Old Testament prophets, John could see the rich getting richer and the poor poorer. A start had to be made to get things back on track.

The special cases are doubly interesting. Nobody likes paying taxes at the best of times, and some of the tolls were levied simply at the whim of local rulers, shamelessly lining their pockets and giving the collectors tacit licence to do the same. John doesn't say they should stop working for the hated rulers; he's not going to recommend unemployment. But they must earn their living and no more. No getting rich at the expense of their own people. We shall meet more tax- and toll-collectors later on in Luke's gospel.

The soldiers are probably from Herod's own troops; they are unlikely to be Roman soldiers, coming to a Jewish prophet for a ritual that only made sense within Israel's national story. Like the toll-collectors, they aren't told to abandon their careers, but they must avoid abusing their position, as was evidently commonplace. No thuggery, using their brute force to rob people with impunity. 'Be content with your wages' isn't a way of telling them not to campaign for higher wages from their employers; the steady creeping inflation that modern Western economies experience was virtually unknown in the first-century Roman world, and annual pay rises would not have been an issue. Rather, the soldiers are not to use a complaint about low pay as an excuse to rob and pillage ('Herod doesn't pay us enough, so we have no choice').

Simple, clear commands; but if they were obeyed they would demonstrate that people meant business. None of these things happens by chance; they only occur when people have genuinely repented of the small-scale injustices which turn a society sour. But there is more. John is not just a moral reformer; he is not just announcing that the time has arrived for the great liberation, the great new **Exodus**. He is the herald of the **Messiah**.

There was already, of course, a 'king of the Jews'. Herod Antipas, though officially a 'tetrarch' – a kind of second-rank prince – was working on rebuilding the **Temple**, which was itself a way of claiming royal status. King Solomon, after all, had been the first Temple builder, and some of Israel's greatest kings had rebuilt or restored the Temple. Herod was hoping to inherit his father's title, king of the Jews.

But John had other ideas. The true Messiah, the true king of the Jews, was coming, and his coming would bring devastating judgment. The idea of the Messiah as judge as well as saviour is an important part of mainstream Jewish expectation; the Messiah would bring God's justice to the world, and this would involve naming and dealing with evil. John speaks of him in terms of the fork and the fire: the farmer's fork, to separate the wheat from the chaff, and the fire that burns up the chaff once it's been separated. It's not exactly the picture of Jesus that many Western Christians want, but unless we are to step right outside the biblical witness, it's one aspect of the truth we have to take seriously.

Herod Antipas had had an affair with Herodias, the wife of his brother Philip, after which she had divorced Philip (it was unheard of in Jewish **law** for a wife to divorce her husband) and married Antipas. John's denunciation of this flagrant and incestuous adultery was not simply a moral criticism. Part of the point was that if Herod had any pretensions to being the true king of the Jews, behaviour like that would prove him a sham. The Lord's anointed would never do such a thing. Like Elijah opposing Ahab (1 Kings 17—18), John spoke out fearlessly against Herod, and took the consequences.

Jesus himself would give more detailed teaching than John, and we shall look at it in due course. But he never retreated from the two things John was saying here. On the one hand, he too was just as committed as John to God's justice working its way out into the world in the behaviour of his followers. On the other hand, he like John was solidly opposed to the house of Herod, and spent his public career quietly subverting it by establishing his own network of supporters and followers. His vision of God's kingdom differed radically from Herod's: for him, God's justice would be displayed not through riches and royalty of worldly style, but through the love and justice that would finally be combined on the cross.

LUKE 3.21–38

Jesus' Baptism and Genealogy

[21]So it happened that, as all the people were being baptized, Jesus too was baptized, and was praying. The heaven was opened, [22]and the holy spirit descended in a bodily form, like a dove, upon him. There came a voice from heaven: 'You are my son, my dear son! I'm delighted with you.'

[23]Jesus was about thirty years old at the start of his work. He was, as people thought, the son of Joseph, from whom his ancestry proceeds back in the following line: Heli, [24]Matthat, Levi, Melchi, Jannai, Joseph, [25]Mattathias, Amos, Nahum, Esli, Naggai, [26]Maath, Mattathias, Semein, Josech, Joda, [27]Johanan, Rhesa, Zerubbabel, Shealtiel, Neri, [28]Melchi, Addi, Kosam, Elmadam, Er, [29]Joshua, Eliezer, Jorim, Matthat, Levi, [30]Simeon, Judah, Joseph, Jonam, Eliakim, [31]Melea, Menna, Mattatha, Nathan, David, [32]Jesse, Obed, Boaz, Sala, Nahshon, [33]Amminadab, Admin, Arni, Hezron, Perez, Judah, [34]Jacob, Isaac, Abraham, Terah,

Nahor, ³⁵Serug, Reu, Peleg, Eber, Shela, ³⁶Kainan, Arphachsad, Shem, Noah, Lamech, ³⁷Methuselah, Enoch, Jared, Mahalaleel, Kainan, ³⁸Enosh, Seth, Adam, and God.

When I visited New Zealand some years ago, I was taught how to greet an audience in the traditional Maori fashion. I much enjoyed and appreciated the welcome I was given by this ancient people, many of whom are now devout Christians, and the chance to learn something of their history and culture.

Many of the Maori people in New Zealand can tell you which of the original eight long canoes their ancestors arrived in when they first arrived in the country between 800 and 1,000 years ago. There is every reason to suppose that this memory of family trees and origins is reasonably accurate. Many peoples in today's world, and perhaps still more in the ancient world, regularly told and tell stories of family history, and though these may be embellished from time to time, they are often to be seen as trustworthy. Only in the modern Western world, or where there have been huge social disruptions from war and migration, have people lost touch with ancestry beyond a generation or two.

The Jews were particularly conscious of ancestry, with good reason. God had made promises to Abraham and his family for ever, and through wars, enforced **exile**, and attempted genocide, they clung (as they still do) to their memories and stories of ancestry as to a lifeline. The books of Chronicles in the Old Testament begin with several chapters of names, which seem very tedious to a modern reader, but were vital for people at the time. They needed to know who they were, which meant knowing which part of the people of Israel they belonged to.

So to begin with it seems surprising that we have not one but two quite different family trees for Jesus. Matthew begins his book with a list of names from Abraham to Jesus; Luke now includes a list of names working back from Jesus, through Abraham, to Adam and thence to God himself. And the odd thing is that the lists don't match. Luke has considerably more generations between Abraham and Jesus; and, though some of the stages are the same, the lists part company altogether between David (around 1000 BC) and Salathiel and his son Zerubbabel (after the exile), and then again between Zerubbabel and Joseph. Even the name of Joseph's father is different. In any case, what is the point of a genealogy of *Joseph*, when both Luke and Matthew insist that he was not in fact Jesus' physical father?

Ever since the early days of the church, learned scholars have struggled to give good answers to these questions, and most have admitted defeat. Obviously, in a small and close-knit community, there is every probability that someone could trace their descent from the same source by two or more different routes. The Maori themselves can give several different genealogies for themselves, depending on which ancestor they want to highlight and how much intermarrying has taken place. Different tribal subunits can trace their descent in different ways for different purposes, resulting in criss-crossing links of all sorts.

This is so even in modern Western society. After my own parents married, they discovered that they were distant cousins, with one remove of generation. Think of the little country of Israel in the period between David and Jesus; similar things could easily have happened. Many could have traced their descent to the same ancestors by at least two routes.

Luke, it seems, has come upon a family tree which he presents without comment, simply to declare that Jesus was indeed not only a true Jew but a descendant of David and Zerubbabel – part of the genuinely royal family. He was counted as Joseph's adopted son, which served, it seems, for this purpose (we are never told whether Mary was of royal descent; since she was a cousin of Elisabeth it may be that she was from a priestly family). If there were other motives in the arrangement of names as they came to Luke (some have suggested that the 77 names should be seen as eleven groups of seven), he doesn't draw our attention to them.

The one link between the family tree and what goes before and comes after is the final phrase: Jesus is the **son of God**. Of course, by that reckoning so is everyone else in the list, from Joseph right back to Adam. Luke certainly means more than this when he uses the phrase 'son of God' as a title for Jesus (1.35; 3.22; 4.3, 9). Perhaps it is best to see the family tree, stretching back to the creation of the world, as a way of saying that, though Jesus is indeed the **Messiah** of Israel (another meaning of 'son of God'), he is so precisely for the whole world. All creation, the whole human race, will benefit from what he has come to do.

This global scope to God's purposes is in the background as Jesus comes to the Jordan to be baptized by **John**. Luke adds here, as in one or two other key points, the fact that Jesus was praying when the crucial revelation occurred. Part of his constant picture of Jesus is that he was a man of prayer. It's often suggested that the **baptism** was the moment when Jesus received his first inkling of a messianic calling, but this can hardly be correct; the voice from heaven comes to confirm and give direction to something that has been true all along, as Luke has already told us (2.49). The **spirit** and the word together give Jesus the encouragement and strength he needs to begin his short public career.

They also give an indication of where that career will take him. The heavenly voice echoes words of Isaiah the prophet (42.1), commissioning the Messiah as the Servant, the one who will suffer and die for the people and the world. Behind that again are echoes of Genesis 22.2, when Abraham was commanded to kill his beloved only son, Isaac. The voice is at the same time a wonderful affirmation of Jesus' vocation and a clear reminder of where it is to lead.

Together the baptism story and the family tree tell us where Jesus has come from, who he is, and where he is going. As we make his story our own in our own prayers, and indeed in our own baptism, we too should expect both the fresh energy of the spirit and the quiet voice which reminds us of God's amazing, affirming love and of the path of vocation which lies ahead.

LUKE 4.1–13

Temptation in the Wilderness

¹Jesus returned from the Jordan, filled with the spirit. The spirit took him off into the wilderness ²for forty days, to be tested by the devil. He ate nothing during that time, and at the end of it he was hungry.

³'If you are God's son,' said the devil, 'tell this stone to become a loaf of bread.'

⁴'It is written,' replied Jesus, '"It isn't only bread that keeps you alive."'

⁵The devil then took him up and showed him, in an instant, all the kingdoms of the world.

⁶'I will give you authority over all of this,' said the devil, 'and all the prestige that goes with it. It's been given to me, you see, and I give it to anyone I like. ⁷So it can all be yours . . . if you will just worship me.'

⁸'It is written,' replied Jesus, '"The Lord your God is the one you must worship; he is the only one you must serve."'

⁹Then the devil took him to Jerusalem, and stood him on a pinnacle of the Temple.

'If you are God's son,' he said, 'throw yourself down from here; ¹⁰it's written, after all, that "He will give his angels a command about you, to look after you"; ¹¹and "They will carry you in their hands, so that you won't hit your foot against a stone."'

¹²'It has been said,' replied Jesus, '"You mustn't put the Lord your God to the test."'

¹³When the devil had finished each temptation, he left him until another opportunity.

Jesus was not Superman. Many today, including some devout Christians, see him as a kind of Christian version of the movie character, able to do whatever he wanted, to 'zap' reality into any shape he liked. In the movies, Superman looks like an ordinary human being, but really he isn't. Underneath the disguise he is all-powerful, a kind of computer-age super-magician. That's not the picture of Jesus we get in the New Testament.

Luke has just reminded us of Jesus' membership in the family of Adam. If there had been any doubt about his being really human, Luke underlines his sharing of our flesh and blood in this vivid scene of temptation. If Jesus is the descendant of Adam, he must now face not only what Adam faced but the powers that had been unleashed through human rebellion and sin. Long years of habitual rebellion against the creator God had brought about a situation in which the world, the flesh and the devil had become used to twisting human beings into whatever shape they wanted.

In particular, after his **baptism**, Jesus faced the double question: what does it mean to be God's son in this special, unique way? And what sort of messiahship was he to pursue? There had, after all, been many royal movements in his time, not only the well-known house of Herod but also other lesser-known figures whom we meet in the historian Josephus. Characters like Simon (not one of the Simons we know in the Bible) and Athronges gathered followers and were hailed as kings, only to be cut down by Roman or Herodian troops. There were would-be prophets who promised their followers signs from heaven, great miracles to show God's saving power. They too didn't last long. What was Jesus to do?

The three temptations can be read as possible answers to this question. The story does not envisage Jesus engaged in conversation with a visible figure to whom he could talk as one to another; the devil's voice appears as a string of natural ideas in his own head. They are plausible, attractive, and make, as we would say, a lot of sense. God can't want his beloved son to be famished with hunger, can he? If God wants Jesus to become sovereign over the world (that, after all, is what Gabriel had told Mary), then why not go for it in one easy stride? If Jesus is Israel's **Messiah**, why not prove it by spectacular displays of power?

If there are in this story echoes of Adam and Eve in the garden, with the serpent whispering plausible lies about God, his purposes and his commands, there are also echoes of Israel in the wilderness. Israel came out of Egypt through the Red Sea, with God declaring that Israel was his son, his firstborn. There then followed the 40-year wandering in the wilderness, where Israel grumbled for bread, flirted disastrously with idolatry, and put God continually to the test. Now Jesus, coming through the waters of baptism as God's unique son, the one through whom Israel's destiny was to be fulfilled, faces the question: how is he to be Israel's representative, her rightful king? How can he deliver Israel, and thereby the world, from the grip of the enemy? How can he bring about the real liberation, not just from Rome and other political foes, but from the arch-enemy, the devil himself?

The answer is that he must begin by defeating him at the most personal and intimate level. Christian leaders today sometimes make the mistake of thinking that as long as they are pursuing the right aims in their public life, what they do in private doesn't matter so much. That is a typical lie whispered by the same voice that Jesus heard in the desert. If God is working by his **spirit** through a person, that person's own life will be increasingly formed by that spirit, through testing at every level. If Jesus could not win the victory there, there was little point carrying on.

Jesus responds to the devil, not by attempting to argue (arguing with temptation is often a way of playing with the idea until it becomes too attractive to resist), but by quoting scripture. The passages he draws on come from the story of Israel in the wilderness: he is going to succeed where Israel failed. Physical needs and wants are important, but loyalty to God is more important still. Jesus is indeed to become the world's true lord, but the path to that status, and the mode of it when it arrives, is humble service, not a devilish seeking after status and power. Trust in God doesn't mean acting stupidly to force God into doing a spectacular rescue. The power that Jesus already has, which he will shortly display in healings in particular, is to be used for restoring others to **life** and strength, not for cheap stunts. His status as God's son commits him, not to showy prestige, but to the strange path of humility, service and finally death. The enemy will return to test this resolve again. For the moment, an initial victory is won, and Jesus can begin his public career knowing that though struggles lie ahead the foe has been beaten on the first field that really matters.

We are unlikely to be tempted in exactly the same way as Jesus was, but every Christian will be tested at the points which matter most in her or his life and vocation. It is a central part of Christian vocation to learn to recognize the voices that whisper attractive lies, to distinguish them from the voice of God, and to use the simple but direct weapons provided in scripture to rebut the lies with truth.

The Christian discipline of fighting temptation is not about self-hatred, or rejecting parts of our God-given humanity. It is about celebrating God's gift of full humanity and, like someone learning a musical instrument, discovering how to tune it and play it to its best possibility. At the heart of our resistance to temptation is love and loyalty to the God who has already called us his beloved children in Christ, and who holds out before us the calling to follow him in the path which leads to the true glory. In that glory lies the true happiness, the true fulfilment, which neither world, nor flesh, nor devil can begin to imitate.

LUKE 4.14–30

Opposition to Jesus in Nazareth

[14]Jesus returned to Galilee in the power of the spirit. His reputation spread throughout the whole district. [15]He taught in their synagogues to universal acclaim.

[16]He came to Nazareth, where he had been brought up. On the sabbath, as was his regular practice, he went into the synagogue and stood up to read. [17]They gave him the scroll of the prophet Isaiah. He unrolled the scroll and found the place where it was written:

[18]'The spirit of the Lord is upon me
because he has anointed me
to tell the poor the good news.
He has sent me to announce release to the prisoners
and sight to the blind,
to set the wounded victims free,
[19]to announce the year of God's special favour.'

[20]He rolled up the scroll, gave it to the attendant, and sat down. All eyes in the synagogue were fixed on him.

[21]'Today,' he began, 'this scripture is fulfilled in your own hearing.'

[22]Everyone remarked at him; they were astonished at the words coming out of his mouth – words of sheer grace.

'Isn't this Joseph's son?' they said.

[23]'I know what you're going to say', Jesus said. 'You're going to tell me the old riddle: "Heal yourself, doctor!" "We heard of great happenings in Capernaum; do things like that here in your own country!"

[24]'Let me tell you the truth', he went on. 'Prophets never get accepted in their own country. [25]This is the solemn truth: there were plenty of widows in Israel in the time of Elijah, when heaven was shut up for three years and six months, and there was a great famine over all the land. [26]Elijah was sent to none of them, only to a widow in the Sidonian town of Zarephath.

[27]'And there were plenty of people with virulent skin diseases in Israel in the time of Elisha the prophet, and none of them was healed – only Naaman, the Syrian.'

[28]When they heard this, everyone in the synagogue flew into a rage. [29]They got up and threw him out of town. They took him to the top of the hill on which their town was built, meaning to fling him off. [30]But he slipped through the middle of them and went away.

The commentators were ecstatic after the game. 'He played like a man inspired', they said. What images does that conjure up for you?

A sports star, perhaps, running rings round the opposition and scoring a brilliant goal.

Or, from a different world, a musician: eyes closed, fingers flying to and fro on an instrument, filling the air with wonderful jazz.

'Inspiration': we use the word loosely. We imply that 'it just came over them', that they suddenly became someone different. Of course we know that it didn't happen like that. The brilliant athlete has been training and practising, hour after hour and week after week. The musician has been playing exercises, perfecting technique for long hours out of the public eye. Then, when the moment comes, a surge of adrenalin produces a performance which we call 'inspired' – but which is actually the fruit of long, patient hard work.

When Jesus said 'the **spirit** of the Lord is upon me', Luke has already let us into the secret. His years of silent preparation. His life of prayer leading up to his **baptism**. The confirmation of his vocation – and then its testing in the wilderness. Then, at last, going public with early deeds in Capernaum (as the exchange in the Nazareth synagogue makes clear, people had already heard of what he'd done elsewhere). Now, with years of prayer, thought and the study of scripture behind him, he stands before his own town. He knew everybody there and they knew him. He preached like a man inspired; indeed, in his sermon that's what he claimed. But what he said was the opposite of what they were expecting. If this was inspiration, they didn't want it.

What was so wrong with what he said? What made them kick him out of the synagogue, hustle him out of the town, and take him off to the cliff edge to throw him over? (Note the irony: the devil invited Jesus to throw himself down because God would protect him; Jesus, having refused, found himself in a similar predicament. Perhaps Luke is telling us that God did protect him, because it came about not through self-advertisement but through commitment to his true vocation.)

The crucial part comes in Jesus' comments to his hearers. He senses that they aren't following him; they are ready to taunt him with proverbs, to challenge him to do some mighty deeds for the sake of show. Perhaps they, too, appear in Jesus' mind like the devil, suggesting that Jesus should do magic tricks for the sake of it. 'Heal yourself, doctor!' – the challenge is not too far removed from the taunt, 'He saved others, but he can't save himself' (23.35). But why? What was so wrong with what he was saying?

By way of defence and explanation for the line he had been taking, Jesus points out what happened in the days of the great prophets Elijah and Elisha, and in doing so identifies himself with the prophets. Elijah was sent to help a widow – but not a Jewish one. Elisha healed one solitary **leper** – and the leper was the commander of the enemy army.

35

That's what did it. That's what drove them to fury. Israel's God was rescuing the wrong people.

The earlier part of Jesus' address must have been hammering home the same point. His hearers were, after all, waiting for God to liberate Israel from pagan enemies. In several Jewish texts of the time, we find a longing that God would condemn the wicked nations, would pour out wrath and destruction on them. Instead, Jesus is pointing out that when the great prophets were active, it wasn't Israel who benefited, but only the pagans. That's like someone in Britain or France during the Second World War speaking of God's healing and restoration for Adolf Hitler. It's not what people wanted to hear.

What, then, was the earlier part of his address about?

Luke says that the people 'were astonished at the words that were coming out of his mouth – words of sheer grace'. Sometimes people have understood this simply to mean, 'they were astonished at what a good speaker he was'. But it seems more likely that he means 'they were astonished that he was speaking about God's grace – grace for everybody, including the nations – instead of grace for Israel and fierce judgment for everyone else'. That fits perfectly with what followed.

Why then did Jesus begin his address with the long quotation from Isaiah (61.1–2)?

The passage he quotes is about the **Messiah**. Throughout Isaiah there are pictures of a strange 'anointed' figure who will perform the Lord's will. But, though this text goes on to speak of vengeance on evildoers, Jesus doesn't quote that bit. Instead, he seems to have drawn on the larger picture in Isaiah and elsewhere which speaks of Israel being called to be the light of the nations, a theme which Luke has already highlighted in chapter 2. The servant-Messiah has not come to inflict punishment on the nations, but to bring God's love and mercy to them. And that will be the fulfilment of a central theme in Israel's own scriptures.

This message was, and remains, shocking. Jesus' claim to be reaching out with healing to all people, though itself a vital Jewish idea, was not what most first-century Jews wanted or expected. As we shall see, Jesus coupled it with severe warnings to his own countrymen. Unless they could see that this was the time for their God to be gracious, unless they abandoned their futile dreams of a military victory over their national enemies, they would suffer defeat themselves at every level – military, political and theological.

Here, as at the climax of the gospel story, Jesus' challenge and warning brings about a violent reaction. The **gospel** still does this today, when it challenges all interests and agendas with the news of God's surprising grace.

LUKE 4.31–44

Jesus' Authoritative Healings

[31]Jesus went down to Capernaum, a town of Galilee. He used to teach them every sabbath. [32]They were astonished at his teaching, because his message was powerful and authoritative.

[33]There was a man in the synagogue who had the spirit of an unclean demon.

[34]'Hey, you!' he yelled out at the top of his voice. 'What's going on with you and me, Jesus of Nazareth? Have you come to destroy us? I know who you are – you're God's Holy One!'

[35]'Shut up!' Jesus rebuked him. 'Come out of him!'

The demon threw the man down right there in front of them, and came out without harming him. [36]Fear came over them all. 'What's all this?' they started to say to one another. 'He's got power! He's got authority! He tells the unclean spirits what to do, and they come out!' [37]Word about him went out to the whole surrounding region.

[38]He left the synagogue and went into Simon's house. Simon's mother-in-law was sick with a high fever, and they asked him about her. [39]He stood in front of her, rebuked the fever, and it left her. And straight away she got up and waited on them.

[40]When the sun went down, everyone who had sick people – all kinds of sicknesses – brought them to him. He laid his hands on each one in turn, and healed them. [41]Demons came out of many people, shouting out, 'You are the son of God!' He sternly forbade them to speak, because they knew he was the Messiah.

[42]When day dawned he left the town and went off to a deserted place. The crowds hunted for him, and when they caught up with him they begged him not to leave them.

[43]'I must tell the good news of God's kingdom to the other towns', he said. 'That's what I was sent for.' [44]And he was announcing the message to the synagogues of Judaea.

Last time I went to Capernaum you could hardly move because of the people. There were coaches full of pilgrims coming and going, parties of tourists with guides talking in several different languages, people taking photographs, people trying to give little lectures, people wanting to say a prayer, people squeezing through to get a better look at the old buildings – and the new ones, too, especially the church built where they think Peter's house may have been.

The reason there was such a crowd was that the Pope was in Galilee. He was making an official visit to the Holy Land, and Roman Catholic pilgrims from all over the world, many of whom were there for the first time, had come to be with him, particularly at a huge service up on the hill a little way north of the Sea of Galilee. Our own little party were not put out. As someone said, it made it a bit more like what happened once word got out that Jesus was in town.

But they didn't have to bring pilgrims in by public transport, even if such a thing had existed in those days. People came in a hurry, because Jesus began doing remarkable healings. The little town of Capernaum, a fishing village on the north shore of the Sea of Galilee, had never seen anything like it. Jesus had evidently decided to make it his base of operations, after he'd left Nazareth. It was where the two pairs of brothers, Peter and Andrew, and James and John, had their homes and their small fishing businesses.

You can still walk into the ruined synagogue there, where some of Jesus' first remarkable healings took place. The buildings you can see date from some while after Jesus' time, but it's the correct site and you can get a sense of it all: a small town, gathering in its main public meeting place. (Synagogues were used for public gatherings as well as what we think of as 'worship'; indeed, for a loyal Jew worship and community were and are so intertwined that it's hard to imagine the one without the other.) That's where we find Jesus' first encounter with a shrieking, yelling, demon-possessed man.

Many people in the modern world don't believe in **demons**. They are inclined to say that this sort of thing was simply a medical condition that people hadn't diagnosed in Jesus' day. Many others, however, in several parts of today's world know only too well that strange forces seem able to invade a personality, so that the person talks with a strange voice and has a peculiar, one might say haunted, look in the eye. It's more than just an illness of the mind, though some of the signs are similar. And sometimes people in that condition do seem to know things that nobody else does.

Whatever we say about such a condition, there is no historical doubt that Jesus dramatically healed a good many people who were regarded as 'possessed'. Such cures were not unusual. Elsewhere in the **gospels**, and in Acts, we find mention of exorcists working from within Judaism. But the strange thing about Jesus, here and elsewhere, is that he did what he did by simple commands. No magic formulae; no (what we would call) mumbo-jumbo. He just told the spirits to go, and they went. That was what astonished people. He didn't have to summon up stronger powers than his own; he just used the authority he already possessed in himself. And, as this passage makes clear, he did the same with 'ordinary' diseases as well, like the raging fever of Simon's mother-in-law.

Once again Luke wants us to recognize what all this is saying about Jesus. Those with special insight can see behind his work and teaching, where he appeared to most people as a prophet. He was 'the **son of God**', here in the sense of 'the **Messiah**'. He was God's anointed.

The Lord's **spirit** was indeed resting on him, as he said at Nazareth, to release the oppressed, to give sight to the blind, to unloose the chains of the prisoners.

Though Capernaum was his base of operations, he spent most of his time on the move. This may have been partly for the sake of the village itself; it couldn't have sustained having more and more people come there for healing. Some have suggested that Jesus didn't want to risk people setting up a kind of local industry around him. But the main reason is that he had to go to where other people were. He had to tell people that God was becoming king in a new way, that God's long-awaited salvation was breaking into the world, even though it didn't look like they had expected it would. And in doing this he had to stay one jump ahead of the authorities. It isn't too long before we find opposition following him. Crowds and healings, powerful teaching about God's **kingdom**: many found it threatening then, and many find it threatening still.

LUKE 5.1–11

The Miraculous Catch of Fish

[1]One day, as the crowds were pressing close to him to hear the word of God, Jesus was standing by the lake of Gennesaret. [2]He saw two boats moored by the land; the fishermen had gone ashore and were washing their nets. [3]He got into one of the boats – it was Simon's – and asked him to put out a little way from the land. Then he sat down in the boat and began to teach the crowd.

[4]When he had finished speaking, he said to Simon, 'Put out into the deeper part, and let down your nets for a catch.'

[5]'Master,' replied Simon, 'we were working hard all night and caught nothing at all. But if you say so, I'll let down the nets.'

[6]When they did so, they caught such a huge number of fish that their nets began to break. [7]They signalled to their partners in the other boat to come and help them. So they came, and filled both the boats, and they began to sink.

[8]When Simon Peter saw it, he fell down at Jesus' knees.

'Leave me alone, Lord!' he said. 'I'm a sinner!' [9]He and all his companions were gripped with amazement at the catch of fish they had taken. [10]This included James and John, the sons of Zebedee, who were partners with Simon.

'Don't be afraid', said Jesus to Simon. 'From now on you'll be catching people.'

[11]They brought the boats in to land. Then they abandoned everything and followed him.

'When Christ calls a person,' declared Dietrich Bonhoeffer, 'he tells them to come and die.' Bonhoeffer, of course, did exactly that, hanged by the Nazis for resistance to Hitler. But when Simon Peter first met Jesus, he didn't realize this. If he could have seen a movie of what would happen to him in the next year or two, he might well have repeated his plea that Jesus leave him in peace. But that's not how Jesus worked; it's not how God works. Peter clearly had a sense that life was never going to be the same again, that he was going to face new demands and challenges; but he couldn't help being swept off his feet by what had happened.

It had started as a neat bit of resourcefulness on Jesus' part. It seems that he'd begun to teach a group by the shore, but the crowd got bigger and bigger and there simply wasn't room. So he improvised. Along the lakeshore close to Capernaum there is a sequence of steep inlets, a zigzagging shoreline with each inlet forming a natural amphitheatre. To this day, if you get in a boat and push out a little from the shore, you can talk in quite a natural voice, and anyone on the slopes of the inlet can hear you clearly – more clearly, in fact, than if you were right there on the shore with them. Jesus was simply exploiting the geography of the area and the ready availability of a boat.

Having commandeered the boat, with the fishermen listening to his every word, he puts them on the spot. Last time I tried to fish in that part of the world it was broad daylight and we caught nothing at all, though the previous night the fishermen had taken plenty. The fish are more likely to be caught after dark. On this occasion the men had worked all night for nothing; the last thing they would normally do would be to start again by daylight. But Jesus told them to, so they did. He made that sort of impression on people, even hard-working, no-nonsense fishermen.

The rest, as they say, is history. A huge catch. Quick messages for help to the other boat. A struggle to get boats and fish back to land before they all went under with the weight. And then the moment of truth. Peter finds himself right out of his league. Jesus promises that the same sort of thing will happen, only now it will be people, not fish. And the fishermen become followers, going off into a new life with only the sketchiest idea of where it will take them.

This is the kind of story it helps to get inside. Become Peter for a few moments; pause and ponder what you normally do, day after day, and then imagine Jesus suddenly appearing, asking for your help with his own work, and then telling you to do something in your own line of work which seems pointless, a waste of time and effort. You do it, grumbling perhaps under your breath; and suddenly everything clicks into place, everything succeeds on a scale you'd never dreamed of. What's going on? How did it happen? Feel the sense of awe, terror even, as you come to terms with the power of Jesus. Then feel that sense of terror increase as he turns to you with what looks like a question in his eyes, though it proves to be a command. 'You and I are going to be working together from now on', he says. And you realize you have no choice. If this man isn't worth following, nobody is.

Or maybe you're not at that stage yet. Maybe you're somewhere back in the crowd by the shore. You've heard something of what Jesus has been saying. You know those fishermen – everybody knows them, they're the hard-working fellows you see coming back from a night's work just when you're getting up. Big, strong men, hands like shovels. From the shore you watch as Jesus talks to them. You see them shrug their shoulders, put out a little, and let down the nets. You hear the shouting, you see the flurry of activity. Then you see big Peter kneeling down in front of Jesus. And then they all go off together. What goes through your mind?

Many people – perhaps many who read this – are in that position in relation to God's **kingdom** today. They have heard enough to know that something's going on. They see other people suddenly changed, their lives turned around. Maybe they're a bit jealous, but also perhaps relieved that the spotlight hasn't been turned on them. But the spotlight, though it does show things up (Peter's instant reaction was to see himself in the light of God's holiness, and to draw the necessary conclusions), shines in order to show the way to life.

Jesus doesn't want to leave anybody out. His call to Peter and the others – that they should now help him in catching people – came precisely in order that the **good news** would go out wider and wider, reaching as many as possible. Ultimately, there are no bystanders in the kingdom of God. We are reading Luke's **gospel** today because Jesus kept his promise to Peter, despite Peter's initial reluctance and subsequent failures. When Jesus calls, he certainly does demand everything, but only because he has already given everything himself, and has plans in store, for us and the world, that we would never have dreamed of.

LUKE 5.12–16

The Healing of the Leper

¹²It so happened that, as Jesus was in one particular town, there was a man whose skin was covered all over with a virulent disease. When he saw Jesus, he fell on his face.

'Lord,' he begged, 'if you want, you can make me clean.'

¹³Jesus stretched out his hand and touched him.

'I do want to', he said. 'Be clean.'

And the skin disease disappeared immediately. [14]Jesus instructed the man not to tell anyone. 'Go and show yourself to the priest', he said, 'and make the offering commanded by Moses in connection with your healing, as evidence for them.'

[15]The news about Jesus, though, spread all round, and large crowds came to hear and to be healed from their diseases. [16]He used to slip away to remote places and pray.

Imagine a man in prison for serious fraud. When he has served his sentence, and re-emerged into the community, what will happen if he goes to his old employer and asks for his job back? What will happen, indeed, if he goes to *any* employer and asks for a job at all, especially one which involves looking after money? Will anyone believe him if he says he's learnt his lesson?

Now imagine someone in the first century who has a powerful and highly infectious disease. Everybody knows that his body is full of it. For years he has had to live away from the town. His family leave food out for him but stay well clear when he comes to collect it. Then one day he shows up in the middle of town, and claims that he's met a wandering preacher who has cured him. Will anyone believe him?

When Jesus healed people, it was often not simply a matter of that person's bodily health. Often the diseases from which people suffered, in a world long before modern medicine, were subject to quite strict regulations. The ancient Jewish purity laws weren't peculiar taboos thought up by legalistically minded law-makers; they were the equivalent of what today we think of as normal hygienic practice, such as our regular washing of hands after using the toilet and before handling food. The regulations that isolated those with serious skin diseases were not idle prohibitions. They were necessary to prevent the spread of disease. Most of the regulations about 'clean' and 'unclean' originate with this motive.

This explains why Jesus, on this occasion and the similar one in 17.12–19, told the sufferer(s) to go and show themselves to the **priests**. Local priests in all the towns and villages acted as teachers and administrators of the law. If someone wanted a clean bill of health, there was a standard procedure laid down in the law (set out in Leviticus 13), and it was the priest's job to examine the person and declare them clean or unclean. Jesus intends to cure the man; but he also intends, of course, that he will be able to rejoin his family, his village and his community as a full and accepted member. He must therefore go to the priest; and, when opportunity occurs (that is, the next time he goes to Jerusalem on pilgrimage), he must make the offering laid down in the law to show his gratitude to God in the appropriate way.

42

But the heart of the story doesn't lie in the command to go to the priest, but in Jesus' simple but profound action. He stretched out his hand and touched the man. We know today, from studies of psychology, what powerful and long-lasting effects result from appropriate human contact. Parents and children, brothers and sisters, lovers and spouses, friends and neighbours – all in their different ways will touch each other, in a hug, a handshake, an embrace, a kiss, a light touch on the arm. A good deal of human communication takes place, not in words, but in gestures like that. To be cut off from all such contact is therefore almost as serious as losing one's sight or hearing. So much sheer love is conveyed by touch.

Nobody had touched this man, we may suppose, for years. His body was now riddled with the disease; it had clearly been, quite literally, eating away at him for a long time. And now Jesus reached out and touched him. We can only imagine the sense of awe and joy that this brought to the **leper**.

In theory, this action should have made Jesus both ceremonially unclean and liable to contract the actual disease. But, as with so many of his healings, it worked the other way round. His cleanness, his healing power, 'infected' the man, just as the love and grace of his touch must have gone through his whole personality like a hot drink on a cold day.

Luke concludes the story by, once more, drawing our attention to Jesus' source of strength. He used to slip away from the crowds to somewhere where he could be alone, and pray. If we even begin to do the same, we may discover that we are enabled, and challenged, to find ways of bringing the same love-in-action to those who need it. Circumstances change, but there are plenty of people in today's world who need the touch of Jesus, literally and metaphorically, and are waiting for us to provide it.

LUKE 5.17–26

The Healing of the Paralytic Lowered through the Roof

[17]One day, as Jesus was teaching, there were Pharisees and legal experts sitting there who had come from every village of Galilee, and from Judaea and Jerusalem. The power of the Lord was with Jesus, enabling him to heal. [18]Just then some men appeared, carrying a paralysed man on a mattress; they were trying to bring him in and lay him before Jesus. [19]The crowd made it impossible for them to get through, so they went up on the roof and let him down through the tiles, mattress and all, so that he landed right in the middle, in front of Jesus.
[20]Jesus saw what trust they had.
'My friend,' he said, 'your sins are forgiven.'

43

²¹The legal experts and Pharisees began to argue. 'Who does he think he is?' they said. 'He's blaspheming! Nobody can forgive sins – only God can do that!'

²²Jesus knew their line of thought.

'Why are you complaining in your hearts?' he replied. ²³'Which is easier, to say, "Your sins are forgiven", or to say, "Get up and walk"? ²⁴But if you want to be convinced that the son of man has authority on earth to forgive sins –' (here he turned to the paralysed man) '– I say to you, get up, pick up your mattress, and go home.'

²⁵At once he got up in front of them all, picked up what he'd been lying on, and went off home, praising God.

²⁶A sense of awe came over everyone. They praised God, and were filled with fear. 'We've seen extraordinary things today', they said.

The day I am writing this, protesters are gathering in trucks and vans, getting ready to drive slowly down the long main road to the capital. Their aim is to cause as much disruption as possible to normal traffic, so that the whole country will be reminded of the cause they represent – a protest against the very high tax on fuel, which, they say, has made it difficult for many companies to stay in business.

Modern democracies tolerate pressure groups like this, provided they don't overstep the mark. They are a way of making feelings known. Though governments don't by any means always do what they want, they are wise to take note of strongly and widely held opinions. If enough people want something badly enough, governments have to take notice, even though the protesters are entirely unofficial, responsible to nobody but themselves. They may claim, of course, to have the best interests of the country at heart, but since nobody has elected them this can't be proved.

The **Pharisees** were a pressure group, not an official body. This is the first time Luke has introduced us to them, and here they are in force, from all over the small country. This may seem a bit excessive; why should they gather like this to check out a young prophet who is doing and saying strange things? The answer is that their particular cause – for which they were from time to time prepared to take drastic action – was the coming **kingdom of God**; and if someone else appeared on the scene who seemed to be talking about the same thing *but getting it all wrong*, they wanted to know about it. It is as though the protesters, driving slowly southwards through England, were suddenly to meet another group, driving slowly northwards, and blocking *their* path.

The Pharisees' kingdom-plan, in line with plenty of earlier Jewish aims and ideals, was to intensify observance of the Jewish law, the **Torah**. That, they believed, would create the conditions for God to act, as he had promised, to judge the pagans who were oppressing Israel and to liberate his people. In addition, some of the more militant believed that it was their God-given duty to take the law into their own hands, and to use violence to kick-start the process of revolution. Jesus' kingdom-vision was very different – almost diametrically opposite, in fact. Since he was drawing crowds and becoming well known, they needed to find out what was going on.

Luke emphasizes that Jesus was powerful, and that it was God's power at work in him. This, of course, was why people came in such numbers that when the unwieldy little procession of people arrived at the door, carrying a paralysed friend on a makeshift stretcher or mattress, they couldn't get in. Jesus saw their resourcefulness, in opening up the roof tiles and letting him down, as a sign that they really believed God was at work and that all this effort would be worthwhile. Again and again Jesus makes a connection between **faith** and the power of God.

In fact, when people don't believe, they can look even at the evidence of their senses, as the Pharisees did that day, and still grumble that something must be wrong. 'Your sins are forgiven'; that did it. Only God can forgive sins, and the normal way he did it, within their system, was through the **Temple** and all that went on there – the sacrificial system, the rituals of cleansing, the great festivals, not least the Day of Atonement. If anyone could speak for God, declaring to the people that God had forgiven their sins, it would be the **priests**, particularly the **high priest**, once sacrificial atonement had been made.

Jesus is slicing through all of that, and declaring on his own authority that this particular man is now right with God – all because of his friends' faith. It isn't so much that Jesus is 'claiming to be God' (though Luke will soon make it clear that when people met Jesus they were indeed meeting God); he is claiming to *speak for* God, in a way which undercuts the normal channels of authority. From the Pharisees' point of view, this is worse than they had feared.

But still worse is to come. Jesus explains what he is doing by the mysterious phrase 'the **son of man**'. In Daniel 7 'one like a son of man' is brought before God, after a time of great persecution, and is given authority over the world. The phrase could simply mean 'a human being'; but the way Daniel 7 was read by many Jews in Jesus' day gave the figure a much more specific meaning. This would be the **Messiah**, the one through whom God would set up his kingdom at last after Israel's long suffering.

Perhaps not all of Jesus' hearers would have understood this, but many would see that he was making a huge claim to authority. His actions and words were God's real kingdom-work, and God would vindicate him, despite the persecutions that he would suffer. At a stroke,

Jesus has summoned up a lively element from contemporary Jewish thought and hope, and has pressed it into service in his own case. The healing of the paralysed man functions, as he intended it to, as a sign that this authority was real. It worked.

No wonder the crowds were amazed. The combination of healing, authority claims, and the sharp dispute with the leading pressure group of the time, was beyond anything they'd known before. The word for 'extraordinary things' in the last line is *paradoxa*, 'paradoxes', things you wouldn't normally expect. There were plenty more to come. As with the 'son of man' scene in Daniel, Jesus' whole public career consisted in standing things the other way up from how people had expected. When people come to him today with even a grain of faith, the unexpected still can and does occur.

LUKE 5.27–39

Questions about Table-Company and Fasting

[27]After this Jesus went out and saw a tax-collector called Levi, sitting at the tax-office. 'Follow me', he said. [28]And he left everything, got up, and followed him.

[29]Levi made a great feast for him in his house, and a large crowd of tax-collectors and others were there reclining at table. [30]The Pharisees and the legal experts began to grumble to Jesus' disciples.

'Why do you lot eat and drink', they asked, 'with tax-collectors and sinners?'

[31]'Healthy people don't need a doctor', replied Jesus. 'It's sick people who do! [32]I haven't come to call the righteous; I'm calling sinners to repentance.'

[33]'John's disciples often fast, and say prayers', they said to him, 'and so do the Pharisees' followers – but your disciples eat and drink.'

[34]'Can you make the wedding guests fast', replied Jesus, 'while the bridegroom is with them? [35]But the time will come when the bridegroom is taken away from them. That's when they will fast.'

[36]He added this parable. 'Nobody tears a piece of cloth from a new coat to make a patch on an old one. If they do, they tear the new, and the patch from it won't fit the old one anyway. [37]And nobody puts new wine into old wineskins. If they do, the new wine will burst the skins: it will go to waste, and the skins will be ruined too. [38]You have to put new wine in new skins. [39]And nobody who drinks old wine wants new. "I prefer the old", they say.'

Technology advances so fast that most of us can't keep up. If you buy a computer today, by tomorrow it will be getting out of date. Within a year or two you won't be able to get spare parts for it. Teams of engineers are working hard all the time to make electronic equipment that can perform more tasks at higher speed. What looks brand new this year, and surprises you with what it can do, will look old and slow next year.

This is particularly frustrating if, like me, you don't move that fast, and end up with software that used to work perfectly happily on your old machine but can't be transferred to the new one. The new machine sends you messages saying it doesn't recognize what you're putting into it. Suddenly the old material you felt comfortable with simply doesn't fit.

That is one modern illustration of what Jesus is saying by way of reply to his critics. There is, though, one obvious drawback with this particular example. When you're buying computers (or farm equipment, or medication, or whatever it is) you know that the process of research and development is going on and on. Everything that is new will soon be old. But in the world of Jesus and his followers, the expectation and hope was that God's new age would come in once for all, and never again be outdated. The old would pass away, the new would come, and that would be that. It would be a one-off transition, not to be repeated.

With that warning, the illustration applies very well. What Jesus is doing is putting into effect the new world that God is bringing about – and the old ways just don't fit. They are obsolete, not because they were bad in themselves but because God's new age has new power, new possibilities and new hope that simply weren't there before. Novelty is deeply threatening, especially when people have built their lives around the old way. Think how people felt when their business of making and mending horse-drawn stagecoaches was quite suddenly undermined by the arrival, first of steam trains, and then of motor cars. Or how the whole shipbuilding industry shuddered when aeroplanes became the normal method of intercontinental travel. That's the sort of change Jesus claims to be introducing.

It all starts, as often in Luke (and with Jesus, if it comes to that) with a very human situation. Tax-collectors are never popular, but in Jesus' day it was worse. They were extortionists. And, more than that: they were working for the Romans, or for Herod, and their necessary contact with **Gentiles** put them under political suspicion (collaborating with the enemy) and ritual exclusion (they might well be unclean). It's significant that when Levi throws a party, most of the others present are, like him, tax-collectors. They had to befriend each other, since most ordinary folk wouldn't have anything to do with them.

Jesus broke into that world, as he broke into the leper's sealed-off universe with a single touch, summoning Levi to leave his work and follow him. And he explains what he's doing, to the predictable grumblers, with what we today would call a mission statement: he is like a doctor who can't do his work unless he associates with the sick. His job is to call sinners to repentance. No longer are people to be placed in two categories, with no movement possible between them (except, of course, when a 'righteous' person commits sin). The new age is breaking in, and this new age is the time of forgiveness. That's what God had always promised. This is the new **covenant** spoken of by the prophets; forgiveness is here, walking down the street, and when people repent it is theirs. Never mind if it upsets the tidy classifications of the old system. This is a party – the first of many in Luke's **gospel** – and like all Jesus' parties it is a sign of the new age. It is, for those with eyes to see, a miniature **messianic** banquet.

Luke, following Mark at this point, attaches to this story a string of short sayings about just how new this kingdom-message is. For a start, it rules out fasting. Fasting in Judaism, and in the various sects and groups of Jesus' day, was a sign of waiting, of bewailing the present time when God's **kingdom** still had not arrived. It was a way of looking back to the disasters that had befallen Israel, and humbling oneself in repentance to pray for God's mercy. But what if God's mercy was now alive and active, healing, celebrating, creating a new world and inviting you to enjoy it? Once again, the party theme: this is like a wedding feast (a regular Jewish image for God's coming new age), and the last thing you do at a wedding is abstain from food or drink. It's a celebration of life itself. Yes, there is a dark note to this as well: one day the bridegroom will be taken away, and then it will be time to fast once more. But it won't be for long. Luke's gospel ends with two Easter meals, one in Emmaus and one in the upper room. The bridegroom returns, and his risen life means that God's new age has been well and truly launched.

Luke's version of the sayings is slightly different from Mark's. In Mark's, the point about the new cloth is that it's unshrunk, so when it shrinks it will ruin the patching job. In Luke's version, the point is that by cutting out a new piece of cloth you will both ruin the new coat and not help the old one. There's no use, in other words, trying to see if you can fit some bits of Jesus' kingdom-programme into the programmes of John's disciples and the **Pharisees**. Take one element of Jesus' work, and you miss the whole; and you can't, in any case, fit that one element into the old ways of thinking. You have to take the new thing whole or not at all.

So too with the wine and the skins. Try to fit Jesus' new work into the thought-forms and behaviour patterns of John's movement, or the Pharisees' movement, and all you'll get is an explosion (it had already started to happen). But – the last line is unique to Luke, and it's a solemn warning – don't expect the people who have given their lives to the old movements to be happy about switching allegiance. They are likely to stay with what they know. They have got used to the old wine and are frightened they won't like the new.

That's a perennial problem faced by all reformers, but of course this passage isn't about any and every innovation and reformation that people may dream up. People sometimes use this passage to justify every bright idea and to mock every tradition, but that's not the idea. Jesus is doing a new thing; this new thing still forms the basis of Christianity today. The real challenge of this passage is to see where in the world – and, of course, in the church too – people are living today as though the old age was still the norm, as though the new life of the gospel had never burst in upon us. The task then is to live out the new life, the new energy, which was at the heart of Jesus' teaching and work.

LUKE 6.1–11

Teachings on the Sabbath

¹One sabbath, Jesus was walking through some cornfields. His disciples were plucking and eating ears of grain, rubbing them with their hands.

²'Why', asked some Pharisees, 'are you doing something that isn't permitted on the sabbath?'

³'Haven't you read what David did?' replied Jesus. 'When he and his men were hungry, ⁴he went into God's house and took the "bread of the Presence", which no one but the priests was allowed to eat. He ate some, and gave it to his companions.

⁵'The son of man', he declared, 'is Lord of the sabbath.'

⁶On another sabbath he went into the synagogue and was teaching. A man was there whose right hand was withered. ⁷The scribes and Pharisees were watching him, to see if he would heal him on the sabbath, so that they could find an accusation against him.

⁸He knew what they were thinking.

'Get up', he said to the man with the withered hand, 'and come out here in the middle.' He got up and came out.

⁹'Let me ask you something', Jesus said to them. 'Is it lawful to do good on the sabbath or to do evil? To save life or to destroy it?'

¹⁰He looked round at all of them.

'Stretch out your hand', he said to the man.

He did so; and his hand was restored. ¹¹But they were filled with rage, and discussed with each other what they might do to Jesus.

A relative of mine likes to tell of an occasion when he flew, with some business friends, to Ireland to watch a rugby match. When they got off the plane, there were no customs officers waiting to receive them.

So two or three of them went into the official booths, put on the caps they found there, and inspected the passports of the other people who were arriving. They had no official authority, but it seemed to work. I have often wondered, hearing that story, what happened when the real customs officers arrived; but at that point history, as so often, remains silent.

That must have been how Jesus appeared to many onlookers. He held no public office. He wasn't a priest (**priests** had the job of teaching people the **law**). He wasn't part of any well-known pressure group, such as the **Pharisees**, who had their own opinions on how the law should be kept, which they tried to insist on for society as a whole. He hadn't had any formal training as a teacher.

And yet there he was, so to speak, in the airport arrivals zone telling people what to do, giving some people permission to do things they were not normally supposed to. Who did he think he was? That is, in fact, the main question Luke wants us to ask. Luke is not so interested in asking, 'Do we or don't we keep the **sabbath**?' but rather, 'Who did Jesus think he was?'

The first little incident seems complicated until we see to the heart of it. Jesus' point is that he and his men are in the same position as David and his men had been. They were an exception to the normal rule, and so is he. Normally only priests in the sanctuary ate the 'bread of the Presence' (the bread which was set aside to symbolize God's presence in fellowship with his people); but David claimed the right to do so. Why? Presumably because he was the rightful king of Israel. Samuel had anointed him when he was only a lad, and had proclaimed him king; but Saul was still on the throne. At the time of the story, David was leading a ragtag group of followers, keeping away from Saul, waiting for the time when his kingship would come true.

This speaks volumes about Jesus. He, too, as Luke has been at pains to tell us, has been anointed as Israel's king. He, too, is waiting for the time when this kingship will come true. He, too, is on the move with his odd little group of followers. And now – picking up a biblical image which some of his hearers might have understood, though many probably didn't – he was the sovereign '**son of man**', the one whom Israel's God would prove in due course to be the rightful king, on the day when opponents would be silenced and everything would be put to rights.

What mattered, then, wasn't so much that Jesus' followers were breaking the sabbath. They were and they weren't; it depends which regulations people chose to appeal to, and opinions differed on what precisely you could and couldn't do on the sabbath. What mattered is that Jesus was the coming King, who had the right to suspend even

50

the sacred sabbath law when necessary. And he seems to have thought that it was necessary; God's new world was breaking in, and the rules appropriate for the old one had to be rethought.

For many Christians in today's world, keeping the sabbath has become a quaint memory. Several do still observe it; but for many in the Western world it is remembered as something we used to do a long time ago but don't think much about today. For Jesus' contemporaries, though, it was one of the chief badges of their identity in a hostile world, a sign to them and their neighbours that they were God's special people. It's easy for modern Western Christians to mock the Jews of Jesus' day for fussing about something that doesn't concern us. There are many things in our world, our society, which have become just as central for us – and perhaps just as much under God's judgment – as sabbath-keeping was for them.

The other story–the healing of the man with the withered hand – rams the point home. What counts is that God, the creator, is honoured in what is done. Is this action, Jesus asks, going to save **life** or to destroy it? On this occasion Jesus didn't do anything that either official Jewish **law** or the unofficial codes of the Pharisees would have deemed illegal. He didn't even touch the man. Telling him to stretch out his hand could hardly be counted as 'work', and hence be forbidden. But it was enough that Jesus was doing things which indicated that he regarded himself as being able to act with sovereign freedom in respect of the ancestral laws and traditions. Luke is preparing us for what is to come next: the way in which Jesus began to shape the growing community of his followers, to turn them into God's new Israel, the people who would live in God's new age. This people, defined by their loyalty to Jesus as the true King, the true 'son of man', would already celebrate the new 'week' that was dawning. They would no longer be bound by the sabbath law, part of the old creation that was drawing towards a close.

LUKE 6.12-26

The Beatitudes

¹²It happened around that time that Jesus went up into the mountain to pray, and he spent all night in prayer to God. ¹³When day came, he called his disciples, and chose twelve of them, calling them 'apostles': ¹⁴Simon, whom he called Peter, and Andrew his brother, and James and John, and Philip, Bartholomew, ¹⁵Matthew, Thomas, James son of Alphaeus, Simon who was called 'the hothead', ¹⁶Judas son of James, and Judas Iscariot, who turned traitor.

¹⁷He went down with them, and took up a position on a level plain where there was a large crowd of his followers, with a huge company

of people from all Judaea, from Jerusalem, and from the coastal region of Tyre and Sidon. [18]They came to hear him, and to be cured from their diseases. Those who were troubled by unclean spirits were healed, [19]and the whole crowd tried to touch him, because power was going out from him and healing everybody.

[20]He lifted up his eyes and looked at his disciples, and said:

'Blessings on the poor: God's kingdom belongs to you!

[21]'Blessings on those who are hungry today: you'll have a feast!

'Blessings on those who weep today: you'll be laughing!

[22]'Blessings on you, when people hate you, and shut you out, when they slander you and reject your name as if it was evil, because of the son of man. [23]Celebrate on that day! Jump for joy! Don't you see: in heaven there is a great reward for you! That's what your ancestors did to the prophets.

[24]'But woe betide you rich: you've had your comfort!

[25]'Woe betide you if you're full today: you'll go hungry!

[26]'Woe betide you if you're laughing today: you'll be mourning and weeping!

[27]'Woe betide you when everyone speaks well of you: that's what their ancestors did to the false prophets.'

Let us imagine that you are a schoolteacher. One day, you go out into the school playground, where there are dozens of children kicking footballs around. You go over to where they are, and call for them to gather round. Then you begin, slowly but surely, to select eleven of them. You don't need to say a word. Choose your eleven and lead them off somewhere else. Everyone will know what you're doing. You're picking a football team.

Then supposing you and your team begin to work together, to train for the serious games ahead. What are you going to do? You assume they know something of football, something of the rules. But you want to tell them that some things are quite different now. The game has changed. Things you do in the playground aren't the same as things you do in a real match.

But it's no good lecturing them for hours about how to play. What they need is three or four things to remember to do, and three or four things to remember *not* to do. Then, in the heat of the moment, these basic guidelines will come back to them, or so you hope, and keep them focused on how best to play the game.

Now think what Jesus was doing. They didn't have football teams in his day, and in any case what he was doing was far more serious than that. What they did have was a long memory of the time when God called the twelve tribes of Israel – descended from the twelve sons of Jacob – and made them his special people, so that through them he could fulfil his purposes for the whole world. Now Jesus has come, as it were, out onto the playground where all sorts of people are trying out ways of being God's people – some with new rules to obey, some with new schemes for violent revolution, some with support for Herod and his regime, some with proposals for withdrawing into the desert and praying in private, and no doubt others as well. From the people he has met, he chooses **twelve**. Even if he'd done that without a word, everyone could see what he was doing. He was picking an Israel team. They were to be the nucleus, the centre and starting point, for what God was now going to do. They were the core of God's renewed Israel.

He gave them clear orders as to how his vision of God's work would go forward. Four promises, and four warnings, presented in terms of Israel's great scriptural codes: in the book called Deuteronomy, there were long lists of 'blessings' for those who obeyed the law, and 'curses' for those who didn't. These formed part of the charter, the **covenant**, the binding agreement between God and Israel. Now, with the renewed Israel formed around him, Jesus gives them his own version of the same thing.

And a radical version it is. It's an upside-down code, or perhaps (Jesus might have said) a right-way-up code instead of the upside-down ones people had been following. God is doing something quite new: as Jesus had emphasized in the synagogue at Nazareth, in chapter 4, he is fulfilling his promises at last, and this will mean **good news** for all the people who haven't had any for a long time. The poor, the hungry, those who weep, those who are hated: blessings on them! Not that there's anything virtuous about being poor or hungry in itself. But when injustice is reigning, the world will have to be turned once more the right way up for God's justice and **kingdom** to come to birth. And that will provoke opposition from people who like things the way they are. Jesus' message of promise and warning, of blessing and curse, rang with echoes of the Hebrew prophets of old, and he knew that the reaction would be the same.

So if Jesus comes to our 'playgrounds' today, where we have fun with ideas and schemes, where we try out different ways of making sense of life, usually with only mixed success – what sort of a team is he going to choose? Who is he calling, and to what sort of a task? What are his promises and warnings for our world, for people who will hear his call and follow him? We must all answer for ourselves. But as Christians we believe that what Jesus began with the call of the Twelve and the sharp-edged teaching of blessings and curses remains in force today. This is the shape of the kingdom: the kingdom which still today turns the world upside down, or perhaps the right way up, as much as ever it did.

LUKE 6.27–38

Loving Your Enemies

[27]'But this is my word', Jesus continued, 'for those of you who are listening: love your enemies! Do good to people who hate you! [28]Bless people who curse you! Pray for people who treat you badly! [29]'If someone hits you on the cheek – offer him the other one! If someone takes away your coat – don't stop him taking your shirt! [30]Give to everyone who asks you, and don't ask for things back when people have taken them.

[31]'Whatever you want people to do to you, do that to them. [32]If you love those who love you, what credit is that to you? Think about it: even sinners love people who love them. [33]Or again, if you do good only to people who do good to you, what credit is that to you? Sinners do that too. [34]If you lend only to people you expect to get things back from, what credit is that to you? Even sinners lend to sinners to get paid back. [35]No: love your enemies, do good and lend without expecting any return. Your reward will be great! You will be children of the Highest! He is generous, you see, to the stingy and wicked. [36]You must be merciful, just as your father is merciful.

[37]'Don't judge, and you won't be judged. Don't condemn, and you won't be condemned. Forgive, and you'll be forgiven. [38]Give, and it will be given to you: a good helping, squashed down, shaken in, and overflowing – that's what will land in your lap. Yes: the ration you give to others is the ration you'll get back for yourself.'

One of the greatest Jewish scholars to write about Jesus in the modern age was David Flusser, who taught for many years at the Hebrew University in Jerusalem. But not everyone approved of his scholarship; one of his most brilliant students, visiting a university elsewhere, was once given a very low mark by the professor simply because of being associated with Flusser himself. Then, some time later, a student of that other professor came to study with Flusser. His work was not very good, but Flusser insisted on grading it with an 'A'. His teaching assistant protested: how could he do that, particularly after what the other professor had done? 'Give him an A', insisted Flusser. 'This I have learned from Jesus.'

The **kingdom** that Jesus preached and lived was all about a glorious, uproarious, absurd generosity. Think of the best thing you can do for the worst person, and go ahead and do it. Think of what you'd really like someone to do for you, and do it for them. Think of the people to whom you are tempted to be nasty, and lavish generosity on them instead. These instructions have a fresh, spring-like quality. They are all about new **life** bursting out energetically, like flowers growing through concrete and startling everyone with their colour and vigour.

But are they possible? Well, yes and no. Jesus' point was not to provide his followers with a new rulebook, a list of dos and don'ts that you could tick off one by one, and sit back satisfied at the end of a successful moral day. The point was to inculcate, and illustrate, an attitude of heart, a lightness of spirit in the face of all that the world can throw at you. And at the centre of it is the thing that motivates and gives colour to the whole: you are to be like this *because that's what God is like*. God is generous to all people, generous (in the eyes of the stingy) to a fault: he provides good things for all to enjoy, the undeserving as well as the deserving. He is astonishingly merciful (anyone who knows their own heart truly, and still goes on experiencing God's grace and love, will agree with this); how can we, his forgiven children, be any less? Only when people discover that this is the sort of God they are dealing with will they have any chance of making this way of life their own.

In fact, this list of instructions is all about which God you believe in – and about the way of life that follows as a result. We must admit with shame that large sections of Christianity down the years seem to have known little or nothing of the God Jesus was talking about. Much that has called itself by the name of Jesus seems to have believed instead in a gloomy God, a penny-pinching God, a God whose only concern is to make life difficult, and salvation nearly impossible. But, by the same token, this passage gives the lie to the old idea (which was around in Jesus' day as well as our own) that all religions are really the same, that all gods are really variations on the same theme. This God is different. If you lived in a society where everyone believed in this God, there wouldn't be any violence. There wouldn't be any revenge. There wouldn't be any divisions of class or caste. Property and possessions wouldn't be nearly as important as making sure your neighbour was all right. Imagine if even a few people around you took Jesus seriously and lived like that. Life would be exuberant, different, astonishing. People would stare.

And of course people did stare when Jesus did it himself. The reason why crowds gathered, as Luke told us earlier, was that power was flowing out of Jesus, and people were being healed. His whole life was one of exuberant generosity, giving all he'd got to give to everyone who needed it. He was speaking of what he knew: the extravagant love of his Father, and the call to live a lavish human life in response. And finally, when they struck him on the cheek and ripped the coat and shirt off his back, he went on loving and forgiving, as Luke will tell us later (23.34, 43). He didn't show love only to his friends, but to his enemies, weeping over the city that had rejected his plea for peace. He was the true embodiment of the God of whom he spoke.

There are two particularly astonishing things about these instructions. First, their simplicity: they are obvious, clear, direct and memorable. Second, their scarcity. How many people do you know who really live like this? How many communities do you know where these guidelines are rules of life? What's gone wrong? Has God changed? Or have we forgotten who he really is?

LUKE 6.39–49

Judging Others and True Obedience

³⁹Jesus told them this riddle. 'What do you get when one blind man guides another? Both of them falling in a ditch! ⁴⁰Students can't do better than the teacher; when the course is done, they'll all be just like the teacher.

⁴¹'Why look at the speck of dust in your brother's eye, when you haven't noticed the plank in your own eye? ⁴²How can you say to your brother, "Dear brother, let me take the speck out of your eye", when you can't see the plank in your own? You're a fraud! First take the plank out of your own eye, and then you'll see clearly to take the speck out of your brother's eye.

⁴³'You see, no good tree bears bad fruit; nor can a bad tree produce good fruit. ⁴⁴Every tree is known by its fruit. You don't pick figs from thorns; nor do you get grapes from a briar-bush. ⁴⁵The good person brings good things out of the good treasure of the heart; the evil person brings evil things out of evil. What comes out of the mouth is what's overflowing in the heart.

⁴⁶'Why do you call me, "Lord, Lord", and don't do what I say? ⁴⁷I'll show you what people are like when they come to me, and hear my words, and do them. ⁴⁸They are like a wise man building a house: he dug, he went down deep, and he laid a foundation on rock. When a flood came, the river burst its banks all over the house, but it couldn't shake it because it was well built. ⁴⁹But when people hear but don't obey – that's like a man who built a house on the ground, without a foundation. When the river burst over it, it fell down at once. The ruin of that house was devastating.'

One picture is worth a thousand words. Here, in quick succession, are four of Jesus' most vivid word-sketches. They are meant to be funny. Try reading them like that, and you'll see a dry, perhaps typically Jewish, humour coming through; the Bible is full of humour if we know how to recognize it. But what these little scenes have to say is deadly

56

serious. Jesus intended people to remember these lessons. They were going to need to.

Each is a warning about rival teachings, rival visions of the **kingdom**, about 'solutions' which leave the depths of the problem untouched. They applied to rival teachings in Jesus' day, but they apply just as well to some of today's theories about what human **life** should be like.

The sequence begins with the riddle about the blind leading the blind. Beware, Jesus is saying, of other teachings which look as though they're offering guidance but will in fact put you all in the ditch. The next saying seems to be a comment on this point: students can't advance beyond their teachers. There's no point studying with the **Pharisees**; all you'll be at the end of the day is another Pharisee. Jesus is challenging his hearers to break out of the moulds they are being offered, and to come to the startling new way he is pioneering.

The next riddle, about the speck of dust in the other person's eye and the plank in one's own (it is meant to sound ridiculous; Jesus was deliberately sketching a verbal cartoon, a caricature) is also a warning against a certain type of teaching. As with the blind in the previous saying, the question is: can you see clearly enough to lead, let alone criticize, someone else? What people criticize in others is frequently, though not always, what they are subconsciously aware of (or afraid of) in themselves. The speck and the plank are a classic case of what psychologists call 'projection'. The person knows there's something seriously wrong with his or her own eye, so tries to avoid the problem by telling someone else there's a tiny problem with theirs.

How did the rival teachers in Jesus' day fit this model? Perhaps because, with so many of their rules and regulations, they were trying to fine-tune obedience to the law down to the last possible detail, while missing the law's major point. They were trying to make Israel holier and holier as a way of separating their nation *from* other nations; but the point of the law and the prophets was to make Israel the light *to* the nations. They were hunting for specks in each other's eyes with magnifying glasses, but couldn't see that there was a plank – a single massive disobedience – in their own.

But of course Jesus' picture continues to be relevant to new situations long after his own day. There must be many churches where a huge fuss is made about small details, while the main point of the **gospel**, and of radical Christian witness in the world, is missed altogether. It has been claimed that the leaders of the Russian Orthodox Church in 1917 were having a long debate about vestments at the very moment when the Bolsheviks were launching their revolution. Whether that is true or not, the very thought of it serves as a dire warning to other churches at other times. There's nothing wrong with getting the details in place; the story ends with removing the speck, after all; but first you've got to deal with the plank.

The point of it all – the point of being a Jew, of God's call to Israel, of God's call to every individual – is in fact to produce truly human beings. That's the thrust of the riddle about trees and fruit. Moral reformation which leaves the heart untouched is about as useful as tying bunches of grapes on to a briar-bush. Jesus is inviting his hearers to a way of life which is so completely new that it will need a change of heart, a change deep down in the personality. There are many alternatives to Jesus' invitation on the market today, just as there were in his time, but they don't touch the real problem.

The sermon ends with a stern warning, expressed as another vivid story. Listening to true wisdom and not putting it into practice is like building without foundations. Sooner or later the floods will come, and then it will be apparent what sort of building you're living in. Jesus' contemporaries may have heard a hint here about the great building project of their day, the completion of Herod's rebuilding of the **Temple** in Jerusalem. Certainly Luke makes it clear later on that the Temple was under God's judgment because its rulers hadn't obeyed Jesus' call to a different way of obedience. But the message applies to all sorts of people and situations. One of the lasting achievements of Jesus was to tell such vivid and easily memorable stories that people of every age, and in every part of the world, can hear a word for themselves.

The question is, of course: are we today so keen on looking for specks in other people's eyes that we can't see the planks in our own? Do our plans and schemes look good on the outside but leave the heart untouched? Are we building without a foundation? As we ask those questions about ourselves, and watch out in case we are lured into those traps by others, we must maintain, as our basic rule of life, the generous, free-spirited approach of the previous parts of the sermon. Jesus' radical offer of new and abundant life is so all-embracing, and hence so all-demanding, that people try to find alternative ways. But they must be resisted, or the house will come down with a crash.

LUKE 7.1–10

The Healing of the Centurion's Servant

¹When Jesus had finished saying all these words in the hearing of the people, he went into Capernaum.

²There was a centurion who had a slave who was particularly precious to him. This slave was ill, at the point of death. ³The centurion heard about Jesus, and sent some Jewish elders to him, to ask him to

come and rescue his slave. ⁴They approached Jesus and begged him eagerly.

'He deserves a favour like this from you', they said. ⁵'He loves our people, and he himself built us our synagogue.'

⁶Jesus went with them.

When he was not far off from the house, the centurion sent friends to him with a further message.

'Master,' he said, 'don't trouble yourself. I don't deserve to have you come under my roof. ⁷That's why I didn't think myself worthy to come to you in person. But – just say the word, and my slave will be healed. ⁸You see, I'm used to living under authority, and I have soldiers reporting to me. I say to this one, "Go", and he goes; to another one, "Come", and he comes; and to my slave, "Do this", and he does it.'

⁹When Jesus heard this he was astonished.

'Let me tell you,' he said, turning to the crowd that was following him, 'I haven't found faith of this kind, even in Israel.'

¹⁰The people who had been sent to him went back to the house. There they found the slave in good health.

The soldier walks forward slowly into the jungle. His task is to protect villagers from terrorists; every step means danger. Suddenly a command reaches him on his radio. His senior officer has seen where the enemy are hiding. He must obey instantly, not only for his own sake but in order to get the job done. It isn't what he was expecting, but he has been trained to do what he's told without hesitation.

That kind of clear authority and automatic obedience is vital in certain dangerous jobs. Authority like this works almost like a machine: an order goes out from the top, and each rank underneath does what they are told, passing on the word to those below them.

Most of us don't live in very tight or clear authority structures. There are always people that we respect; in our places of work, there are people whose decisions we accept and go along with, and whose instructions we carry out. But we can then make the mistake of thinking that God's authority is somewhat less definite, more like the less direct models of authority we have known in other aspects of our own lives.

It's true, of course, that God's sovereignty over the world is exercised with such love and compassion that the image of a commanding officer organizing a battle or a route march is hardly the best picture to use. But if we see God's authority, at work in Jesus Christ, as any less absolute than that of a military officer, we are, according to the passage, not only mistaken but also lacking **faith** itself.

The heart of the story is not the healing of the slave; that's important, because without it the story wouldn't exist, but it's just the framework for what Luke wants to highlight. What matters is the centurion's faith. Here he was, a middle-ranking military officer, stationed in Capernaum. He would be receiving regular orders from a commander, probably in Caesarea, about fifty miles away. And he would have soldiers responsible to him for performing tasks locally, perhaps including peacekeeping.

Often soldiers in that position would despise the local people as an inferior race, but this man didn't. He had come to love and respect the Jewish people, and had even paid for the building of the local synagogue. Luke presents him to us, as he does with another centurion in Acts 10, as a humble **Gentile**, looking in at Israel and Israel's God from the outside, liking what he sees, and opening himself to learning new truth from this strange, ancient way of life. Matthew's version of the story (8.5–13) is shorter, and omits the elaborate detail with which Luke emphasizes his respect and humility, sending two groups of messengers to Jesus.

Jesus is astonished at the second message; and we are astonished at his astonishment! Normally in the **gospels** Jesus does and says things that surprise people; this is one of the few places where Jesus himself is surprised. And the reason is the sheer quality of the man's faith. This faith isn't an abstract belief about God, or the learning of dogmas. It is the simple, clear belief that when Jesus commands that something be done, it will be done. He regards Jesus like a military officer, with authority over sickness and health. If Jesus says that someone is to get well, they will. What could be simpler?

Where he got this faith, we don't know. If he had lived in Capernaum for a while, he had no doubt heard of Jesus and perhaps seen him perform remarkable cures already. He recognized that there was a power at work in Jesus that could carry all before it. Like yet another centurion, later on (23.47), he looked at Jesus and was prepared to risk more than Jesus' own fellow-Jews had done, and declare that God was at work in him.

The story thus opens up in a practical way some of what the sermon of the previous chapter had highlighted. There was no need for Jesus' fellow-Jews to protect themselves from a Gentile like this, by drawing tighter and tighter circles of holiness around themselves. For all his lack of appropriate religious background, he had grasped the very centre of the Jewish faith: that the one true God, the God of Israel, was the sovereign one, the Lord of **heaven** and earth. And he had grasped it in its shocking new form: *this one true God was personally present and active in Jesus of Nazareth*. Luke presents this Gentile as a model for all those who will come in by faith from outside God's ancient people, to share the blessings of healing and salvation.

Contrast the prayer of this centurion with the prayers we all too often pray ourselves. 'Lord,' we say (not out loud, of course, but this is what we often think), 'I might perhaps like you to do this . . . but I know you may not want to, or it might be too difficult, or perhaps impossible . . .' and we go on our way puzzled, not sure whether we've really asked for something or not. Of course, sometimes we ask for something and the answer is No. God reserves the right to give that answer. But this story shows that we should have no hesitation in asking. Is Jesus the Lord of the world, or isn't he?

LUKE 7.11–17

The Raising of the Widow's Son

¹¹Not long afterwards, Jesus went to a town called Nain. His disciples went with him, and so did a large crowd. ¹²As he got near to the gate of the city, a young man was being carried out dead. He was the only son of his mother, and she was a widow. There was a substantial crowd of the townspeople with her.

¹³When the master saw her, he was very sorry for her. 'Don't cry', he said to her. ¹⁴Then he went up and touched the bier, and the people carrying it stood still.

'Young fellow', he said, 'I'm telling you – get up!' ¹⁵The dead man sat up and began to speak, and he gave him to his mother.

¹⁶Terror came over all of them. They praised God.

'A great prophet has risen among us!' they said. 'God has visited his people!'

¹⁷This report went out about him in the whole of Judaea and the surrounding countryside.

So where was the **faith** this time? The centurion's servant was healed because of his owner's faith, but in this story the only person who has any faith that the dead man can be raised is Jesus himself. Though Jesus loves to see the signs of faith, he isn't always bound by it, and in this case he acts freely, from sheer compassion, to do something nobody had imagined he could or would.

Luke certainly wants us to make a connection between this scene and the later one, when Jesus is himself carried off, his widowed mother's eldest son, for burial outside Jerusalem. In the present case, of course, the young man is brought back to ordinary **life** and will have to die again one day. Luke will eventually tell of Jesus' new life in which death is left behind for good.

Come inside the story and allow its force to sweep over you. Walk in the crowd a few paces behind the bier, on a hot day in Galilee, with the bright sun sparkling on the tears which are streaming down everyone's cheeks. Death is common enough, and everybody knows what to do. The professional mourners and wailers are there, making plenty of noise so that friends and relatives, and particularly the poor mother, can cry their hearts out without the embarrassment of making a scene all by themselves. (How much kinder a system than the clinical, detached solemnity of a modern Western funeral!) People are coming along with spices to anoint the body, ready to wrap them up in the grave-clothes to offset the smell of decomposition.

You make your way from the family home, through the streets, to the town gate. A death in a small Middle Eastern community touches everyone. The family burial plot will be a little way outside the town: probably a small cave in the side of a hill, where the husband and father had been buried some time before, and where now his bones, folded with care and devotion, lie stored in a bone-box, leaving the main shelf clear for the next burial. That's where the procession is going.

Then, quite suddenly, some strangers arrive. A man leading a small group of followers. He seems vaguely familiar: Upper Galilee isn't such a large place, and perhaps he grew up in a neighbouring village (Nain is about five miles south-east of Nazareth). He is looking at the widowed and now doubly bereaved mother, and something inside him seems to be stirring. He comes up and says something to her – and then, to everyone's surprise and horror, he touches the bier. (Nobody would normally do that except the official bearers; touching a corpse or the bier, or even the bearers themselves, would make you unclean.) Then – the biggest shock of all – he's telling the lad to get up . . . and he's getting up. The whole funeral procession goes wild with astonishment, delight, disbelief.

They don't know which one to look at, the no-longer-dead boy, his amazed and ecstatic mother, or this stranger who has done what the old prophets, Elijah and Elisha, used to do. (Luke has told the story with deliberate echoes of 1 Kings 17 and 2 Kings 4.) 'God has visited his people', they say: not in the sense of paying them a social visit, but in the old biblical sense, where this phrase was used to refer to God 'visiting' Israel at the time of the **Exodus** and other great events. It means, 'God has come near to us, to save and rescue us'. It means, 'This is the time we've been waiting for'.

Now go through the scene again; but this time, instead of it being a funeral procession in a small first-century Galilean town, make it the moment you most dread in this next week or next year. Maybe it's something that you know is going to happen, like a traumatic move of house or job. Maybe it's something you are always afraid of, a sudden accident or illness, a tragedy or scandal. Come into the middle of the scene, if you can, in prayer; feel its sorrow and frustration, its bitterness and anger. Then watch as Jesus comes to join you in the middle of it. Take time in prayer and let him approach, speak, touch, command. He may not say what you expect. He may not do what you want. But if his presence comes to be with you there that is what you most need. Once he is in the middle of it all with you, you will be able to come through it.

These two stories at the start of Luke 7 – the centurion's servant and the widow's son – do two things in particular as Luke's larger narrative develops. They take the commands of the great sermon in chapter 6 and they show what this life looks like on the ground, with God's love going out in new, unexpected, healing generosity. And they prepare us for the question that is now emerging as the central one. Who does Jesus think he is? What do these actions say about his own role, his vocation and mission?

LUKE 7.18–35

Jesus and John the Baptist

[18]The disciples of John the Baptist told him about all these things. John called two of these followers [19]and sent them to the master with this message: 'Are you the Coming One, or should we expect someone else?'

[20]The men arrived where Jesus was. 'John the Baptist', they said, 'has sent us to you to say, "Are you the Coming One, or should we expect someone else?"'

[21]Then and there Jesus healed several people of diseases, plagues and possession by unclean spirits; and he restored the sight of several blind people. [22]Then he answered them:

'Go and tell John what you have seen and heard: the blind see, the lame walk, people with virulent skin diseases are cleansed, the deaf hear, the dead are raised, the poor hear the gospel. [23]And a blessing on the person who isn't shocked by me!'

[24]So off went John's messengers.

Jesus then began to talk to the crowds about John.

'Why did you go out into the desert?' he asked. 'What were you looking for? A reed swaying in the breeze? [25]Well then, what did you go out to see? Someone dressed in silks and satins? See here, if you want to find people wearing fine clothes and living in luxury, you'd better look in royal palaces. [26]So what did you go out to see? A prophet? Yes indeed, and more than a prophet. [27]This is the one of whom the Bible says, "Look: I send my messenger before my face; he will get my path ready ahead of me."

[28]'Let me tell you this', he went on. 'Nobody greater than John has ever been born of women. But the one who is least in God's kingdom is greater than he is.'

²⁹When all the people, and the tax-collectors, heard that, they praised God for his faithfulness; they had been baptized with John's baptism. ³⁰But the Pharisees and the lawyers, who had not been baptized by John, rejected God's plan for them.

³¹'What picture can I use', Jesus continued, 'for the people of this generation? What are they like? ³²They're like children sitting in the square and calling this old riddle to each other:

We piped for you and you didn't dance;
we wailed for you and you didn't cry!

³³'When John the Baptist came, he didn't eat bread or drink wine, and you say, "He's got a demon!" ³⁴When the son of man came, eating and drinking, you say, "Look! A glutton and a drunkard, a friend of tax-collectors and sinners!" ³⁵Well, wisdom is justified by all her children.'

Pull a coin out of your pocket and look at it. What does it tell you?

I don't mean, how rich does it say you are. Nor am I thinking about the actual words that are engraved on it. I'm referring to the pictures, the symbols.

The last two countries I visited before writing this were Greece and the United States; as usual, some of their coins came home with me. The Greek ones have pictures of ancient heroes: Alexander the Great on a 100-drachma coin, Democritus the philosopher on a 10-drachma one. On the other side they have symbols: the sun with its bright rays on the first, the sun and the solar system on the other. The American coins have heroes, too, though not quite so old: Abraham Lincoln on one, George Washington on another. And the symbols, for those who bother to look at them, are powerful too: Monticello, Thomas Jefferson's home in Virginia, on the back of the 1-cent piece, the great eagle on the quarter, and so on.

Now imagine that you had never seen a book, a newspaper, a photograph or even a stained-glass window. The only pictures you would know would be occasional paintings, carvings, mosaic floors (if you were, or worked for, someone very rich) – and coins. And coins were the only ones you would see regularly. They were the only mass medium in the ancient world. They were the principal way of getting across a symbolic message to ordinary people. For Jews, who (at least in theory) weren't allowed to make pictures of human beings, the choice of symbols for coins was very important indeed.

When Herod Antipas chose the symbols for his coins, just a few years before the time of Jesus' public ministry, his favourite was a typical Galilean reed. You would see whole beds of them swaying in the breeze by the shores of the sea of Galilee. A reed would symbolize the beauty and fertility of that area.

'What did you go out to see?' asked Jesus to the crowds who had gone to be baptized by **John**, and were now following him. 'A reed swaying in the breeze?' They would have got the message. Were you looking for a new king – another one like old so-and-so up the road? If they missed the point, the next line brought it closer home. Were you looking for someone wearing the latest splendid fashions? If so, you were looking in the wrong place: the royal palace is the place for luxurious clothes. Well then, what were you looking for? A prophet! Yes indeed, but something more than just 'a' prophet. This was a special prophet indeed. This was the Advance Guard, the Preparer.

This whole long passage, the discussion between Jesus and John's messengers, and then Jesus' cryptic comments to the crowd, highlight one question in particular: who does Jesus think he is? To talk about Herod on the one hand, even by implication, and to talk about John on the other, are ways of talking about the figure who stands in between them. Is Jesus just a powerful prophet? Is he the new king, God's anointed, destined to replace Herod? Or what is he?

John, in prison, was clearly puzzled. Jesus wasn't doing what he had expected. If Jesus really was the **Messiah**, why wasn't he establishing the sort of messianic **kingdom** John wanted – presumably including liberation for prisoners like himself? Jesus is far too astute, with listening ears all around, to say openly, 'Yes, I'm the Messiah'. We hear a few chapters later that Herod wanted to kill him (13.31), and a clear statement would have been an unnecessary risk. Instead, he heals all sorts of people before the eyes of the messengers, and suggests that they draw their conclusions – with a helping shove in the right direction provided by the quotation of various passages of Isaiah. (Some Jews already saw this sort of list as a prediction of what the Messiah would do when he came; one such list occurs in an ancient scroll found in **Qumran**.) This is the kind of Messiah Jesus intends to be: not a straightforward rival to Herod (though his kingdom will eventually challenge and outlast all the Herods in the world), but a kingdom operating in a different mode altogether, healing people and the world at every level.

But if Jesus is a different sort of king, John is a different sort of prophet. He isn't just one prophet among many. He is the one spoken of by Malachi, the one whose task is to prepare the way for the coming Lord. In Malachi 3.1, the messenger clears the path for the Master to come to the **Temple** and cleanse it of all unholiness, to bring God's judgment and mercy to bear on Israel as a whole. And in this passage the Master in question doesn't seem to be simply the Messiah; he is YHWH himself, Israel's God in person. That, we may suppose, is why (though initially it sounds surprising) the least in God's kingdom is greater than John. The least of those who belong to the new movement initiated by Jesus is greater than the greatest man who was ever born up to that time. This is a strong claim indeed, though still too indirect for anyone to take it back as a hostile report to Herod. Those who sat down and chewed it over, though, would realize what was being said. Those who didn't would still look and look but never see the point.

Many of Jesus' contemporaries were like that: complaining that John was too austere, complaining in the next breath that Jesus was too much the life and soul of the party. But wisdom will out, and those who had understood what was going on would see that this was how it had to be.

People today still judge Jesus by their expectations, instead of pausing and probing into the evidence to see what was really going on. They do the same, often enough, with Jesus' followers – criticizing some for being too strict, others for being too soft, some for being too intellectual, others for being too down-to-earth. Yet wisdom can still be glimpsed by those with eyes to see. Following the Messiah who is different to what we imagined is always demanding; but this is the only way to the kingdom of God.

LUKE 7.36–50

Jesus Anointed by a Sinful Woman

[36]A Pharisee asked Jesus to dine with him, and he went into the Pharisee's house and reclined at table. [37]A woman from the town, a known bad character, discovered that he was there at table in the Pharisee's house. She brought an alabaster jar of ointment. [38]Then she stood behind Jesus' feet, crying, and began to wet his feet with her tears. She wiped them with her hair, kissed his feet, and anointed them with the ointment.

[39]The Pharisee who had invited Jesus saw what was going on.

'If this fellow really was a prophet,' he said to himself, 'he'd know what sort of a woman this is who is touching him! She's a sinner!'

[40]'Simon,' replied Jesus, 'I have something to say to you.'

'Go ahead, Teacher', he replied.

[41]'Once upon a time there was a moneylender who had two debtors. The first owed him five hundred dinars, the second fifty. [42]Neither of them could pay him, and he let them both off. So which of them will love him more?'

[43]'The one he let off the more, I suppose', replied Simon.

'Quite right', said Jesus.

[44]Then, turning towards the woman, he said to Simon, 'You see this woman? When I came into your house, you didn't give me water to wash my feet – but she has washed my feet with her tears, and wiped

them with her hair. ⁴⁵You didn't give me a kiss, but she hasn't stopped kissing my feet from the moment I came in. ⁴⁶You didn't anoint my head with oil, but she has anointed my feet with ointment.

⁴⁷'So the conclusion I draw is this: she must have been forgiven many sins! Her great love proves it! But if someone has been forgiven only a little, they will love only a little.'

⁴⁸Then he said to the woman, 'Your sins are forgiven.'

⁴⁹'Who is this', the other guests began to say among themselves, 'who even forgives sins?'

⁵⁰'Your faith has saved you', said Jesus to the woman. 'Go in peace.'

When you look at a painting, what do you look for first?

Some people stand well back and let the full sweep of it wash over them: the glorious colours, the contrasts, the light and shade.

Some people focus at once on the characters, the people in the scene. Are they happy or sad, noble or wicked, quiet or agitated? What are they thinking?

Others like to look for the way in which the artist has used the picture to comment on the world of his or her day, on its social or perhaps political issues.

Others again – perhaps artists themselves – may begin by coming up close and seeing how, with each individual brushstroke, the artist has built up to an overall effect.

The scene now before us is another of Luke's great 'paintings', and each of the possible lines of approach will work. The story of Jesus at the house of Simon the **Pharisee** is as full of meaning, of **gospel**, as any story in the New Testament. But it's also full of sheer artistry that brings the gospel up in three-dimensional, vivid reality.

Consider first the overall effect. Though several others are mentioned, three characters dominate the stage: Simon the Pharisee, Jesus and the unnamed woman. (People have often supposed that this is the same scene as the one we find in Mark 14.3–9 and the similar passages in Matthew 26 and John 12, but it probably isn't.) The balance of the scene is superb, with Jesus keeping his poise between the outrageous adoration of the woman and the equally outrageous rudeness of his host – and yet coming up with something fresh, something which, to the onlookers, was just as outrageous as the behaviour of the other two. The story sweeps to and fro between the three of them with passion and power.

The central characters, though sketched in only a few strokes, are vivid and credible. The host is a Pharisee who was presumably not completely opposed to Jesus – at least, not to start with. There were several different positions within the Pharisaic movement. The majority were what we would call hard-line right-wingers, but several,

67

including perhaps this Simon, may have been prepared to give Jesus a fair hearing. He has heard the rumours that maybe Jesus is a prophet (7.16), and he is keen to see for himself. He thinks he's found the answer (Jesus can't be a prophet because he hasn't realized what sort of a woman this is), only to be proved doubly wrong (Jesus knows what she has been and what she now is – a forgiven sinner – *and* what he, Simon, is thinking). Luke, telling the story, has emphasized three times in the first two sentences that he is a Pharisee, and that it is to his house that both Jesus and this woman have come.

The woman is an uninvited guest. What we think of as 'private life' in the modern West was largely unknown in Jesus' world: doors would often remain open, allowing beggars, extra friends, or simply curious passers-by to wander in. The woman intends, it seems, to anoint Jesus; we learn finally that this is an expression of grateful love because she has received God's overflowing forgiveness; but when she finds herself before him she is overcome, and his feet are wet with her tears before she can get the ointment jar open. Then, trying to make things better, she makes them worse as far as the onlookers are concerned: she lets down her hair, something no decent woman would do in public, and wipes his feet, kissing them all the while, and finally doing what she came for, anointing them.

Now look at this painting through the eyes of the artist, describing his world – in other words, for Luke, showing what happens when God's love in the gospel impacts on a human situation. Luke has shown us how Jesus, in Nazareth and then in the great sermon, stands on its head the normal expectation of what would happen when God brought in his **kingdom**. It would be a time of exuberant generosity, surprising grace, and at the same time fierce opposition which would meet God's judgment. Now we see, in a single incident, what this looks like in practice. Social convention is thrown out of the window; forgiveness and love set new standards and raise new expectations; human beings appear, not as society has 'constructed' them, but as God sees them. Several of the **parables** in Luke have a similar 'reversal' at their heart: think of the 'prodigal son' in Luke 15, or the 'Pharisee and tax-collector' in Luke 18. Luke lived in a church which was coming to terms with God's astonishing reversal of fortune. Many Jews had rejected the message about Jesus, but many non-Jews were accepting it and flooding into the church, delighted (as was this woman) that their sins were forgiven by the God of generous love.

When we look closer at the detail of the story, one of the things we notice is the way in which Jesus turns the tables on the Pharisee. *He* is the one who is guilty of poor hospitality – almost as much of a social blunder as the woman's letting down of her hair. The Pharisee has never come to terms with the depths of his own heart, and so doesn't appreciate God's generous love when it sits in person at his own table. For Luke, true **faith** is what happens when someone looks at Jesus and discovers God's forgiveness; and the sign and proof of this faith is love.

LUKE 8.1–15

The Parable of the Sower

[1]Soon afterwards, Jesus went about in person, with the Twelve, through the towns and villages, announcing and proclaiming the good news of God's kingdom. [2]They were accompanied by various women who had been healed from evil spirits and diseases: Mary who was called 'Magdalene', from whom seven demons had gone out, [3]Joanna the wife of Chouza (Herod's steward), and Susanna, and many others. They looked after the needs of Jesus and his companions out of their own pockets.

[4]A large crowd came together, and people came to him from town after town. He spoke to them in parables:

[5]'A sower went out to sow his seed. As he was sowing, some fell by the road, and was trodden on, and the birds of the air ate it up. [6]Other seed fell on stony ground, and when it came up it withered, because it didn't have any moisture. [7]Other seed fell in among thorns, and when the thorns grew up they choked it. [8]Other seed again fell into good soil, and came up, and gave a yield of a hundredfold.'

As he said this, he called out: 'If you've got ears to hear, then hear!'

[9]His disciples asked him what this parable was about.

[10]'You are being let in on the secrets of God's kingdom,' he said, 'but to the rest it happens in parables, so that "they may see but not perceive, and hear but not understand."

[11]'This is the parable: the seed is the word of God. [12]Those by the roadside are people who hear, but then the devil comes and takes away the word from their hearts, so that they won't believe it and be saved. [13]Those on the stony ground are those who hear the word and receive it with delight – but they don't have any root, and so they believe only for a time, and then, when a time of testing comes, they draw back. [14]The seed that falls in among thorns represents people who hear, but as they go on their way they are choked by the cares and riches and pleasures of life, and they don't bear proper, ripening fruit. [15]But those in the good soil are the ones who hear the word and hold on to it with an upright and good heart, and who patiently produce fruit.'

If Jesus was telling this story today, he might well include other categories as well. What about the seeds that were planted in good soil but were ruined by acid rain? What about the plants that were coming up nicely but were bulldozed by occupying forces to make room for a new road? There's plenty of room to develop different lines of thought.

But of course what Jesus was doing was not commenting on farming problems but explaining the strange way in which the **kingdom of God** was arriving. Many of his hearers were expecting something big and obvious to happen: for a new king to overthrow Herod, a new and legitimate priest to oust the present **high priest**, and in particular for a Jewish movement to get rid of the hated pagans who were their ultimate masters. None of that was happening, certainly not in the way they thought. Jesus was keen to open their eyes and ears to see and hear what God was actually doing.

Luke has already told us enough about Jesus' public career for us to be able to see the sort of people he's talking about. Here are the villagers in the synagogue at Nazareth, hearing Jesus' sermon on Isaiah, but unwilling to accept what he's saying. The word is trampled underfoot, and the birds of the air are snatching it away. Here is the **Pharisee** at table: he has invited Jesus to dine, and obviously wants to give him a hearing, but what Jesus does and says is so unexpected and shocking that he tries to distance himself from it as far as he can. The seed has landed in among the stones of his prejudice, and nothing can get near it to nurture it and allow it to grow. Here are the people of 'this generation' (7.31), who have other things on their minds, and don't want a prophet like either **John** or Jesus. The seed has landed among thorns, and is being choked.

But here is a **Gentile** centurion who believes that Jesus has authority to command even serious illness to depart. Here is Levi the tax-collector leaving his shady business and following Jesus. Here is the unnamed woman whose extravagant behaviour shows that she has experienced God's forgiveness and new **life** deep within her heart. Here are many, many more, already in the first few weeks of Jesus' kingdom-project, who show that the word he is speaking is producing fruit. Here, indeed, are the **Twelve**, whom we shall gradually come to know in Luke's story. Though he doesn't highlight their weaknesses as relentlessly as Mark, he still shows them as muddled and puzzled, needing, often enough, help and new direction. The plants are growing up, but they are not yet mature enough to 'produce fruit patiently' ('patience' occurs here only in Luke: we may suppose that, from his perspective, the promised fruit did indeed take time to appear).

And here, too, is a group of women (8.1–3) whom the other **gospel**-writers don't mention until much later – until, in fact, they turn up at the foot of the cross, lend a hand with the burial, and then are the first at the tomb. They have heard the **word**, and been healed by it (Luke implies that they had all been healed, not simply Mary Magdalene).

And they have done the unthinkable: they have left the well-defined social space of home and family, where they had a role and a duty, and have chosen to accompany Jesus and his followers on the road from place to place, looking after their needs and doing so, moreover, out of their own pockets.

This is every bit as shocking, from a first-century Palestinian point of view, as the story of the woman letting her hair down and kissing Jesus' feet. (The fact that Mary Magdalene is mentioned in this way so soon after that incident may be Luke's hint that she was the unnamed woman, but there is no firm reason to say that she must have been.) One can only imagine the looks they would get, and the things people might say about such a company. But one can also imagine Jesus thinking of them not least as people in whose hearts and lives the word had had its effect, people who were already bearing fruit, putting life, reputation and property at the disposal of this extraordinary new kingdom-movement.

Look out of the window at the people walking by. What sort of soil is the seed being sown in today? What can we do to plough up the rough ground, to remove the stones, to weed out the thorns? What can we do to sow the word more successfully? The answers will vary from place to place and time to time. But perhaps the first and most important answer is to ask ourselves how much mature growth, how much fruit, the word is producing in our own lives. If we have ears, we must learn to hear.

LUKE 8.16–25

Jesus Calms the Storm

[16]'Nobody lights a lamp', continued Jesus, 'and then hides it under a pot or a bed. They put it on a lampstand, so that people who come in can see the light. [17]You see, nothing is hidden which won't become visible. Nothing is concealed that won't come to light.

[18]'So be careful how you listen. If you've got something, more will be given to you; if you haven't, even what you imagine you have will be taken away from you.'

[19]His mother and brothers came to him, and couldn't get near him because of the crowd. [20]So they sent a message to him: 'Your mother and your brothers are standing outside, wanting to see you.'

[21]'Mother and brothers, indeed?' replied Jesus. 'Here are my mother and brothers – people who hear God's word and do it!'

[22]One day he got into a boat with his disciples, and suggested that they cross to the other shore. So they set off. [23]As they were sailing, he

fell asleep. A violent wind swept down on the lake, and the boat began to fill dangerously with water.

²⁴'Master, Master!' shouted the disciples, coming and waking him up. 'Master, we're lost!'

He got up and scolded the wind and the waves. They stopped, and there was a flat calm.

²⁵'Where's your faith?' he asked them.

They were afraid and astonished. 'Who is this, then,' they asked one another, 'if he can give orders to wind and water, and they do what he says?'

The chairman of the board looked around the room. This was a big decision and everyone knew it. 'Can we agree on this plan, then?' he asked. 'We need to decide.' Twenty serious faces looked back at him, each with their own portfolio to consider, each with their own hopes and fears.

At that minute the secretary came into the room. 'Sorry, Mr Chairman,' she said, 'but you told me you wanted to take this call as soon as it came.'

He left the room to answer the phone. Twenty pairs of eyes followed him. What could be so important as to make this decision wait? Five minutes passed.

'It was my daughter,' he explained cheerfully, as he returned. 'She was in an under-nines swimming race this afternoon. And she won! It's a great day!' And, to a stunned silence, he continued the meeting.

Does that seem shocking? Perhaps a pleasant surprise? Certainly, in terms of the way business has been run in the Western world for the last century, it would be startling, to say the least, to have a senior businessman postpone a vital decision because of a child's swimming race. It goes against the normal expectations.

And only when we've felt the force of that can we appreciate the shock waves that Jesus sent through his followers, and the whole society, with *his* response to a sudden request for attention from his family. If we, deep down, would like our families to be more important to us than sometimes they are, we can be sure that in Jesus' world family unity and solidarity were far, far more important. But this just highlights the earth-shaking effect of his response when his mother Mary and his brothers – James and the others – came to see him.

Mark tells us at one point (3.21) that they were afraid Jesus was out of his mind. John explains elsewhere (7.5) that they didn't believe in him and what he was doing. Luke offers no such explanation. All we have is an apparently normal visit from the family, and a stunning slap in the face from Jesus. 'Mother? Brothers?' (Two of the most sacred relationships anyone, not least a Jew, could have.) 'Here they are –'

looking around at the motley crew crowding into the house: 'Anyone who hears God's word and does it!'

We shouldn't miss the echoes of the **parable** of the sower in the previous passage. These ones sitting around him are the people who are like seed sown on good soil, who hear God's **word**, and produce fruit. That's how important the **kingdom** is: it's even more important than the claims of family, which are themselves the most important normal claims a person can have. It isn't that Jesus is being like a careless businessman who undervalues his family because he's so focused on the next big decision. Jesus is like the most caring family person you can imagine, who nevertheless knows that hearing and doing God's word is even more important. Woe betide preachers, pastors or theologians who make this saying an excuse for neglecting their families because they're busy with God's work. Often that's just an excuse for careerism and selfish attention to 'my work', as though one's work was the principal source of identity and status. But there is danger in store, too, for those who allow any claims whatever to modify or water down the absolute claim of God's word on their lives. Jesus, knowing that his family didn't understand his vocation (but hoping that they would come to do so in time), couldn't allow them to distract and divert him from the vital and urgent work he was undertaking.

This shocking tension between the old world of family ties and the new world of the **gospel** lies underneath the warnings at the start of this passage. God is doing something new, and it mustn't be hidden away or kept in secret. Even if you try, it won't work, because the time is coming when secrets will be published, when dark becomes light, when God's kingdom is unveiled in all its glory, and then things at present hidden will be known to all. From Luke's point of view, the events of Jesus' cross and **resurrection**, of the gift of the **spirit**, the mission and consolidation of the church, and the fall of Jerusalem – all of these are the unveiling of what was hidden in Jesus' early ministry. This is what God was doing all along, and the truth – who was really listening, who was really following? – would emerge all too soon.

The lesson is made plain for the **disciples** on the lake, as it is for us whenever we come to the end of our own resources and discover that we have to throw ourselves on the mercy of Jesus because there's no one and nothing else that will help. The choice of **faith** is absolute. Either we trust him or we are left at the mercy of the storm. Luke uses this story to take one further step with the question, 'Who then is this?', which reaches its first main answer in the next chapter. But this story also poses the question of faith. We will only give the right answer to the question of who Jesus is when we realize that to give it commits us to total trust and obedience.

LUKE 8.26–39

The Healing of the Demoniac

²⁶They sailed to the land of the Gerasenes, which is on the other side from Galilee. ²⁷As he got out on land, a demon-possessed man from the town met him. For a long time he had worn no clothes, and he didn't live in a house but among the tombs. ²⁸When he saw Jesus he screamed and fell down in front of him.

'You and me, Jesus – you and me!' he yelled at the top of his voice. 'What is it with you and me, you son of the Most High God? Don't torture me – please, please don't torment me!' ²⁹Jesus was commanding the unclean spirit to come out of the man. Many times over it had seized him, and he was kept under guard with chains and manacles; but he used to break the shackles, and the demon would drive him into the desert.

³⁰'What's your name?' Jesus asked him.

'Regiment!' replied the man – for many demons had entered him. ³¹And they begged him not to order them to be sent into the pit.

³²A sizeable herd of pigs was feeding on the hillside, and the demons begged him to allow them to go into them. He gave them permission. ³³The demons went out of the man and entered the pigs, and the herd rushed down the steep slope into the lake and was drowned.

³⁴The herdsmen saw what had happened. They took to their heels and spread the news in town and country, ³⁵and people came out to see what had happened. They came to Jesus, and found the man from whom the demons had gone out sitting there at Jesus' feet, clothed and in his right mind. They were afraid. ³⁶People who had seen how the demoniac had been healed explained it to them. ³⁷The whole crowd, from the surrounding country of the Gerasenes, asked him to go away from them, because great terror had seized them. So he got into the boat and returned.

³⁸The man who had been demon-possessed begged Jesus to let him stay with him. But he sent him away. ³⁹'Go back to your home,' he said, 'and tell them what God has done for you.' And he went off round every town, declaring what Jesus had done for him.

I have a photograph, framed above my mantelpiece, of the Sea of Galilee seen from the top of the Golan Heights. I took it on a sunny day in late autumn: the scene is tranquil and clear, with the town of Tiberias just visible on the opposite shore. You would hardly think that fierce battles have raged up there in our own day. It looks like a place you might go for a country holiday, to get away from it all.

We don't know why Jesus decided to go there, across the lake from the main part of Galilee (the word 'Galilee' referred to various parts of the area, depending on how the borders were redrawn with successive

74

political settlements; but it mostly meant the area to the north and west of the lake). Then, as now, the area to the south and east of the lake was disputed territory. In Jesus' day, the north-east shore of the lake was part of 'Gaulanitis' (the same root word as 'Golan'), and the south-east was the area of the Ten Towns, in Greek the 'Decapolis'. There is still disagreement over exactly where the present incident is supposed to have taken place, but we assume the **gospel**-writers are thinking of either the southern part of Gaulanitis or the northern extremity of the Decapolis. Either way, it was on the eastern side of the lake, and for most of that shore the land does indeed rise steeply from close to the water.

The point of all this is that the area was largely **Gentile** territory, though many Jews would live there as well. Jesus had chosen to cross over on to foreign soil, perhaps to escape the immediate pressure of travelling around under the nose of Herod Antipas. There was, however, to be no peace there either. This violent man, possessed, it seems, by a multitude of spirits, at once confronts him and fills the air with screaming and yelling. The **disciples** must have wanted to get straight back in the boat and head for home again.

Jesus remains calm before this human storm, as he had before the wind and the waves on the lake. The same quiet authority will deal with the one as with the other. The bizarre scene with the pigs (another sign of Gentile territory; Jews didn't eat, or keep, pigs) has sometimes been seen as picture-language for what many Jews, and other inhabitants of the region including perhaps the possessed man, wanted to do with the hated foreign Romans: drive them back into the sea. To dismiss a 'regiment' or 'squadron' of Roman soldiers in that way was the dream of several revolutionary leaders in the first century. But Luke's focus in telling this story is on the man himself, and, as always, on Jesus.

For Luke, what has happened to this man isn't just a remarkable healing; it is 'salvation' (verse 36). The salvation which God promised long ago, which has appeared in Jesus, and which has already reached many in Israel, is now starting to spread further afield.

But the real point of the story comes at the close. The man, quite understandably, wants to be allowed to stay with Jesus. Not only is he now bonded to him by the astonishing rescue he has experienced; he may well assume that things would not be easy back in his home territory, where everyone knew the tragic tale of his recent life. There might be considerable reluctance to accept him again as a member of a family or a village. He would have to stand up and take responsibility for himself; he couldn't rely on being able, as it were, to hide behind Jesus. He is one of those to whom Jesus does *not* say 'follow me' in any literal sense; he is one of those (the majority we may suppose) to whom he said 'go home and tell them'. Having experienced the **good news** in action, he must now tell it himself.

Luke reserves the real point for the last words – in Greek, the last word of the story. 'Go home', says Jesus, 'and tell them what *God* has done for you'. And the man goes off and tells everyone what *Jesus* has done for him. Luke is not offering us, or not yet, any formula, or carefully worked-out doctrine, of how 'God was in Christ'. At the moment it is simply something people discover in their experience: what Jesus does, God does. Or, to put it the other way round, if you want to tell people what God has done, tell them what Jesus has done. The best brains in two thousand years of Christianity have struggled to find adequate words to explain how this can be; but it is a truth known to many, at a level too deep for mere theory, from the moment they discover God's saving power in the person and work of Jesus.

LUKE 8.40–56

Jairus's Daughter and the Woman with Chronic Bleeding

⁴⁰Jesus returned. A large crowd was waiting for him, and welcomed him back. ⁴¹A man named Jairus, a ruler of the synagogue, came and fell down in front of his feet. He pleaded with him to come to his house, ⁴²because he had an only daughter, twelve years old, who was dying. So they set off, and the crowd pressed close in around him.

⁴³There was a woman who had had an internal haemorrhage for twelve years. She had spent all she had on doctors, but had not been able to find a cure from anyone. ⁴⁴She came up behind Jesus and touched the hem of his robe. Immediately her flow of blood dried up.

⁴⁵'Who touched me?' asked Jesus.

Everybody denied it. 'Master', said Peter, 'the crowds are crushing you and pressing you!'

⁴⁶'Somebody touched me', said Jesus. 'Power went out from me, and I knew it'.

⁴⁷When the woman saw that she couldn't remain hidden, she came up, trembling, and fell down in front of him. She told him, in front of everyone, why she had touched him, and how she had been healed instantly.

⁴⁸'Daughter', said Jesus, 'your faith has saved you. Go in peace'.

⁴⁹While he was still speaking, someone arrived from the synagogue-ruler's house. 'Your daughter's dead', he said. 'Don't bother the teacher any longer'.

⁵⁰'Don't be afraid', said Jesus when he heard it. 'Just believe, and she will be rescued'.

⁵¹When they got to the house, he didn't let anyone come in with them except Peter, John and James, and the child's father and mother. ⁵²Everyone was weeping and wailing for her.

'Don't cry', said Jesus. 'She isn't dead; she's asleep.' ⁵³They laughed at him, knowing that she was dead.

⁵⁴But he took her by the hand. 'Get up, child', he called. ⁵⁵Her spirit returned, and she got up at once. He told them to give her something to eat. ⁵⁶Her parents were astounded, but he told them to tell nobody what had happened.

We don't know for sure that Luke was a doctor, though there are several things in his work that make it likely, as well as Paul's mention of him as 'Luke, the beloved doctor' (Colossians 4.14). But if he was, there must have been a wry smile on his face when he wrote verse 43. Perhaps he knew of patients like that, who had spent everything they had on medical attention and it still didn't make any difference. In a world without modern medicine, and also without any form of state-funded medical aid or private insurance schemes, good health was a precious but fragile commodity. If you didn't have it, you might easily find that sickness and poverty followed each other in a downward spiral from which no return was possible.

Luke has followed Mark in fitting the story of the woman and her twelve-year ailment inside the story of Jairus's twelve-year-old daughter. (Is there, perhaps, an echo of Luke's own earlier story of the twelve-year-old Jesus?) The two parts of the story are joined in several other ways, too, particularly in Jesus' command to Jairus to have **faith**, which comes immediately after he has told the woman that her faith has brought her salvation. If Jairus's faith was to help in the healing of his daughter, then that faith was itself helped by seeing Jesus declare that power had gone out from him even before he knew who had been healed. (The phrase itself is striking, and says a lot about what it was like for Jesus to be instrumental in so much healing.) If touching Jesus could have that effect, who knows what might happen if Jesus himself came and touched a dead little girl?

Of course, touching was itself very important in both cases. In the world before modern hygiene (soap as we know it wasn't invented until the Middle Ages, and of course many things we take for granted today, such as running water and proper drains, were barely thought of then), purity taboos were vital simply to maintain public health. The Jewish scriptures and subsequent traditions had codified and elaborated them into almost an art form. And two of the most obvious sources of pollution were: corpses, and women with internal bleeding.

In other words, a first-century reader coming upon this double story would know very well that Jesus was, apparently, incurring double pollution. In the first case he couldn't help it; the woman came and touched him without his knowing either that she was doing it or what she was suffering from; but officially he had become 'unclean' nonetheless. That is partly why the woman hoped to remain hidden, and why she was shy about coming forward, and then crushingly embarrassed when eventually she had to. In the second case, though, Jesus deliberately went and touched a dead body. As we saw with the widow's son at Nain (7.11–17), that very act was breaking through a taboo; and in this case as well the result was instant and breathtaking.

In both cases, the woman and the girl, we find further signs of Luke's care about, and interest in, the stories of women; as is well known, he highlights their role more than the other **gospels**. But in both, as well, we also find foreshadowings of what is to come in Jesus' story. Luke has been patiently pointing out, through one story after another, who Jesus really is. He is also, at the same time, opening the way for his central explanation of what Jesus has come to achieve. When Luke tells of Jesus' arrival in Jerusalem, and his arrest and death, his main theme is of how Jesus, innocent of anything that would condemn him to crucifixion, takes the place of the guilty, those who had courted that fate all along. Already in these incidents we see the same pattern emerging. Jesus shares the pollution of sickness and death, but the power of his own love – and it is love, above all, that shines through these stories – turns that pollution into wholeness and hope.

This is the message that Luke would repeat to us today, in whatever problem or suffering we face. The presence of Jesus, getting his hands dirty with the problems of the world, is what we need, and what in the gospel we are promised. As we live inside Luke's developing story, we find Jesus quietly coming alongside us in our own muddle and fear. He welcomes our trembling touch, and responds with that central biblical command: 'Don't be afraid.'

LUKE 9.1–17

The Twelve Sent Out and the Feeding of the Five Thousand

[1]Jesus called together the Twelve, and gave them power and authority over all demons, and to cure diseases. [2]He sent them out to announce God's kingdom and cure the sick.

[3]'Don't take anything for the journey,' he said to them, 'no stick, no bag, no bread, no money, no second cloak. [4]Whenever you go into a house, stay there and leave from there. [5]If anyone won't receive you,

go out of that town and wipe the dust off your feet as evidence against them.'

⁶So off they went, and travelled through the villages, announcing the good news and healing people everywhere.

⁷Herod the Tetrarch heard what was going on, and was very puzzled. Some people were saying that John had been raised from the dead. ⁸Others were saying that Elijah had appeared; still others, that one of the old prophets had arisen.

⁹'I beheaded John,' said Herod, 'but I keep hearing all these things about this other fellow. Who is he?' And he tried to get to see him.

¹⁰The apostles returned and told Jesus what they had done. He took them off and went away privately to a town called Bethsaida. ¹¹When the crowds discovered, they followed him. He welcomed them and spoke to them about the kingdom of God, and he healed those who needed it.

¹²As the day wore on, the Twelve came to Jesus.

'Send the crowd away,' they said, 'so that they can go into the villages and countryside nearby, find somewhere to stay, and get something to eat. We're in quite a lonely spot here.'

¹³'You give them something to eat,' he replied.

'All we've got here', they said, 'is five loaves and a couple of fishes – unless you mean we should go ourselves and buy food for all these people?' ¹⁴(There were about five thousand men.)

'Get them to sit down,' Jesus said to them, 'in groups of around fifty each.'

¹⁵They did so, and everyone sat down. ¹⁶Then Jesus took the five loaves and the two fish. He looked up to heaven, blessed the food, divided it and gave it to the disciples to pass around the crowd. ¹⁷Everyone ate, and was satisfied. They took up twelve baskets of broken bits left over.

When a new business starts up, it's often the dream of one person that makes it happen. But if the business succeeds, more people need to come on board. Not just to do the detailed work that the founder hasn't got time for, but to share in the planning, to take responsibility. Often this is difficult and painful for the visionary who began it all. But it's necessary: one person can't do it all, and can't be there for ever.

How much more vital was it that Jesus share his life and work with his closest followers. He knew, though they didn't yet, that he wouldn't be with them very long. He knew he was shortly to meet a terrible fate. By the end of Luke 9 he will have begun to explain this to his followers – though they never understood it, or believed it, until afterwards. But already he was beginning to share his vocation with them. They needed to learn to do what he was doing, to trust God like he trusted

God. Of course, when they tell people about God's **kingdom**, they will be talking about Jesus, not themselves. But Jesus has commissioned them to share his work.

That in itself gives them a certain status. This is strange, because at first they seem the very opposite of the ambassadors of a king. They are to go in complete poverty, relying entirely on what people give them as they continue Jesus' own work of announcing the **good news** and healing those in need. Though in some respects they might have looked like the wandering philosophers who appeared from time to time in the Middle East, Jesus forbade them to take the money-bag in which such travelling teachers would store what they had got through begging. This was to be a venture of **faith** from first to last.

This preaching and healing tour both was and wasn't a model for the life of the church after Pentecost. Nowhere do we hear that the early church acted like this. They needed great faith to attempt the things they did; the Jerusalem community, in selling property and pooling resources, gave themselves to God's kingdom just as fully as the **Twelve** on this occasion. But Luke, telling this story, doesn't mention the particular strategy adopted in that part of Acts. This was, it seems, part of the urgent, unique mission of Jesus.

Jesus invites the **disciples** into partnership here by telling them to give the crowds something to eat. They are naturally puzzled: what can he mean? Even if they were to buy bread themselves, how could they afford enough for such a huge number? What Jesus then does is a kind of close-up, sharply focused version of what they themselves had been doing when travelling round relying on God's provision. Jesus takes it one radical stage further. Invoking the power of the God through whom the whole physical world is created and sustained in **life**, he calmly thanks God for what he has provided, blesses the food, breaks it and gives it – again involving the astonished disciples, this time in distributing the food to the equally amazed crowd.

People often find this story incredible. They suggest that maybe when Jesus made everyone sit down, and gave them a tiny bit of food, that prompted them to produce the food they had all brought anyway. That's one explanation; there are several others, all attempting to explain away what each of the four **gospels** says quite explicitly. Of course, if the disciples had known that even a few people had food with them there wouldn't have been a problem in the first place. No: at this point today's reader is invited, like the disciples at the start of the chapter, to go out into the unknown, into a world where things aren't normally like that, and to trust God completely. In terms of our knowledge of how the world normally works, this is like asking us to

80

set off without stick or bag, food or money. We aren't even allowed the frequent fall-back position which sounds good but avoids the issue ('the real **miracle** was in people's hearts'). Christians who intend to make the gospel story their own are living a venture of faith from first to last.

Not, however, blind faith. We aren't called to believe that Jesus can, as it were, do tricks to order. He wasn't a magician. What he did on this rare occasion was to allow God's creative power to flow through him in a special way, as with his healings only more so. And, as the gospel-writers describe this incident with words so familiar in the later church from celebrations of the Lord's supper (he 'took the bread, blessed it, broke it and gave it'), we Christians are invited to invoke that same healing, creative power in all that we do, in everything that flows from our life of worship.

Meanwhile, a storm cloud appears on the horizon. Jesus had kept out of Herod's way up to now, but sending the disciples on a wider mission meant that the grumpy Tetrarch was bound to take notice. When he asks 'Who is Jesus?', this isn't the question of an innocent enquirer. If Jesus was in the same category as **John the Baptist** or Elijah, no rich and oppressive king of the Jews would remain unscathed. Unless, of course, he struck first.

LUKE 9.18–27

Peter's Declaration of Jesus' Messiahship

[18]When Jesus was praying alone, his disciples gathered around him. 'Who do the crowds say I am?' he asked them.

[19]'John the Baptist', they responded. 'And others say Elijah. Others say that one of the ancient prophets has arisen.'

[20]'What about you?' said Jesus. 'Who do you say I am?'

'God's Messiah', answered Peter.

[21]He gave them strict and careful instructions not to tell this to anyone.

[22]'The son of man', he said, 'must suffer many things, and be rejected by the elders, and the chief priests and the legal experts. He must be killed, and raised up on the third day.'

[23]He then spoke to them all. 'If any of you want to come after me,' he said, 'you must say No to yourselves, and pick up your cross every day, and follow me. [24]If you want to save your life, you'll lose it; but if you lose your life because of me, you'll save it. [25]What good will it do you if you win the entire world, but lose or forfeit your own self? [26]If you're ashamed of me and my words, the son of man will be ashamed of you,

when he comes in the glory which belongs to him, and to the father, and to the holy angels.
²⁷'Let me tell you,' he concluded, 'there are some standing here who won't experience death until they see God's kingdom.'

'When did you first know', I asked my friend, 'that you wanted to be a philosopher?' (He was at this time already a senior professor of philosophy.)

'Oh, that's easy', he replied. 'I knew when I was sitting in my first lecture in the undergraduate programme. I sat there and knew that this was what I wanted to do with my life.'

That is, perhaps, unusual – though many people do report such moments of clarity, vision and, yes, vocation. But there's another side to the story. When did *other* people know that he was to be a philosopher? It wouldn't have done any good if he'd gone to his teachers after that first class and said, 'That's it: this is the life for me!' They would have told him to get on with the first week's assignments, then the second week's, and so on. After several months they might, perhaps, tell him he was doing well. Perhaps after a year or so his fellow-students might tell him he had what it took to get to the top. But only after several years, studying different branches of the subject, writing lengthy dissertations, taking part in seminars, and so on – only after a long time would the academic seniors tell a bright student that it was time he applied for a job. A long time can elapse between feeling called and being recognized.

In Jesus' case, we know that his vocation had been dramatically confirmed at his **baptism**. Luke has made it clear that it stretched way back beyond that, so that already at the age of 12 he was exploring, not whether he had such a calling, but what it might mean.

But part of the calling meant that Jesus would have to engage in a strange public career, without starting off by saying 'I'm the **Messiah**!' His style of messiahship was to be so different from what people expected that, as Luke has already indicated, it cost him dear and nearly got him lynched in Nazareth. It caused even **John the Baptist** to be puzzled about what exactly was going on.

Jesus was known as a prophet, and when people asked what he was up to they went for models to prophets old and new, from Elijah to John the Baptist. Some may have been trying to identify Jesus with the Elijah who, according to Malachi 4.5, would return to herald 'the great and terrible day of the Lord'. Certainly they believed that Jesus was behaving like someone through whom some great act of God was about to take place.

But Jesus was more than that. Prophet he certainly was; but he was not simply pointing to God's **kingdom** some way off in the future, he was causing it to appear before people's eyes, and was setting in motion the events through which it would become firmly established. And sooner or later he had to put the question to the **disciples**. They marked themselves out from the crowd by piercing the disguise; even though Jesus wasn't doing everything they had expected a Messiah to do, the combination of authority, power, insight and fulfilment of the scriptures that they had seen in him was too potent to mean anything else. To have called them, as the deeply symbolic **Twelve**, was important, too; but anyone could have done that, and been mistaken. To have equipped them to go out and do what he was doing was something else again. Their own identity had come to depend on his, and there was only one answer they could give: You're the Messiah, God's anointed king.

If we have understood Luke's story so far, with its strong hints of opposition from the **Pharisees** on the one hand and Herod on the other, it will come as no surprise that Jesus at once tells not just the Twelve but anyone who wants to follow him that there is a dark and dangerous time ahead. The world is being turned upside down, and anyone who wants to come through and be present when God's kingdom appears will have to be prepared to be turned upside down and inside out with it. Despite what many well-meaning evangelists and preachers have said, Jesus didn't come with the message that if we followed him we would have an easy life, with everything happening exactly as we would like it. Just the reverse. To save your life, you have to lose it. To avoid having 'the **son of man**' be ashamed of you, you have to acknowledge him. In other words, when the Messiah is installed as judge of God's world, which was a central part of the Jewish expectation, then only those who have been prepared to follow him when it was dangerous and shameful to do so will be acknowledged by him in return.

Jesus' swift movement, from asking who they think he is to summoning them to follow him even to the death, shows clearly enough that we cannot separate thinking from action in the Christian faith. As Jesus said earlier, it's no use saying 'Lord, Lord,' if you don't *do* what he says. Jesus' identity and his vocation are tied so tightly together that if you want to have anything to do with him you have to take the whole package or nothing at all. There are no half measures in the kingdom of God. And, as we contemplate that challenge, let's be careful to note something that Luke emphasizes at the start of this passage and the next one. These momentous revelations of truth and vocation took place as Jesus had been praying. No half measures there either.

LUKE 9.28–45

The Transfiguration

²⁸About eight days after this conversation, Jesus took Peter, John and James and went up a mountain to pray. ²⁹And, as he was praying, the appearance of his face changed, and his clothes became shining white. ³⁰Two men appeared, talking with him: it was Moses and Elijah, ³¹who appeared in glory and were speaking of his departure, which he was going to fulfil in Jerusalem.

³²Peter and those who were with him were heavy with sleep, but they managed to stay awake. They saw his glory, and the two men who were standing there with him.

³³As they were going away from him, Peter said to Jesus, 'Master, it's wonderful for us to be here! Let's make three tents, one for you, one for Moses, and one for Elijah!' He didn't know what he was saying; ³⁴but as the words were coming out of his mouth a cloud appeared and overshadowed them. They were afraid as they entered the cloud. ³⁵And a voice came from the cloud: 'This is my son, my chosen one: listen to him.' ³⁶As the voice spoke, there was Jesus by himself. They kept silent, and told nobody at that time anything of what they had seen.

³⁷The next day, as they were going down from the mountain, a large crowd met them. ³⁸A man from the crowd shouted out, 'Teacher! Please, please have a look at my son! He's my only child, ³⁹and look what's happening to him! A spirit seizes him, and suddenly it shrieks and convulses him, so that he foams at the mouth. It goes on savaging him, and it's almost impossible to get it to leave him. ⁴⁰I begged your disciples to cast it out, but they couldn't.'

⁴¹'You faithless and depraved generation!' said Jesus in reply. 'How long shall I be with you and have to put up with you? Bring your son here.'

⁴²While he was on the way, the demon tore at him and threw him into convulsions. Jesus rebuked the unclean spirit, healed the child, and gave him back to his father. ⁴³Everyone was astonished at the greatness of God.

While they were all still expressing amazement at everything he had done, Jesus said to his disciples, ⁴⁴'Let these words go right down into your ears: the son of man is to be given over into human hands.' ⁴⁵They had no idea what he was talking about. It was hidden from them, so that they wouldn't perceive it, and they were afraid to ask him about what he had said.

The Oscar-winning movie *Chariots of Fire* tells the story of two athletes at the 1920 Paris Olympics. Harold Abrahams, after a gigantic struggle as much against himself as against the other runners, achieved the gold medal in the 100 yards. Eric Liddell, the devout Christian who had refused to run on a Sunday, switched events and won the gold in the 440 yards. It is a moving double story, all the more so for being true.

After the 1920 Games were over, the movie shows all the athletes returning on the boat train to London, and spilling out excitedly into Waterloo station. All except Harold Abrahams. His girlfriend waits anxiously as the crowd thins out. Only when they have all gone does Harold emerge slowly from the train. He has achieved what he set out to do. He has the long-coveted prize in his hand. He has been up the mountain, and is realizing that whatever he does now he will never stand there again. He has to come down from the giddy heights and face reality.

All the **gospel**-writers follow the story of the transfiguration with the story of a boy who is desperately ill, so sick that the **disciples** hadn't been able to cure him. They seem to be telling us that the two go together: the mountaintop experience and the shrieking, stubborn **demon**. Many people prefer to live their lives without either, to be people of the plateau, undramatic and unexciting. God seems to call some to that kind of **life**. But, for many, dramatic visions and spiritual experiences are balanced by huge demands. The more open we are to God, and to the different dimensions of God's glory, the more we seem to be open to the pain of the world. We are right to be wary when we return from some great worship service, when we rise from a time of prayer in which God has seemed close and his love real and powerful. These things are never given for their own sake, but so that, as we are equipped by them, God can use us within his needy world.

Luke has highlighted, throughout this passage, the way in which the transfiguration was preparing Jesus himself not just for one human tragedy but for the greatest threat of all. Moses and Elijah, says Luke, were speaking with Jesus about 'his departure, which he was going to fulfil in Jerusalem'. The word for 'departure' is *exodus*, and Luke means us to understand that in several senses. It can mean, like 'exodus' in the Old Testament, 'departure', 'going away'. It can also serve as a euphemism for 'death', as when someone says 'when I am no longer here', referring to their own death. But the reason Luke has chosen this word – not least in connection with Moses! – is that in his death Jesus will enact an event just like the great **Exodus** from Egypt, only more so. In the first Exodus, Moses led the Israelites out of slavery in Egypt and home to the promised land. In the new Exodus, Jesus will lead all God's people out of the slavery of sin and death, and home to their promised inheritance – the new creation in which the whole world will be redeemed.

Jesus himself, then, went through the mountaintop experience, knowing that it was preparing him to follow where the law and the prophets

85

(here represented by Moses and Elijah) had pointed: down into the valley, to the place of despair and death, the place where demons shriek and sufferers weep, the place where the **son of man** will be handed over to sinners (which here means '**Gentiles**'). The disciples were overwhelmed by the transfiguration, and blurted out things they didn't mean (Peter seems to have thought it would be good to keep Moses, Elijah and Jesus there for ever–but things don't work like that). They were unable to understand how it was that the glory which they had glimpsed on the mountain, the glory of God's chosen son, the Servant who was carrying in himself the promise of redemption, would finally be unveiled on a very different hill, an ugly little hill outside Jerusalem.

We, too, often find it completely bewildering to know how to understand all that God is doing and saying, both in our times of great joy and our times of great sadness. But the word that comes to us, leading us on to follow Jesus even when we haven't a clue what's going on, is the word that came from the cloud on that strange day in Galilee: 'This is my son, my chosen one: listen to him.'

LUKE 9.46–62

The Nature of Discipleship

[46]A dispute arose among them about which of them was the greatest. [47]Jesus knew this quarrel was going on in their hearts, so he took a child and stood it beside him.

[48]'If you receive this child in my name,' he said, 'you receive me. And anyone who receives me, receives the one who sent me. Whoever is the least among you – that's the one who is great.'

[49]'Master,' commented John, 'we saw someone casting out demons in your name. We told him to stop, because he wasn't part of our company.'

[50]'Don't stop him', replied Jesus. 'Anyone who isn't against you is on your side.'

[51]As the time came nearer for Jesus to be taken up, he settled it in his mind to go to Jerusalem. [52]He sent messengers ahead of him. They came into a Samaritan village to get them ready, [53]and they refused to receive him, because his mind was set on going to Jerusalem. [54]When the disciples James and John saw it, they said, 'Master, do you want us to call down fire from heaven and burn them up?' [55]He turned and rebuked them, [56]and they went on to another village.

[57]As they were going along the road a man addressed Jesus. 'Wherever you're going,' he said, 'I'll follow you!'

[58]'Foxes have lairs,' Jesus replied, 'and the birds in the sky have nests; but the son of man doesn't have anywhere to lay his head.'

[59]To another person he said, 'Follow me.'

'Master,' he replied, 'let me first go and bury my father.'

⁶⁰'Let the dead bury their dead,' said Jesus. 'You must go and announce God's kingdom.'

⁶¹'I will follow you, Master,' said another, 'but first let me say good-bye to the people at home.'

⁶²'Nobody,' replied Jesus, 'who begins to plough and then looks over his shoulder is fit for God's kingdom.'

The most famous work of early English literature is Chaucer's *Canterbury Tales*. As we read it today, we get a sudden and vivid picture of life in the fourteenth century, and of the rich and diverse human characters of the time, with their joys and sorrows, their sins and their saintliness. It is almost as if we knew them for ourselves.

But there is one thing about the book which Chaucer's own contemporaries would have found fascinating but which is commonplace for us. They seldom if ever travelled anywhere; the pilgrims were doing something almost as unusual, in their world, as flying to the moon is for us. Travel used to be a rare luxury. As recently as the nineteenth century, only the idle rich from England could afford the time and money to visit the sights of Europe. In Chaucer's world, as in most of the world for most of human history, most people didn't travel at all. Those rich enough to afford horses could go some distance, but often wouldn't, because of all sorts of dangers. They stayed in their local neighbourhood all their lives.

This was true for most people in Jesus' world, too, with one major exception. Jews in Galilee regularly made one journey: the pilgrimage to Jerusalem (about three or four days' walk). And all Jews, wherever they were, would tell the story of the great journey of the **Exodus**, when their ancestors travelled from Egypt to the promised land. As they did so, they would tell other biblical stories as well – stories about kings and prophets, about God's dealings with Israel in bygone days.

Luke has all this in mind as he tells us about Jesus' plans to go to Jerusalem, where (as we saw in verse 31) he was to 'fulfil' his 'exodus'. It wasn't the moment yet for an official pilgrimage, and the journey which begins with 9.51 will continue – providing a frame for most of Luke's **gospel** – until 19.41; but from now on Jerusalem is the goal, and Jesus is constantly on the move. Luke's other great book, the Acts of the Apostles, also includes a long travel sequence (the journeys of St Paul, eventually arriving in Rome). Travelling in obedience to God's call is one of Luke's central pictures for what it means to be a Christian. Following Jesus is what it's all about.

The first thing he makes clear about following Jesus is that it's not easy. Before they even set off, the **disciples** are having a private row about which of them is the greatest. Whenever any project is launched, people discover that their own ambitions get mixed up with it. That has to be dealt with before you can start; the problem will recur, but markers must be put down right away. Then the disciples have to learn that God's **kingdom** may be going forward through people they don't know, who aren't part of their group. Things are not always straightforward.

When they start, Jesus 'sends messengers (the word can also mean 'angels') ahead of him'. Luke wants to remind us that this is indeed an Exodus journey: in the book of Exodus itself (23.20) God 'sends his angel before you' to guide the people into the land. But this is also a *new* Exodus journey: the prophet Malachi (3.1) declares that God will send his angel, or messenger, before him, so that when he arrives to judge and save, the people will be ready. All of this is built into Jesus' strange new journey. This is the road to the real promised land; it is also the road by which God himself is returning to his people.

All James and John can think of is that they are now in the same position as Elijah in the Old Testament. If they meet opposition, they want to call down fire from **heaven** (2 Kings 1.10–12). But that's not what Jesus' journey is like. It's not a triumphant march, sweeping all resistance aside. It is the progress of the gospel of the kingdom, and as we know from Luke 4 that means the message of love – of a grace so strong, so wide-ranging, and so surprising, that many will find it shocking.

Including, it seems, many who see Jesus and think it would be a fine thing to follow him. The people who speak to Jesus on the road are like the seed sown on rocky ground, or among thorns, in Luke 8. They want to follow, but have conditions attached. Are they ready to drop what they're doing and come right away? The obligation to bury one's father was regarded by many Jews of the time as the most holy and binding duty of a son; but Jesus says that that, too, is secondary to the call to follow him and announce God's kingdom.

The challenge to move forward, to journey on with Jesus, comes over loud and clear in the last line. Many today don't work the land, and perhaps don't appreciate what happens if you're trying to plough a straight furrow and then look back to see how you did. Even if what you see is a straight line, the act of looking back will mean that the next bit will become crooked. Think of other pictures. If you're singing a song, it's no good wondering whether you sang the previous line all right. You've got to concentrate on the next line. If you're on a journey, the map you need is the one which tells you where to go next, not the one for the road you've just travelled.

The question comes home to us with renewed force. Where is Jesus asking us to travel, not yesterday but tomorrow? Are we ready to follow him wherever he goes?

LUKE 10.1–16

Jesus Sends Out the Seventy

¹After this the master commissioned seventy others, and sent them ahead of him in pairs to every town and place where he was intending to come.

²'There's a great harvest out there,' he said to them, 'but there aren't many workers. So plead with the harvest-master to send out workers for the harvest.

³'Off you go now. Remember, I'm sending you out like lambs among wolves. ⁴Take no money-bag, no pack, no sandals – and don't stop to pass the time with anyone on the road. ⁵Whenever you go into a house, first say, "Peace on this house." ⁶If a child of peace lives there, your peace will rest on them; but if not, it will return to you.

⁷'Stay in the same house, and eat and drink what they provide. The worker deserves to be paid, you see. Don't go from house to house. ⁸If you go into a town and they welcome you, eat what is provided, ⁹heal the sick who are there, and say to them, "God's kingdom has come close to you." ¹⁰But if you go into a town and they don't welcome you, go out into the streets of the town and say, ¹¹"Here is the very dust of your town clinging to our feet – and we're wiping it off in front of your eyes! ¹²But you should know this: God's kingdom has come close to you!" Let me tell you, on that day it will be more tolerable for Sodom than for that town.

¹³'Woe betide you, Chorazin! Woe betide you, Bethsaida! If the powerful deeds done in you had been done in Tyre and Sidon, they would have repented long ago, sitting in sackcloth and ashes. ¹⁴But it will be more tolerable for Tyre and Sidon in the judgment than for you. ¹⁵And you, Capernaum – you want to be lifted up to heaven, do you? No: you'll be sent down to Hades!

¹⁶'Anyone who hears you, hears me; anyone who rejects you, rejects me; and anyone who rejects me, rejects the one who sent me.'

I had lunch with a friend who told me how, earlier in the year, his teenage son had been taken seriously ill. For weeks he had been going to doctors and specialists, all of whom had been puzzled by his symptoms. Finally he went to a senior specialist, who put an end to the speculation. 'Take him to the hospital at once,' he said. 'We'll operate tomorrow.' He had discovered a brain tumour, which was removed with great skill and without lasting damage. Had they waited another day it might have been too late.

Something of that mood hangs over the story of Jesus' second sending out of followers. This time, when Jesus sends messengers to the places he intends to visit, there is a note of real urgency. He knows he will not pass this way again; if people don't respond to his mission this time, it may be too late. He is the last herald before the great debacle that will come on the nation if they don't pay attention. If they reject him, there can be no subsequent warning. If they delay, it may be too late.

Only Luke tells us of a mission of seventy, and there are two puzzles about this. First, some manuscripts read 'seventy-two', instead of 'seventy', and there has been much discussion about which is correct. Second, whichever it is, why was this number chosen (either by Jesus or Luke)? Was there a symbolic meaning for it?

The answer to both questions may be that once again Luke is seeing Jesus in the light of Moses, who on one occasion chose seventy elders of Israel, who were given a share in God's **spirit**, and were thereby equipped to help him lead the people of Israel (Numbers 11.16, 25). On that occasion, not unlike what we saw in Luke 9.49–50, two others who were not part of the original seventy also received the spirit, to the alarm of some. The point will then be that Jesus is sending out assistants to help in leading the new **Exodus**.

But in the original Exodus the Israelites rebelled, grumbled and didn't want to go the way God was leading. That, indeed, was the main reason why Moses needed extra help. In Jesus' work, too, many if not most of his contemporaries simply didn't want to know. Despite all his healings, and the power and shrewdness of his teaching, the way he wanted them to follow – the way which he knew would lead them to God's true Exodus – was simply not the way they wanted. Thus it had been since his first sermon at Nazareth; thus it was to be right up to his last days in Jerusalem.

At the heart of his call was the message of peace. 'Peace to this house', the messengers were to say, looking to see whether there was a 'child of peace' there. Jesus' contemporaries were for the most part not wanting peace – peace with their traditional enemies the Samaritans (about whom one of Jesus' most famous **parables** will occupy us later in this chapter), or peace with the feared and hated Romans. They wanted an all-out war that would bring God's justice swiftly to their aid and get rid of their enemies once and for all.

But Jesus' vision of God's **kingdom** was going in the opposite direction. As far as he was concerned, the idea of fighting evil with evil was like the children of Israel wanting to go back to Egypt. Other movements had tried the way of violence, with disastrous results. But his rejection of that way was not based simply on pragmatic considerations. It grew directly out of his knowledge and love of Israel's God as the God of generous grace and astonishing, powerful, healing love. This was the God whose life-giving power flowed through him to heal; this was the God to whose kingdom he was committed.

His messengers therefore had to go with a word of warning as well as of invitation. To refuse this message would mean courting the disaster of going the opposite way from God himself; and that would mean, as always, throwing oneself into the hands of pagan power. The judgment that would fall on Chorazin and Bethsaida in central Galilee, and on Jesus' own town of Capernaum, would be more terrible than that suffered by the wicked cities of the Old Testament, but it would not consist of fire falling from **heaven**. It would take the form of Roman invasion and destruction. Rome's punishment for rebel subjects would be the direct result of God's people turning away from God's way of peace.

This explains the urgency and sternness of Jesus' charge to the seventy. They were not offering people a new religious option which might have a gentle effect on their lives. They were holding out the last chance for people to turn away from Israel's flight into ruin, and to accept God's way of peace. God's kingdom – God's sovereign and saving rule, longing to enfold his people and the whole world with love and new creation – had come close to them. Jesus was on his way to Jerusalem for the showdown with the forces of evil. To reject him now, or even to reject his messengers, was to reject God himself.

LUKE 10.17–24

The Celebration of Jesus

[17]The seventy came back exhilarated.

'Master,' they said, 'even the demons obey us in your name!'

[18]'I saw the satan fall like lightning from heaven,' he replied. [19]'Look: I've given you authority to tread on snakes and scorpions, and over every power of the enemy. Nothing will ever be able to harm you. [20]But – don't celebrate having spirits under your authority. Celebrate this, that your names are written in heaven.'

[21]Then and there Jesus celebrated in the holy spirit.

'I thank you, father,' he said, 'Lord of heaven and earth! You hid these things from the wise and intelligent, and revealed them to babies. Yes, father, that was what you graciously decided. [22]Everything has been given me by my father. Nobody knows who the son is except the father, and nobody knows who the father is except the son, and anyone to whom the son wishes to reveal him.'

[23]Jesus then turned to the disciples privately.

'A blessing on the eyes', he said, 'which see what you see! [24]Let me tell you, many prophets and kings wanted to see what you see, and they didn't see it; and to hear what you hear, and they didn't hear it!'

What was it like being Jesus? That's one of the hardest questions for anyone reading the **gospels**, but this passage gives us some clues.

It's all too easy for Christians to make the mistake of thinking that he just sailed through life with ease; being divine, we sometimes suppose, meant that he never faced problems, never had to wrestle with difficulties. Of course, the gospels themselves give us a very different picture. But, as we said earlier, we are easily fooled into thinking of Jesus as a kind of Superman.

That sort of understanding might seem, to begin with, to be supported by this passage. Jesus speaks of seeing **the satan** fall like lightning from **heaven**. He gives the seventy power over all evil. He celebrates his unique relationship with the Father. He speaks of a fulfilment which the great ones of old had longed to see. Surely, we think, this is Jesus the superhero, striding through the world winning victories at every turn, able to do anything at all? And surely, we often think, this Jesus is remarkably irrelevant to our own lives, where we face problems and puzzles and severe tests of **faith**, where despite our prayers and struggles things often go just plain wrong?

Luke has no intention of describing Jesus as Superman. The rest of his gospel makes that quite clear, and this passage fits in much better with his overall portrait than with the one we project back from our shallow modern culture. What we find here, in fact, is the unveiling of the true nature of the battle Jesus was facing and fighting.

He has now determined to go to Jerusalem, and, as we have seen, a new note of urgency comes in as he sends the seventy ahead of him. The depth of this urgency appears in the discussion, with the seventy, of their role and mission. Jesus began his public career with a private battle against the real enemy; this battle will continue until its last great showdown, as the powers of darkness gather for their final assault (22.53). But the initial victory which Jesus won in the desert is already being implemented through the work of his followers, and this points in turn to the victory which will come through the last battle.

We must remind ourselves who or what 'the satan' is in Jewish thinking. The word 'satan' literally means 'accuser', and 'the satan' appears in scripture as the director of public prosecutions in God's heavenly council (Job 1.6–12; 2.1–7; Zechariah 3.1–2). At some point he seems to have overstepped the role, not only bringing unfounded accusations, but inciting people to do things for which he can then accuse them. Finally, in flagrant rebellion against God and his plans of salvation for the world, the satan seeks to pervert, distort and overthrow Israel, the chosen bearers of God's promise, and to turn aside from his task Israel's true **Messiah**, the bringer of fulfilment. He has gained enormous power because the world in general, and Israel's leaders too, have been tricked by his cunning.

Jesus' task is therefore not simply to teach people a new way of life; not simply to offer a new depth of spirituality; not simply to enable them to go to heaven after death. Jesus' task is to defeat the satan, to break his power, to win the decisive victory which will open the way to God's new creation in which evil, and even death itself, will be banished.

So what did Jesus see, and what did it mean? 'I saw the satan fall like lightning from heaven', he said. As the seventy were going about their urgent mission, Jesus in prayer had seen a vision, echoing the prophetic visions of the downfall of the ancient enemy (Isaiah 14.4–23; Ezekiel 28.1–19). Jesus had seen, in mystical sight, the heavenly reality which corresponded to the earthly victories won by the seventy. He knew, and could assure the seventy, that their work was indeed part of the great victory begun in the desert and to be completed on the cross. They must not imagine, though, that they can now sit back and enjoy their new powers. What matters is that God's purpose is going forward, and that they are already enrolled in it. There is shortly coming a time, after all, when even the **Twelve**, even Peter, will be sifted like wheat by the satan, before the final victory can be accomplished (22.31–32).

In the same moment of vision and delight, Jesus celebrates what he realizes as God's strange purpose. If you needed to have privilege, learning and intelligence in order to enter the **kingdom of God**, it would simply be another elite organization run for the benefit of the top people. At every stage the gospel overturns this idea. Jesus sees that the intimate knowledge which he has of the Father is not shared by Israel's rulers, leaders and self-appointed teachers; but he can and does share it with his followers, the diverse and motley group he has chosen as his associates. God, says St Paul, chose what is foolish in the world to shame the wise, the weak to shame the strong.

As Jesus goes on his way to fight the final battle in Jerusalem, he knows that this strange purpose is already being accomplished. At its heart is the creation of a new people: a people who recognize Jesus as God's true son, the Messiah, and a people who through the work of Jesus are coming to know God for themselves as Father. A people, in other words, who fulfil Israel's destiny; a people who see and hear what prophets and kings longed to see and hear but did not.

LUKE 10.25–37

The Parable of the Good Samaritan

²⁵A lawyer got up and put Jesus on the spot.

'Teacher,' he said, 'what should I do to inherit the life of the coming age?'

²⁶'Well,' replied Jesus, 'what is written in the law? What's your interpretation of it?'

²⁷'You shall love the Lord your God', he replied, 'with all your heart, all your soul, all your strength, and all your understanding; and your neighbour as yourself.'

²⁸'Well said!' replied Jesus. 'Do that and you will live.'

²⁹'Ah,' said the lawyer, wanting to win the point, 'but who is my neighbour?'

³⁰Jesus rose to the challenge. 'Once upon a time,' he said, 'a man was going down from Jerusalem to Jericho, and was set upon by brigands. They stripped him and beat him and ran off leaving him half dead. ³¹A priest happened to be going down that road, and when he saw him he went past on the opposite side. ³²So too a Levite came by the place; he saw him too, and went past on the opposite side.

³³'But a travelling Samaritan came to where he was. When he saw him he was filled with pity. ³⁴He came over to him and bound up his wounds, pouring in oil and wine. Then he put him on his own beast, took him to an inn, and looked after him. ³⁵The next morning, as he was going on his way, he gave the innkeeper two dinars. "Take care of him," he said, "and on my way back I'll pay you whatever else you need to spend on him."

³⁶'Which of these three do you think turned out to be the neighbour of the man who was set upon by the brigands?'

³⁷'The one who showed mercy on him', came the reply.

'Well,' Jesus said to him, 'you go and do the same.'

The best-known stories are sometimes the hardest to understand. 'The good Samaritan' has passed into folklore, and has succeeded, confusingly, in changing the meaning of the word 'Samaritan' itself in modern English. There is now a well-known organization called 'The Samaritans', whose task is to give help to people in the direst need. But that certainly wasn't what people would have meant by the word in Jesus' day.

Often this **parable** is simply taken in a general moral sense: if you see someone in the ditch, go and help them. Sometimes, where people remember that in Jesus' day the Samaritans and the Jews hated each other like poison, this is expanded into a further moral lesson about the wickedness of racial and religious prejudice. But if we are to have any chance of understanding what Jesus himself meant – and what was at stake in the wider conversation with the lawyer – we need to go deeper.

Fortunately this isn't difficult. The hatred between Jews and Samaritans had gone on for hundreds of years – and is still reflected, tragically, in the smouldering tension between Israel and Palestine today. Both sides claimed to be the true inheritors of the promises to Abraham and Moses; both sides, in consequence, regarded themselves as the rightful possessors of the land. Few Israelis today will travel from Galilee to Jerusalem by the direct route, because it will take them through the West Bank and risk violence. In exactly the same way, most first-century pilgrims making the same journey would prefer, as Jesus himself did, to travel down the Jordan valley to Jericho and then turn west up the hill to Jerusalem. It was much safer.

But still not completely safe. The desert road from Jericho to Jerusalem had many turns and twists, and brigands could lurk out of sight in the nearby hills and valleys, ready to strike. A lonely traveller was an easy target. And, when he was left half-dead, those who went by couldn't tell whether he was dead or alive . . . so, since as **Temple** officials it was important for the two in the story not to contract impurity by touching a corpse, it was better that they remain aloof, preserving their purity at the cost of their obedience to God's law of love.

The lawyer's question and Jesus' answer don't quite match up, and that's part of the point. He wants to know who counts as 'neighbour'. For him, God is the God of Israel, and neighbours are Jewish neighbours. For Jesus (and for Luke, who highlights this theme), Israel's God is the God of grace for the whole world, and a neighbour is anybody in need. Jesus' telling question at the end isn't asking who the Samaritan regarded as his neighbour. He asked, instead, who *turned out to be* the neighbour of the half-dead Jew lying in the road. Underneath the apparently straightforward moral lesson ('go and do the same'), we find a much sterner challenge, exactly fitting in with the emphasis of Luke's story so far. Can you recognize the hated Samaritan as your neighbour? If you can't, you might be left for dead.

But even that doesn't get right to the heart of it. Jesus is himself on the road to Jerusalem – it is perhaps significant that the first parable told on the journey is about people coming and going on the road Jesus himself will shortly tread – and his challenge to Israel is to see that the way of confrontation with Samaritans, Romans and pagans of whatever sort is not the way of living and showing God's grace. He is urgently offering the way of peace, and only the 'children of peace' (10.6) will escape the self-inflicted judgment that will befall those bent on violence.

What lies at the heart of the confrontation with the lawyer, then, is a clash between two quite different visions of what it means to be Israel, God's people. The lawyer's question about the key requirements for entering the **age to come** was a standard rabbinic question, to which there were standard answers available. His own summary is exactly the same as that which Jesus himself gives in Mark 12.29–31 and Matthew 22.37–40. But what he had in mind was the way in which the law provided a definition of Israel. He wanted to put Jesus on the spot, and force him into saying something that might appear heretical.

When Jesus makes him reveal his own summary, and then simply agrees with it, the lawyer now aims 'to win the point', 'to justify himself' – not simply meaning 'to show that he hadn't asked a trivial or obvious question', but 'to come out on top in this public confrontation'. The question about the neighbour is designed to smoke out Jesus' supposedly heretical views on God's wider plans for the whole world, and so to show that the lawyer was right to challenge him. It does indeed produce from Jesus an answer about the wide-reaching grace of God, but the story Jesus tells makes it clear that these views are not heretical, but rather the true fulfilment of the commandment which the lawyer claims to regard as vital.

What is at stake, then and now, is the question of whether we will use the God-given revelation of love and grace as a way of boosting our own sense of isolated security and purity, or whether we will see it as a call and challenge to extend that love and grace to the whole world. No church, no Christian, can remain content with easy definitions which allow us to watch most of the world lying half-dead in the road. Today's preachers, and today's defenders of the **gospel**, must find fresh ways of telling the story of God's love which will do for our day what this brilliant parable did for Jesus' first hearers.

LUKE 10.38–42

Martha and Mary

[38]On their journey, Jesus came into a village. There was a woman there named Martha, who welcomed him. [39]She had a sister named Mary, who sat at the master's feet and listened to his teaching.

[40]Martha was frantic with all the work in the kitchen.

'Master,' she said, coming in to where they were, 'don't you care that my sister has left me to do the work all by myself? Tell her to give me a hand!'

[41]'Martha, Martha,' he replied, 'you are fretting and fussing about so many things. [42]Only one thing matters. Mary has chosen the best part, and it's not going to be taken away from her.'

If you thought 'the good Samaritan' was radical, this powerful little story suggests that Luke has plenty more where that came from. In describing Jesus' journey to Jerusalem, he has chosen this incident as part of his introduction. It took place at Bethany, as we know from other accounts of these sisters, and Bethany was not far from Jerusalem – near, in fact, the top of the road described in the **parable** we've just studied. The incident can't, therefore, have taken place at this point in the story, but Luke has placed it here to alert us to something special about Jesus' work. Not only was he redrawing the boundaries of God's people, sending out a clear message about how the **gospel** would reach to those outside the traditional borders. He was redrawing the boundaries between men and women *within* Israel, blurring lines which had been clearly laid down.

The real problem beween Martha and Mary wasn't the workload that Martha had in the kitchen. That, no doubt, was real enough, but it wasn't the main thing that was upsetting Martha. Nor was it (as some have suggested) that both the sisters were romantically attracted to Jesus and Martha was jealous of Mary's adoring posture, sitting at Jesus' feet. If there was any such feeling, Luke neither says nor hints anything about it. No: the real problem was that *Mary was behaving as if she were a man.* In that culture, as in many parts of the world to this day, houses were divided into male 'space' and female 'space', and male and female roles were strictly demarcated as well. Mary had crossed an invisible but very important boundary within the house, and another equally important boundary within the social world.

The public room was where the men would meet; the kitchen, and other quarters unseen by outsiders, belonged to the women. Only outside, where little children would play, and in the married bedroom, would male and female mix. For a woman to settle down comfortably among the men was bordering on the scandalous. Who did she think she was? Only a shameless woman would behave in such a way. She should go back into the women's quarters where she belonged. This wasn't principally a matter of superiority and inferiority, though no doubt it was often perceived and articulated like that. It was a matter of what was thought of as the appropriate division between the two halves of humanity.

In the same way, to sit at the feet of a teacher was a decidedly male role. 'Sitting at someone's feet' doesn't mean (as it might sound to us) a devoted, dog-like adoring posture, as though the teacher were a rock star or a sports idol. When Saul of Tarsus 'sat at the feet of Gamaliel' (Acts 22.3), he wasn't gazing up adoringly and thinking how wonderful the great **rabbi** was; he was listening and learning, focusing on the teaching of his master and putting it together in his mind. To sit at someone's feet meant, quite simply, to be their student. And to sit at the feet of a rabbi was what you did *if you wanted to be a rabbi yourself.* There is no thought here of learning for learning's sake. Mary has quietly taken her place as a would-be teacher and preacher of the **kingdom of God**.

Jesus affirms her right to do so. This has little to do with the women's movements in the modern West. They do have some parallels with Jesus' agenda, and the two can make common cause on several issues; but they should not be confused. Jesus' valuation of each human being is based not on abstract egalitarian ideals, but on the overflowing love of God, which, like a great river breaking its banks into a parched countryside, irrigates those parts of human society which until now had remained barren and unfruitful. Mary stands for all those women who, when they hear Jesus speaking about the kingdom, know that God is calling them to listen carefully so that they can speak of it too.

We would be wrong, then, to see Martha and Mary, as they have so often been seen, as models of the 'active' and the 'contemplative' styles of spirituality. Action and contemplation are of course both important. Without the first you wouldn't eat, without the second you wouldn't worship. And no doubt some people are called to one kind of balance between them, and others to another. But we cannot escape the challenge of this passage by turning it into a comment about different types of Christian lifestyle. It is about the boundary-breaking call of Jesus. As he goes up to Jerusalem, he leaves behind him towns, villages, households and individuals who have glimpsed a new vision of the kingdom, and for whom **life** will never be the same again. God grant that as we read his story the same will be true for us.

LUKE 11.1-13

The Lord's Prayer

[1]Once Jesus was praying in a particular place. When he had finished, one of his disciples approached him.

'Teach us to pray, Master,' he said, 'just like John taught his disciples.'

[2]'When you pray,' replied Jesus, 'this is what to say:

'Father, may your name be honoured; may your kingdom come; [3]give us each day our daily bread; [4]and forgive us our sins, since we too forgive all our debtors; and don't put us to the test.

[5]'Suppose one of you has a friend,' he said, 'and you go to him in the middle of the night and say, "My dear friend, lend me three loaves of bread! [6]A friend of mine is on a journey and has arrived at my house, and I have nothing to put in front of him!" [7]He will answer from

inside his house, "Don't make life difficult for me! The door is already shut, and my children and I are all in bed! I can't get up and give you anything." ⁸Let me tell you, even if he won't get up and give you anything just because you're his friend, because of your shameless persistence he will get up and give you whatever you need.

⁹'So this is my word to you: ask and it will be given you; search and you will find; knock and it will be opened to you. ¹⁰You see, everyone who asks receives! Everyone who searches finds! Everyone who knocks has the door opened for them! ¹¹If your son asks you for a fish, is there a father among you who will give him a snake? ¹²Or if he asks for an egg, will you give him a scorpion? ¹³So if you, evil as you are, know how to give good presents to your children, how much more will your heavenly father give the holy spirit to those who ask him!'

The telephone rang. It was a message that my younger son, a singer, was about to get on an aeroplane to go with his choir to the other side of the world. If I was quick, I might just be able to catch him with a call to wish him well. I phoned, caught him, and we had a good chat. There are times when I wonder where fatherhood ends and friendship begins.

Friendship and fatherhood together teach us something about God and prayer. Actually, the learning can be a two-way street. It isn't just a matter of thinking about earthly friends and fathers and then learning that God is like that. There are times when a father needs to take a long, hard look at what God's fatherhood is all about, and start changing his own fatherhood behaviour to be more like it. And most of our friendships, I suspect, could do with the improvement that some reflection about God as a friend might provide.

It is that picture – of God as a friend, in bed and asleep, with his children around him – which probably strikes us as the more peculiar. (We are used to saying that God is our father, though we may not always ask what exactly that means; but God as our friend is less obvious.) In the sort of house Jesus has in mind, the family would all sleep side by side on the floor, so that if the father got up at midnight the whole family would be woken up. My children are now past that stage (my wife and I are more likely to be woken up when they come home at midnight or later), but it's obvious what a nuisance it is when the knock comes on the door.

Yet the friend outside has a real problem, and the sleeping friend can and will help him. The laws of hospitality in the ancient Middle East were strict, and if a traveller arrived needing food and shelter one was under an obligation to provide it. The friend in the street knows that the friend in bed will understand; he would do the same if the roles were reversed.

What counts is *persistence*. There are all sorts of ways in which God isn't like a sleepy friend, but Jesus is focusing on one point of comparison only: he is encouraging a kind of holy boldness, a sharp knocking on the door, an insistent asking, a search that refuses to give up. That's what our prayer should be like. This isn't just a routine or formal praying, going through the motions as a daily or weekly task. There is a battle on, a fight with the powers of darkness, and those who have glimpsed the light are called to struggle in prayer – for peace, for reconciliation, for wisdom, for a thousand things for the world and the church, perhaps a hundred or two for one's own family, friends and neighbours, and perhaps a dozen or two for oneself.

There are, of course, too many things to pray about. That's why it's important to be disciplined and regular. If you leave it to the whim of the moment you'll never be a true intercessor, somebody through whose prayers God's love is poured out into the world. But because these things are urgent, important and complex there has to be more to prayer than simply discipline and regularity. Formal prayers, including official liturgies for services in church, are vital for most people for their spiritual health, but they are like the metal shell of a car. To be effective it needs fuel for its engine, and to be effective prayers need energy, too: in this case, the kind of dogged and even funny determination that you'd use with a sleepy friend who you hoped would help you out of a tight spot.

The larger picture, though, is the more familiar one of God as Father. This isn't just an illustration drawn from family life, though of course it is that at its heart, and Jesus' illustrations about giving a child real food rather than poisonous snakes make their point. If we are ever tempted to imagine God as a tyrant who would take delight in giving us things that weren't good for us, we should remember these pictures and think again. But the illustration is bigger than that as well. The idea of God as Father goes right back to the time when Israel was in slavery and needed rescuing. 'Israel is my son, my firstborn,' declared God to Pharaoh through Moses and Aaron; 'so let my people go!' From then on, to call on God as 'Father' was to invoke the God of the **Exodus**, the liberating God, the God whose **kingdom** was coming, bringing bread for the hungry, forgiveness for the sinner, and deliverance from the powers of darkness – all themes, we may observe, that Luke has drawn to our attention in the last two chapters we have studied.

The 'Lord's Prayer', as many call it, is therefore not just a loosely connected string of petitions. It is a prayer for people who are following Jesus on the kingdom-journey. Jesus was on the way to Jerusalem, to act on behalf of God's name, which had been dragged in the mud as his people had turned away from him in rebellion. He was on the way to accomplish the 'Exodus' in which the long-awaited kingdom of God would become a reality. He had provided bread for the journey, and 'the breaking of bread' was to become the sign of his presence in the church, and the bond between his followers. He was already offering forgiveness, and would accomplish it completely in his death – and he was already demanding from his followers that they imitate the graciousness of their God in forgiving their enemies, let alone each other. And, as we have already seen and will shortly see in more detail, he was waging war against the powers of evil, a war that would reach its decisive battle on Calvary. This is a prayer which grows out of the mission of Jesus himself. It has been ideally suited, both as it stands and as a framework for wider praying, for his followers ever since.

LUKE 11.14–28

Jesus and Beelzebul

[14]Jesus was casting out a demon that prevented speech. When the demon had gone out, the man who had been silent spoke, and the crowd was amazed. [15]But some of them said, 'He casts out demons by Beelzebul, the prince of demons!' [16]Others, trying to test him out, asked him to produce a sign from heaven.

[17]Jesus knew what they were thinking.

'Every kingdom split down the middle goes to ruin', he said. 'If a house turns in on itself, it falls. [18]Well then: if even the satan is split down the middle, how can his kingdom last? This', he added, 'is because you say that I cast out demons by Beelzebul!

[19]'Now look: supposing I do cast out demons by Beelzebul, whose power are your own people using when they cast them out? Think about it: they will be your judges. [20]But if it's by God's finger that I cast out demons, then God's kingdom has come upon you.

[21]'Imagine a strong man, armed to the teeth, guarding his palace. Everything he owns is safe and sound. [22]But supposing someone stronger comes and overpowers him, and takes away the armour he was trusting in – then he can help himself and start dividing up the plunder! [23]If you're not with me, you're against me. If you're not gathering with me, you're scattering.

[24]'When the unclean spirit goes out of a person, it roams through desert landscapes looking for a place to rest. When it doesn't find anywhere, it says to itself, "I shall go back to the house I left behind." [25]And it finds the place neat and tidy. [26]So it sets off and brings along seven other spirits more evil than itself, and goes back to live there. That person will end up worse off than he began.'

> ^{27}While he was saying these things, a woman from the crowd raised her voice. 'A blessing on the womb that bore you,' she shouted, 'and the breasts that you sucked!'
> ^{28}'On the contrary,' replied Jesus. 'A blessing on those who hear God's word and keep it!'

A friend was telling me about the first years in which she had been a schoolteacher. 'It was very strange,' she said. 'Sometimes a pupil would be doing just fine, and then suddenly their work would get much worse. We wouldn't find out why until the parents came to the school to talk to us. Then suddenly we'd understand what the problem was: a death in the family, a divorce, or something equally traumatic.'

Those of us who can remember being pupils, and who have then been parents of schoolchildren, will understand the point. What you see on the surface in the classroom isn't the whole picture. You need to understand what's going on out of sight as well, in the home or the local village where the student returns at the end of the working day. Only then will the depth of the problem become clear.

Jesus' opponents thought they had seen the hidden truth behind what he was doing. Outwardly, he was rebuking **demons**, and they were obeying him. The spirits did what he told them. People who saw this were faced with two possible interpretations. Either Jesus really was equipped with special power from God, giving him this extraordinary authority. Or he was somehow in league with the source of evil power; perhaps he had struck a bargain with the prince of demons. (The word 'Beelzebul' or 'Beelzebub' was a kind of nickname, originally meaning something like 'Lord of flies'. By Jesus' day it was simply a way of referring to the personal source of evil without giving it, or him, a more precise definition.)

Accusing Jesus like this was, for the opponents, an ideal way not only of rejecting Jesus' message about the **kingdom**, but of launching a propaganda attack against him. 'Ah,' they were saying, 'don't just look at the outward effects! You need to understand what's going on behind. Then you'll see he's a scoundrel – in league with the devil himself!' Those who were not with him were therefore against him (though this proverb-like saying needs balancing with 9.50, and wisdom is required in deciding which applies to which situation).

Jesus would of course have agreed that there was a hidden meaning behind what he was doing, but it was the precise opposite of what they were suggesting. His own explanation indicates what is really going on.

He begins by pointing to a fatal flaw in the opponents' logic. If **the satan** is opposing his own troops, he has already lost the battle: his kingdom is split down the middle. He then invites the accusers to compare him with other Jewish exorcists of the time. Are they, too, in league with the devil? If not, why should he be?

Jesus is not claiming to be simply one exorcist among others. He is not casting out demons by some magic formula, or by using the name of some mighty or holy person. He is doing so 'by the finger of God' – a phrase which Luke hopes will remind his readers of the powerful works which Moses did at Pharaoh's court (Exodus 8.19), and which the magicians of Egypt could not copy. Jesus is acting like someone who has successfully attacked and tied up the strong man who was guarding a house. He has won an initial victory over the satan, and is now able to give orders to his underlings and have them obey him at once.

Jesus is showing, then, that the God of the **Exodus** is alive and well and at work. His journey to Jerusalem is marked at every step by signs of what he must accomplish there. The power which enables him to defeat the demons in the present is the same power by which, through death itself, he will destroy death.

For the moment, though, a warning: Jesus tells a strange story about an evil spirit which returns to the place it left. This can't be a warning about the likely effect of exorcisms; if it was, it would be better not to do them at all, since the poor person ends up worse off than before. It probably means what it seems to in Matthew (12.43–45), applying not to an individual person but to the nation as a whole.

The point of Jesus' exorcisms, after all, was not simply to heal as many individuals as possible. If that were his aim, he wasn't very successful when seen in the longer term. Rather, he was aiming to enact God's kingdom, for Israel and the world. Israel, like a demon-possessed person, had been 'cleansed' by various movements of reform. But unless the living presence of God came to dwell in her midst, Israel would remain vulnerable to the return of the demons. Jesus stood there among his people, embodying as we shall see the return of God to Israel. Unless they turned from accusation to acceptance, the demons that had led them to ruin in former days would come back in full force.

Jesus' powerful teaching evoked a typical cry of admiration from a woman in the crowd. Fancy being the mother of such a son! But Jesus quickly turns the saying around into another warning, as in the earlier comment about his true family (8.21). When the **word** of God is at work, what is required is not applause but obedience.

LUKE 11.29–41

The Sign of Jonah

²⁹The crowds kept increasing. Jesus began to say to them, 'This generation is an evil generation! It looks for a sign, and no sign will be given to it except the sign of Jonah.

³⁰'Jonah was a sign to the people of Nineveh; just so, the son of man will be a sign to this generation. ³¹'The Queen of the South will rise up in the judgment with the men of this generation and will condemn them: she came from the ends of the earth to listen to Solomon's wisdom, and look – something greater than Solomon is here. ³²The men of Nineveh will rise up in the judgment with this generation and will condemn it: they repented at Jonah's preaching, and look – something greater than Jonah is here.

³³'Nobody lights a lamp in order to hide it or put it under a jug. They put it on a lampstand, so that people who come in can see the light.

³⁴'Your eye is the lamp of your body. If your eye is focused, your whole body is full of light. But if it's evil, your body is in darkness. ³⁵Watch out, then, in case the light inside you turns to darkness. ³⁶If your whole body is illuminated, with no part in darkness, everything will be illuminated, just as you are by a flash of lightning.'

³⁷While he was speaking, a Pharisee invited him to have dinner at his house. So he went in and sat down. ³⁸The Pharisee, watching him, was surprised that he didn't first wash before dinner.

³⁹'Now, you Pharisees,' said the master to him, 'you clean the outside of the plate and the cup, but your insides are full of violent robbery and wickedness. ⁴⁰That's stupid! Didn't the one who made the outside make the inside as well? ⁴¹You should give for alms what's inside the bowl and then everything will be clean for you.'

The great church is completely dark. It is almost midnight, and the little crowd outside the west door shuffles round and stamps to keep warm in the chilly April air. Then, as the clock strikes, the fire is lit, with a sudden glow on all the watching faces. A single candle is lit from the fire. The doors swing open, the light moves forward into the pitch-black church, and the Easter celebration begins. Soon the whole place will be full of flickering, glowing candlelight, the light of God's power and love shining in the darkness of the world.

Not every church celebrates Easter this way, but those that do will have no difficulty making the connections that hold together the rather confusing collection of sayings in this passage. The context is still, of course, Jesus' journey to Jerusalem, like a candle going forwards into the darkness.

104

When the light comes, it scatters the darkness; but what if you were rather enjoying the darkness, able to get on unseen with whatever evil purposes you had? Light brings hope and new possibility, but it also brings judgment. Light symbolizes new life in the face of the darkness of death, but it also shows up that darkness for what it is. These sayings, then, though full of hope, are also filled with warnings of judgment. Jesus, on his way to Jerusalem, is constantly saying in one way or another that God's light will shine out and expose the darkness that had taken hold of the hearts and minds of his contemporaries.

It all begins with a sign – the sign of Jonah. Jonah is an almost comic figure in the Old Testament: the prophet who runs away, the problem passenger thrown into the sea, the dinner the whale can't stomach, and the hothead who gets cross with God over a withered plant. In between, though, he told the people of Nineveh to repent, never thinking they would listen and obey. But he was wrong: they did – whether or not, as in Matthew's version of the story, because they had heard about his escapade with the sea and the whale, or whether simply because of the power of the **message**.

Now here is Jesus, anything but a comic figure, telling his own people it's time to repent, and they ignore him. Here is Jesus with a greater wisdom than even the legendary Solomon, and his own people don't listen. There is a straight line from this point that leads to the moment when Jesus weeps over Jerusalem because, unlike Nineveh, it has ignored the warnings, refused the way of peace, and thereby sealed its own fate.

Luke's reader, meanwhile, is left to ponder the way in which Jesus speaks of the foreigners, the Queen of the South and the people of Nineveh, who will 'rise at the judgment'. The two words used to mean 'rise' are both regular early Christian words for the **resurrection**: Luke expects his readers to know about the coming resurrection of the dead, and of the great judgment that will then take place. The light of Easter is the light of judgment as well as hope.

When we read the sayings about light, then, they speak of more than a general wisdom or spiritual illumination. To begin with, Jesus warns that the light that has come into the midst of Israel is designed not to remain hidden but to shine all around. Then, changing the image, he gives another warning, more cryptic for us and easy to miss.

To begin with, it looks like a rather obvious saying about human life: 'If the eye is in working order,' Jesus seems to be saying, 'you can see where you're going; but if it isn't, you can't; so watch out in case your light (that is, your eye) becomes darkened.' Now clearly Jesus isn't giving advice about protecting our physical eyes; nor about the spiritual dangers of looking at the wrong things. Nor, I think, is he just speaking of the spiritual insight of individuals. The passage makes more sense, especially where Luke has placed it, as a warning to 'this generation', his contemporaries. They must watch out in case they fail to see the light that was standing there in their midst.

The final sentence is then an encouragement to embrace and live by the light while there's time. A day is coming when everything will be lit up (compare 17.24), and on that day those who have allowed the light to illuminate them fully will shine brightly.

What this means in practice emerges in the sharp little dinner-table exchange between Jesus and the **Pharisee**. Some Pharisees were concentrating on outward piety to the neglect of the inward devotion which was part of Jesus' main aim. The last phrase literally means 'give for alms those things that are inside', and, as it stands, this seems almost incomprehensible. But if Jesus meant by 'give for alms' something like 'give over to God for his use', the sentence becomes clear. True piety takes as much care about giving to God the thoughts, intentions and motivations of the heart as about handwashing. If you embrace the light, it must illuminate every part.

Where does all this leave us today? The light of Christ has been in the world for 2,000 years. Are we any better at embracing it for ourselves than Jesus' contemporaries were? For that matter, are we shining this light to the world so that they can see the one who is greater than Solomon, greater than Jonah?

LUKE 11.42-54

Woes against the Pharisees

⁴²'But woe betide you Pharisees!' Jesus continued. 'You tithe mint and rue and herbs of all kinds; and you have sidestepped justice and the love of God. You should have done these, without missing out the others.

⁴³'Woe betide you Pharisees! You love the chief seats in the synagogues and greetings in the marketplaces.

⁴⁴'Woe betide you! You are like hidden tombs, and people walk over them without knowing it.'

⁴⁵At this, one of the legal experts spoke up. 'Teacher,' he said, 'when you say this you're insulting us too!'

⁴⁶'Woe betide you lawyers, too!' replied Jesus. 'You give people heavy loads to carry which they can hardly bear, and you yourselves don't lift a finger to help!

⁴⁷'Woe betide you! You build the tombs of the prophets, and your ancestors killed them. ⁴⁸So you bear witness that you approve of what your ancestors did: they killed them, and you build their tombs.

⁴⁹'For all this, God's Wisdom says, "I'm sending you prophets and ambassadors; some of them you will kill and persecute", ⁵⁰so that the blood of all the prophets shed ever since the beginning of the world may be required from this generation – ⁵¹from the blood of Abel to the blood of Zacharias, who died between the altar and the sanctuary. Yes, let me tell you, it will all be required from this generation.

⁵²'Woe betide you lawyers! You have taken away the key of knowledge. You didn't go in yourselves, and when people were trying to get in you stopped them.'

⁵³He went outside, and the scribes and Pharisees began to be very threatening towards him. They interrogated him about several things, ⁵⁴lying in wait for him to catch him in something he might say.

The tennis player came grumpily into the television interview room. He had just lost a vital match in the Wimbledon men's singles tournament, the premier tennis event of the year. He was tired and cross. Worse: in the course of the game, screened on live television, he had lost his temper and sworn at the umpire. It had not been a good day.

The interviewer was more interested in the swearing than in the tennis. Wasn't he sorry now, he asked, for what he had said?

The tennis player rounded on him.

'Are you perfect?' he demanded.

There was a confused splutter from the (unseen) interviewer, caught between the outrageous claim to perfection and the unthinkable admission that he, too, was human.

'Then shut up!' retorted the player, having made his point.

The incident itself became briefly more important than the tennis. The player had broken a law which, although unwritten, had been assumed by many in the media. *He had been rude to a journalist.*

Who are the **Pharisees** in today's society? Who are the lawyers who load heavy burdens on to people's backs but don't themselves lift a finger to shift them? When I was younger, passages like this used to be applied to religious teachers. Some people, we were told, insist on all kinds of religious observances. You should fast on Fridays, you should kneel down and stand up at the right points in church, you should cross yourself. You should earn as many celestial good marks as you could. Or, perhaps, you shouldn't play cards, you shouldn't wear make-up, you shouldn't go to the theatre. You should read your Bible every day. Either way, we were told, people who taught such things tried to make you focus on the things you did, rather than calling you simply to believe and trust God for your salvation.

Well, that sort of teacher does sometimes look like a kind of modern Pharisee. But there are two problems with that as the interpretation.

First, the real Pharisees – the flesh-and-blood first-century Jewish Pharisees – weren't in fact very much like that at all. They held what we would call a strong *political* belief, backed up with religious sanctions: their rules were designed to make people keep the Jewish **law** as best they could, so that Israel would be made holy, and thus God would bring in the **kingdom**. The lawyers weren't trying to set up complex systems as hoops for people to jump through to make sure they were saved; they were trying to codify as much of the Jewish law as they could, working out more and more complex possibilities of situations that might arise when one would need to know what was the right thing to do. Neither of these corresponds very closely to forms of Christian teaching, even degenerate forms, in the modern world.

Second, the Pharisees were a pressure group in what we would call the social and political sphere. They were far more like a group in society who take it upon themselves to urge people to obey particular codes: like those, for instance, who insist upon various 'green' policies for the disposal of garbage. We may agree with the policies, but the point is that these aren't simply 'religious' duties in the old sense. And in particular, at least in the Western world where the press is relatively free, there are many whole newspapers, as well as individual journalists, who take it upon themselves to be the guardians of public morality. They will shriek in mock-horror at all kinds of offences, and take delight in pointing the finger at the rich and respectable. But at the same time many of the journalists who make a living by doing all this are by no means shining examples of moral virtue. In some cases they are the ones who load heavy burdens on people's backs but don't themselves lift a finger to move them.

Now clearly this only goes a little way towards explaining what's going on in this passage, but it's important to loosen ourselves up, away from an older interpretation that sees the Pharisees as simply 'religious leaders' in the sense we mean it today, and so to get out of our minds any idea that Jesus' solemn denunciation of them was simply what we might call 'religious polemic'. Jesus saw very clearly that there were many self-appointed teachers in the world of first-century Judaism who were using their learning partly for their own status and partly for their own political ends. And he, for whom learning and devotion were matters of love for God and for all people (as the best of the Pharisees would have agreed), saw that there was a choice facing the Israel of his day.

It wasn't a matter of *either* following millions of petty rules *or* of a pure, uncluttered religion of love and grace. It was a matter of an agenda which focused on the law as the charter of Israel's national life, on the one hand, and an agenda which demanded **repentance**, turning away from Israel's headlong flight into national rebellion, politically against Rome and theologically against God. There could be no compromise.

When Jesus announced these quite formal 'Woes', then, he wasn't simply saying he *disliked* such attitudes – the detailed outward observance that left the heart untouched, the piety that boosted self-importance, the pollution that appeared as clean and wholesome. It wasn't simply that he happened to disapprove of the objectionable practices of these other groups. It was, rather, that he could see where they would lead: to a terrible conflagration in which the present generation would pull down on its own head the pent-up devastation of the centuries.

'Scribes' refers literally to people trained in writing legal documents; it overlaps quite closely with 'lawyers'. They believed that Israel's law, the Torah, should be applied to every area of life, and so combined in themselves the modern roles of 'lawyer' and 'religious teacher', and much besides. It is small wonder that such people took offence at what Jesus was saying. If he was right, their entire programme was based on a huge mistake. If they were right, the mistake was his. The fierce opposition between them continues on and off right through to the final showdown in Jerusalem. For Luke, continuing the story of Jesus' journey towards his coming death, the warnings to the cities (10.13–15), the battles with the **demons** at several points, and the controversies with these opponents, all form part of Jesus' profile. Jesus is not simply going to Jerusalem to teach. He is going there to bring to its head his whole message of peace: a message which cut across much that passed for traditional teaching, a message which could not but prove fiercely controversial.

Where does the **gospel** of Jesus confront, not just alternative religious or would-be Christian views today, but the strongly held agendas out in the wider world?

LUKE 12.1–12

Further Warnings

[1]Crowds were gathering in their thousands, so much so that they were trampling on each other. Jesus began to say to his disciples, 'Watch out for the leaven of the Pharisees – I mean, their hypocrisy. This is a matter of first importance.

[2]'Nothing is concealed that won't be uncovered; nothing is hidden that won't be made known. [3]So whatever you say in the darkness will be heard in the light, and whatever you speak indoors into someone's ear will be proclaimed from the housetops.

[4]'So, my friends, I have this to say to you: don't be afraid of those who kill the body, and after that have nothing more they can do.

⁵I will show you who to fear: fear the one who starts by killing and then has the right to throw people into Gehenna. Yes, let me tell you, that's the one to fear!

⁶'How much do five sparrows cost? Two copper coins? And not one of them is forgotten in God's presence. ⁷But the hairs of your head have all been counted. Don't be afraid! You are worth more than lots of sparrows.

⁸'Let me tell you: if anyone acknowledges me before others, the son of man will acknowledge that person before God's angels. ⁹But if anyone denies me before others, that person will be denied before God's angels.

¹⁰'Everyone who speaks a word against the son of man will have it forgiven; but the one who blasphemes against the holy spirit will not be forgiven.

¹¹'When they bring you before synagogues, rulers and authorities, don't worry about how to give an answer or what to say. ¹²The holy spirit will teach you what to say at that very moment.'

It started off as an ordinary walk in the country. We decided to head off across open moorland towards a distant crag; the map suggested there might be a good view from the top.

Much of the walk was relaxed. The five of us went at our own paces, in twos and threes, some up ahead and others lagging behind, and it didn't matter. When we got to the crag we assumed it would be a straightforward scramble to the top. But, halfway up, the leader slipped and fell, and though he didn't fall far he'd clearly broken a bone and was in pain.

Suddenly the entire mood of the party changed. Instead of a casual stroll, this had to become a military operation. One of our number, a doctor, took charge and told us what to do. He expected instant obedience and he got it. Whatever we had wanted to do – we'd been looking forward to the view from the crag, which was now forgotten – we suddenly had a different set of priorities. We had to get our injured friend back to the car in one piece, and it would take the complete attention and loyalty of everyone else to achieve it.

Something like this shift takes place between the early chapters of Luke and where we are now. He is allowing us to see how, with Jesus on the long road to Jerusalem, tension is building up, opposition is becoming stronger, and anyone who wants to follow Jesus is going to have to become focused, totally loyal, ready for anything. The mood is not what many think of today as 'religious', where people attend a church service, maybe sense God's presence and love for a few moments, and then return to ordinary life as though little or nothing had happened. This is much more like the concentrated campaign of someone running for high office, in a country where political opponents and their supporters will literally come to blows, and perhaps try to imprison or impeach one another. What Jesus is doing demands total attention. Anything less, and disaster may follow.

Hence the stark warnings about what is whispered today being shouted from the housetops tomorrow. If the **disciples** go gossiping about what they hope Jesus will achieve, word will get round the villages, and before they know it Herod's men will be after them (see 13.31). Not that Herod, or even Rome, are the most dangerous enemy they have. They must be wise in what they say, but they mustn't be afraid of mere mortal enemies. The real enemy is the one who longs to cast people into **Gehenna** ('Gehenna' was the name of Jerusalem's smouldering rubbish-heap, and the word was already in use as an image of hell-fire). This cannot mean that one should fear God, though in some senses that is a good and right thing to do. It means that one should recognize who the ultimate enemy is. In this picture, God is not the enemy to be feared; he is one to trust, the one who values his children more highly than a whole flock of sparrows, who has the very hairs of our head all numbered.

With trust in God on the one hand, and the desperate nature of the battle on the other, Jesus' followers must stand by him. Loyalty must be total. Whatever happens on earth has its counterpart in **heaven**, and those who think to gain temporary earthly advantage by short-term disloyalty may find that whispered denials are broadcast far and wide. However, those who trust God will find that even if they are put on trial for their allegiance to Jesus they will be given words to say. God's own **spirit** will teach them as and when they need it – which is not, of course, an excuse for poor preparation in a regular teaching ministry, but a sure promise for those who find themselves in sudden danger because of their loyalty to the **kingdom**.

In the midst of all this comes a dire warning which many have found disturbing. One may be forgiven for speaking against the **son of man**, but will not be forgiven for blaspheming against the holy spirit. In Mark and Matthew this saying occurs when Jesus has been accused of casting out **demons** by the prince of demons. If you say that the spirit's work is in fact the work of the devil, you have begun to call evil good and good evil, a moral cul-de-sac without turning room. Here in Luke 12 the intention seems broader. Someone who sees Jesus at work and misunderstands what is going on may speak against him, only to discover the truth and repent. But if someone denounces the work of the spirit, such a person is cut off by that very action from profiting from that work. Once you declare that the spring of fresh water is in fact polluted, you will never drink from it. The one sure thing about this saying is that if someone is anxious about having committed the sin against the holy spirit, their anxiety is a clear sign that they have not.

Loyalty, then, is required for disciples, not only when the **Twelve** were following Jesus on the road but when we, today, take it upon ourselves to enlist under his banner and follow where he leads. Luke 12 is a standing rebuke to all casual, half-hearted, relaxed Christianity. The warnings about dangerous foes, and the promise that our God knows and cares about the smallest details of our lives, combine to challenge us to dedicated, single-minded discipleship.

LUKE 12.13–34

The Parable of the Rich Fool

[13]Someone from the crowd said to Jesus, 'Teacher, tell my brother to divide the inheritance with me!'

[14]'Tell me, my good man,' replied Jesus, 'who appointed me as a judge or arbitrator over you?

[15]'Watch out,' he said to them, 'and beware of all greed! Your life doesn't consist of the sum total of your possessions.'

[16]He told them a parable. 'There was a rich man whose land produced a fine harvest. [17]'What shall I do?" he said to himself. "I don't have enough room to store my crops!

[18]'"I know!" he said. "I'll pull down my barns – and I'll build bigger ones! Then I'll be able to store all the corn and all my belongings there. [19]And I shall say to my soul, Soul, you've got many good things stored up for many years. Take it easy! Eat, drink, have a good time!"

[20]'But God said to him, "Fool! This very night your life will be demanded of you! Now who's going to have all the things you've got ready?" [21]That's how it is with someone who stores up things for himself and isn't rich before God.

[22]'So let me tell you this', he said to the disciples. 'Don't be anxious about your life – what you should eat; or about your body – what you should wear. [23]Life is more than food! The body is more than clothing! [24]Think about the ravens: they don't sow seed, they don't gather harvests, they don't have storehouses or barns; and God feeds them. How much more will he feed you! Think of the difference between yourselves and the birds!

[25]'Which of you by being anxious can add a day to your lifetime? [26]So if you can't even do a little thing like that, why worry about anything else? [27]Think about the lilies and the way they grow. They don't work hard, they don't weave cloth; but, let me tell you, not even Solomon in all his glory was dressed up like one of them. [28]So if that's how God clothes the grass in the field – here today, into the fire tomorrow – how much more will he clothe you, you little-faith lot!

²⁹'So don't you go hunting about for what to eat or what to drink, and don't be anxious. ³⁰The nations of the world go searching for all that stuff, and your father knows you need it. ³¹This is what you should search for: God's kingdom! Then all the rest will be given you as well. ³²Don't be afraid, little flock. Your father is delighted to give you the kingdom.

³³'Sell your possessions and give alms. Make yourselves purses that don't wear out, a treasure in heaven that lasts for ever, where the thief doesn't come near and the moth doesn't destroy. ³⁴Yes: where your treasure is, that's where your heart will be too.'

The modern Western world is built on anxiety. You see it on the faces of people hurrying to work. You see it even more as they travel home, tired but without having solved life's problems. The faces are weary, puzzled, living with the unanswerable question as to what it all means. This world thrives on people setting higher and higher goals for themselves, and each other, so that they can worry all day and all year about whether they will reach them. If they do, they will set new ones. If they don't, they will feel they've failed. Was this really how we were supposed to live?

Jesus' warnings indicate that much of the world at least, for much of human history, has faced the same problem. The difference, though, is the level at which anxiety strikes. Many of Jesus' hearers only just had enough to live on, and there was always the prospect that one day they wouldn't have even that. Most of them would have perhaps one spare garment, but not more. As with many in today's non-Western world, one disaster – the family breadwinner being sick or injured, for example – could mean instant destitution. And it was to people like that, not to people worried about affording smart cars and foreign holidays, that Jesus gave his clear and striking commands about not worrying over food and clothing.

We now know that anxiety itself can be a killer. Stress and worry can cause disease, or contribute to it – producing the enchanting prospect of people worrying about worrying, a downward spiral that perhaps only a good sense of humour can break. As with so much of his teaching, what Jesus says here goes to the heart of the way we are. To inhale a bracing lungful of his good sense is health-giving at every level. But his warnings and commands go deeper as well, down to the roots of the problem he faced in confronting his contemporaries with the message of God's **kingdom**. This wasn't just good advice on how to live a happy, carefree life. This was a challenge to the very centre of his world.

The man who wanted Jesus to arbitrate in a property dispute with his brother was typical in his attitude, the attitude that many of Jesus' fellow-Jews took towards the Holy Land itself. The land wasn't just where they happened to live; in the first century, as in the early twenty-first, possession of the land was a vital Jewish symbol. Families clung to their inheritance for religious reasons as well as economic ones.

Jesus was coming with the message that God was changing all that. He wasn't tightening up Israel's defence of the land; he was longing to shower grace and new life on people of every race and place. Israel, as far as he could see, was in danger of becoming like the man in the story who wanted the security of enough possessions to last him a long time. Societies and individuals alike can think themselves into this false position, to which the short answer is God's: 'You fool!' Life isn't like that. The kingdom of God isn't like that.

The kingdom of God is, at its heart, about God's sovereignty sweeping the world with love and power, so that human beings, each made in God's image and each one loved dearly, may relax in the knowledge that God is in control. Reflecting on the birds and the flowers isn't meant to encourage a kind of romantic nature-mysticism, but to stimulate serious understanding: God, the creator, loves to give good gifts, loves to give you the kingdom – loves, that is, to bring his sovereign care and rescue right to your own door. At the heart of the appeal is the difference that Israel should have recognized, between 'the nations of the world' and those who call God 'Father' – that is, between **Gentile** nations and Israel herself. If the gods you worship are distant and removed, or are simply nature-gods without personhood of their own, then of course you will be worried. If your God is the father who calls you his child, what is to stop you trusting him?

The final appeal, which will be repeated at various stages later in Luke, is not necessarily for all followers of Jesus to get rid of all their possessions. Luke himself, in Acts, describes Christian communities in which most members live in their own houses with their own goods around them, and there is no suggestion that they are second-class or rebellious members of God's people. Jesus is returning to the sharing of inheritance with which the passage began, and is advocating the opposite attitude to the grasping and greed which he saw there.

When he speaks of 'treasure in **heaven**', here and elsewhere, this doesn't mean treasure that you will only possess after death. 'Heaven' is God's sphere of created reality, which, as the Lord's Prayer suggests, will one day colonize 'earth', our sphere, completely. What matters is that the kingdom of God is bringing the values and priorities of God himself to bear on the greed and anxiety of the world. Those who welcome Jesus and his kingdom-message must learn to abandon the latter and live by the former.

LUKE 12.35–48

Jesus' Call to Watchfulness

³⁵'Make sure you're dressed and ready with your lamps alight', said Jesus. ³⁶'You need to be like people waiting for their master when he comes back from the wedding feast, so that when he comes and knocks they will be able to open the door for him at once. ³⁷A blessing on the servants whom the master finds awake when he comes! I'm telling you the truth: he will put on an apron and sit them down and come and wait on them. ³⁸A blessing on them if he comes in the second watch of the night, or even the third, and finds them like that!

³⁹'But you should know this: if the householder had known what time the thief was coming, he wouldn't have let his house be broken into. ⁴⁰You too should be ready, because the son of man is coming at a time you don't expect.'

⁴¹'Master', said Peter, 'are you telling this parable for us, or for everyone?'

⁴²'Who then is the faithful and wise servant', said Jesus, 'whom the master will set over all his household, to give them their allowance of food at the proper time? ⁴³A blessing on the servant that his master, when he comes, finds doing just that! ⁴⁴I'm telling you truly, he will install him as manager over all his possessions. ⁴⁵But if that servant says in his heart, "My master is taking his time over coming back", and begins to beat the slaves and slave-girls, to eat and drink and get drunk – ⁴⁶then the master of that servant will come on a day he doesn't expect him to, and at a moment he didn't imagine, and he will cut him in two. He will give him the same place as the unbelievers.

⁴⁷'If a servant knew what the master wanted, and didn't get ready, or do what was wanted, the punishment will be a severe beating. ⁴⁸If the servant didn't know, and did what deserved a beating, it will be a light beating. Much will be required from one who is given much; if someone is entrusted with much, even more will be expected in return.'

My most embarrassing moment of the year came while waiting at an airport to check in for a flight to Tel Aviv. I was leading a small pilgrimage to the Holy Land, and we had risen very early in the morning to get to the airport on time. We had luggage, tickets and . . . only one passport between my wife and myself. It was hers that was missing. We searched bags, coats and pockets. I telephoned my neighbour to go into my house and look there in case I'd left it behind. The other members of our party looked on in a mixture of sympathy and embarrassment. I won't even try to describe what my wife was thinking. Then, just as we were thinking she would have to come on the next day's flight, I moved a suitcase and out fell the missing passport. It had slipped down between two bags while I was checking the tickets, and had stuck there, invisible.

Going on a journey forces you to think carefully about what to take and how to get ready. It's no good suddenly thinking, when the plane is a hundred miles out and five miles high, that you'd like that other pair of shoes rather than the one you've brought! And Jesus' warnings in this passage begin with advice that was originally given to people going on a journey: the people who had to be properly dressed and ready for action were the Israelites getting ready for the sudden **Exodus** from Egypt (Exodus 12.11). As we have seen, Luke highlights the Exodus theme at various points in his story of Jesus' journey to Jerusalem, and the passage in question here points particularly to the first keeping of Passover. The Israelites were to eat that meal already dressed for their journey, so that they could be up and off at a moment's notice.

The way Jesus develops the picture retains this strong sense of urgency, but casts his followers as servants waiting for their master to come home from a particularly long dinner party. (The 'second watch' of the night was around midnight; the 'third watch' was the last stretch before dawn.) As the picture goes on, it becomes more and more clear that Jesus is thinking just as much of the intended application as of the illustration itself. And when we follow the train of thought it is, at some points, quite terrifying.

Not only is Jesus engaged in a running battle with the powers of evil. Not only is he issuing a challenge to total loyalty in the face of opposition. Not only is he saying that God's **kingdom** now demands a complete reordering of priorities. He is now warning that a crisis is coming, a great showdown for which one must be prepared in the same way as servants who listen eagerly for their master's footfall and knock at the door. Jesus seems to have envisaged a coming moment at which the forces of light and darkness would engage in a terrible battle, resulting in his own death, and a devastating catastrophe for Israel in general and Jerusalem in particular. Though this passage and others like it have often been taken as predictions of Jesus' final return, Luke throughout his **gospel** seems to suggest that they refer principally to a complex of events which Jesus knew would happen within the lifetime of his contemporaries.

These events will therefore pose a serious test for the **disciples**. If they start to relax, to assume that because they are Jesus' followers all will be well (Jesus doesn't really imagine they will start to beat their fellow-servants; at this point the illustration is running away with itself), then they will find things will come upon them before they are ready. Jesus knows that the time cannot be far off. In a sense, indeed, he is on his way to Jerusalem to precipitate it. But he also knows that the disciples haven't understood more than a little of what is to come, and he must therefore warn them to be ready. He therefore returns to the picture of the servants and the master from several angles, and with repeated severe warnings.

Peter's question poses a nice point. Jewish stories about a master and servants are often simply about God and Israel, and at least one of Jesus' stories falls into that pattern (Luke 16.1–9). So is this picture of the master coming back home to be understood, from the disciples' point of view, as referring not just to them (as Jesus' 'servants') but to Israel as a whole?

The answer seems to be Yes: it does refer to the nation as a whole. From now on in Luke we shall find several warnings about what will happen to the nation as a whole, and to its central symbol, the **Temple**, if it does not realize that the master is returning. This picture looks forward to 19.11–27, which is not about the second coming of Jesus but about the return of Israel's God to Zion – which was happening, Jesus believed, then and there. The master came back, but the servants were not ready.

At the same time, the passage is often rightly used at ordination or commissioning services, when Christians join together to pray for those who are being entrusted with ministry in God's church. It is an awesome responsibility, and one to which the picture of the servants and the master applies quite well. It is a sobering thought that the one time when Paul talks about Christians facing some kind of negative judgment after their death (mostly he gives nothing but assurance of hope) he is speaking of leaders and teachers who have failed in their task (1 Corinthians 3.12–15). Evangelists and teachers, pastors and theologians alike face this responsibility: when the master comes, will they be found busy at their tasks, or taking their ease and abusing the household?

LUKE 12.49–59

Reading the Signs of the Times

> [49]'I came to throw fire upon the earth,' Jesus continued, 'and I wish it were already alight! [50]I have a baptism to be baptized with, and I am under huge pressure until it's happened!
>
> [51]'Do you suppose I've come to give peace to the earth? No, let me tell you, but rather division. [52]From now on, you see, families will be split down the middle: three against two in a family of five, and two against three, [53]father against son and son against father, mother against daughter and daughter against mother, mother-in-law against daughter-in-law and daughter-in-law against mother-in-law.

54'When you see a cloud rising in the west,' he said to the crowds, 'you say at once, "It's going to rain", and rain it does. 55When you see the south wind getting up, you say, "It's going to be very hot", and that's what happens. 56You impostors! You know how to work out what the earth and the sky are telling you; why can't you work out what's going on at this very moment?

57'Why don't you judge for yourselves what you ought to do? 58When you go with your accuser before a magistrate, do your best to reach a settlement with him. Otherwise he may drag you in front of the judge, and the judge will hand you over to the officer, and the officer will throw you into jail. 59Let me tell you, you won't get out from there until you have paid the very last coin.'

The great composer Ludwig van Beethoven used sometimes to play a trick on polite salon audiences, especially when he guessed that they weren't really interested in serious music. He would perform a piece on the piano, one of his own slow movements perhaps, which would be so gentle and beautiful that everyone would be lulled into thinking the world was a soft, cosy place, where they could think beautiful thoughts and relax into semi-slumber. Then, just as the final notes were dying away, Beethoven would bring his whole forearm down with a crash across the keyboard, and laugh at the shock he gave to the assembled company.

A bit cruel and impolite, perhaps. And of course in many of his own compositions Beethoven found less antisocial ways of telling his hearers that the world was full of pain as well as of beauty – and also of making the transition in the other direction, bringing joy out of tragedy, including his own tragic life, in wonderful and lasting ways. But the shock of that crash of notes interrupting the haunting melody is a good image for what Jesus had to say at the end of Luke 12.

The crisis is coming, we have seen. It poses a challenge to absolute loyalty. But now even what we might have thought the **gospel** was all about is being stood on its head. Prince of Peace, eh? Jesus seems to be saying. No: Prince of Division, more likely! Once this message gets into households there'll be no peace: families will split up over it, just as the prophets had foretold. The warnings about fathers and sons, mothers and daughters, and so on includes a quotation from Micah 7.6, a passage in which the prophet warns of imminent crisis and urges that the only way forward is complete trust in God.

Jesus, then, sees the crisis coming, a crisis of which his own fate will be the central feature (the '**baptism**' which he must still undergo); and he is astonished and dismayed that so few of his contemporaries can see it at all. They are good at local weather forecasts: clouds rolling in from the Mediterranean mean rain, and a wind from the hot and dusty Negev means sultry weather. So why can't they look at what's going on all around them, from the Roman occupation to the oppressive regime of Herod, from the wealthy and arrogant **high priests** in Jerusalem to the false agendas of the **Pharisees** – and, in the middle of it all, a young prophet announcing God's **kingdom** and healing the sick? Why can't they put two and two together, and realize that this is the moment all Israel's history has been waiting for? Why can't they see that the crisis is coming?

If they could, they would be well advised to take action while there was still time. The final paragraph of the chapter is not to be taken as advice to people facing an actual lawsuit. As with several parables in Luke, it is far more likely that Jesus has in mind the crisis that has occupied much of the chapter so far. Israel, rebelling against God's plan that she should be the light of the world, and thus eager for violent uprising against Rome, was liable at any moment to find the magistrate – presumably some Roman official – dragging her off to court to face charges of sedition. Facing the prospect of complete ruin, she should urgently seek ways of coming to terms. In the event, as we know, the warning went unheeded. The Romans came in, magistrates, judges, officers and all, and in AD 70 Israel ended up paying the very last penny.

Jesus' warnings throughout the chapter reach something of a crescendo, and the chapter which follows continues the same theme. But, it might well be asked today, what relevance have these warnings for people who live nearly two thousand years after they all came true?

Part of the answer is that unless we understand the crisis facing Israel in Jesus' day, and the way in which Jesus responded to it, we won't understand what Jesus himself, and Luke as his interpreter, thought about his own death. That will be worked out in later chapters. But there is a further dimension.

The church has from early on read this chapter as a warning that each generation must read the signs of the times, the great movements of people, governments, nations and policies, and must react accordingly. If the kingdom of God is to come on earth as it is in **heaven**, part of the prophetic role of the church is to understand the events of earth and to seek to address them with the message of heaven. And if, like Jesus, we find that we seem to be bringing division, and that we ourselves become caught up in the crisis, so be it. What else would we expect?

In particular, there may come a time when Christian teachers and preachers find, like Beethoven with his salon audiences, that people have become too cosy and comfortable. Sometimes, for instance, the selections of Bible readings for church services omit all the passages that speak of judgment, of warnings, of the stern demands of God's holiness. Maybe there are times when, like Jesus himself on this occasion, we need to wake people up with a crash. There are, after all, plenty of warnings in the Bible about the dangers of going to sleep on the job.

LUKE 13.1–9

The Parable of the Fig Tree

¹At that moment some people came up and told them the news. Some Galileans had been in the Temple, and Pilate had mixed their blood with that of the sacrifices.

²Jesus' response was this. 'Do you suppose', he said, 'that those Galileans suffered such things because they were greater sinners than all other Galileans? ³No, let me tell you! Unless you repent, you will all be destroyed in the same way.

⁴'And what about those eighteen who were killed when the tower in Siloam collapsed on top of them? Do you imagine they were more blameworthy than everyone else who lives in Jerusalem? ⁵No, let me tell you! Unless you repent, you will all be destroyed in the same way.'

⁶He told them this parable. 'Once upon a time there was a man who had a fig tree in his vineyard. He came to it looking for fruit, and didn't find any. ⁷So he said to the gardener, "Look here! I've been coming to this fig tree for three years hoping to find some fruit, and I haven't found any! Cut it down! Why should it use up the soil?"

⁸'"I tell you what, Master," replied the gardener; "let it alone for just this one year more. I'll dig all round it and put on some manure. ⁹Then, if it fruits next year, well and good; and if not, you can cut it down."'

If the New Testament had never been written, we would still know that Pontius Pilate was an unpleasant and unpopular governor of Judaea. The Jewish historian Josephus lists several things he did which upset and irritated the local Jewish population. Sometimes he seemed to be deliberately trying to make them angry. He trampled on their religious sensibilities; once he tried to bring Roman standards (military emblems) into Jerusalem, with their pagan symbols. He flouted their laws and conventions; once he used money from the **Temple** treasury to build an aqueduct, and then brutally crushed the rebellion that resulted. These incidents, and others like them, are recorded outside the New Testament, and help us to understand what sort of person Pilate was.

So it shouldn't surprise us to learn that on another occasion, while some people on pilgrimage from Galilee had been offering sacrifice in the Temple, Pilate sent the troops in, perhaps fearing a riot, and slaughtered them. The present passage simply speaks of their own blood mingling in the Temple courtyard with the blood of their sacrifices – polluting the place, on top of the human horror and tragedy of such an event. It is as though occupying forces were to invade a church and butcher worshippers on Christmas Day.

Remind yourself for a moment where we are in Luke's story. Jesus has decided to go to Jerusalem at the head of a party of Galilean pilgrims. If today I was planning a journey to a town under enemy occupation, and was told on the way there that the local governor was making a habit of killing visiting English clergymen, I suspect I would call my travel agent and book a flight to somewhere less dangerous.

These people, then, aren't simply bringing Jesus information. Two questions hover in the air as they tell their shocking news. First, does Jesus really intend to continue his journey? Isn't he afraid of what may happen to him there? And second, what does this mean? Is this the beginning of something worse? If Jesus has been warning of woe and disaster coming on those who refuse his message, is this a sign that these Galileans were already being punished?

Jesus' stern comments address the second of these questions. (The first remains in the air throughout the chapter, until finally (13.31–35) we discover the answer: Herod is out to kill Jesus in Galilee, but Jesus knows that he must get to Jerusalem. Nowhere is now safe.) Yes, Pilate has killed Galilean pilgrims in Jerusalem; but they were no more sinful than any other Galilean pilgrims. Rather – and he is about to repeat the point – *unless you repent, you will all be destroyed the same way.*

The same way? That's the key. Jesus isn't talking about what happens to people after they die. Many have read this passage and supposed that it was a warning about perishing in **hell** after death, but that is clearly wrong. In line with the warnings he has issued several times already, and will continue to issue right up to his own crucifixion, Jesus is making it clear that those who refuse his summons to change direction, to abandon the crazy flight into national rebellion against Rome, will suffer the consequences. Those who take the sword will perish with the sword.

Or, if not the sword, they will be crushed by buildings in Jerusalem as the siege brings them crashing down. Siloam is a small area of Jerusalem, close to the centre of the ancient city, just to the south of the Temple itself. Building accidents happen; but if the Jerusalemites continue to refuse God's **kingdom**-call to repent, to turn from their present agendas, then those who escape Roman swords will find the very walls collapsing on top of them as the enemy closes in.

This terrifying warning, about the political and military consequences of not heeding his call, is at once amplified by the almost

121

humorous, yet in fact quite sinister, parable of the fig tree in the vineyard. (People often planted fig trees in vineyards; it was good for the grapes.) Underneath the banter between the vineyard owner and the gardener we detect a direct comment on Jesus' own ministry, and a further answer as to what's going to happen when he gets to Jerusalem.

There are two ways of taking the story, both of which give a satisfactory meaning and arrive at the same point. Jesus himself could be seen as the vineyard owner. He has been coming to the Lord's garden, seeking the fruit of **repentance**, throughout his ministry. (We might take the 'three years' of 13.7 as an indication that Jesus' ministry had lasted that long, but it's more likely that it is simply part of the logic of the story.) So far, apart from a very few followers, who are themselves still quite muddled, he has found none: no repentance, not even in the cities where most of his mighty deeds had been done (10.13–15). He is prepared, then, to give Israel, and particularly Jerusalem, the Temple, and the ruling **priests** one more chance. If they still refuse, their doom will be sealed.

Or maybe it is God who has been coming to Israel these many years, seeking fruit. Maybe Jesus is the gardener, the servant who is now trying, as the owner's patience wears thin, to dig around and put on manure, to inject some life and health into the old plant before sentence is passed. Either way the end result is the same: 'If not, you can cut it down.' Luke's arrangement of the material from chapter 10 onwards leaves us in no doubt as to how he saw the matter: when Jerusalem fell in AD 70, it was a direct result of refusing to follow the way of peace which Jesus had urged throughout his ministry.

The passage therefore bristles with a double tension. Will Jerusalem repent and be rescued? And if, as he has been saying, Jesus expects to die himself when he goes there, how do his fate and that of the city relate to one another? What is God up to? And, if we can begin to think about those questions, there are others for us to face ourselves. What is God up to in our world today? In our own lives? Are we bearing fruit for God's kingdom?

LUKE 13.10–21

Jesus Heals a Crippled Woman on the Sabbath

> [10]One sabbath, Jesus was teaching in one of the synagogues. [11]There was a woman there who had had a spirit of weakness for eighteen years. She was bent double, and couldn't stand fully upright. [12]Jesus saw her and called to her.

¹³'Woman,' he said, laying his hands on her, 'you are freed from your affliction.' And at once she stood upright, and praised God.

¹⁴The synagogue president was angry that Jesus had healed on the sabbath.

'Look here,' he said to the crowd, 'there are six days for people to work! Come on one of those days and be healed, not on the sabbath day!'

¹⁵'You bunch of hypocrites!' replied Jesus. 'You would all be quite happy to untie an ox or a donkey from its stall on the sabbath day and lead it out for a drink! ¹⁶And isn't it right that this daughter of Abraham, tied up by the satan for these eighteen years, should be untied from her chains on the sabbath day?'

¹⁷At that, all the people who had been opposing him were ashamed. The whole crowd was overjoyed at all the splendid things he was doing.

¹⁸So Jesus said, 'What is God's kingdom like? What shall we compare it with? ¹⁹It's like a mustard seed that someone took and placed in his garden. It grew, and became a tree, and the birds of the sky made nests in its branches.'

²⁰And again he said, 'What shall we say God's kingdom is like? ²¹It's like leaven that a woman took and hid in three measures of flour, until the whole thing was leavened.'

Let's, for a change, imagine that you are on the edge of the crowd that has followed Jesus so far. You haven't heard everything and haven't understood all you've heard, but you think you've got the general drift of it all and find it both compelling and alarming.

In you go with Jesus to the synagogue on this **sabbath**. What do you see, and what sense does it make to you?

You see – everybody sees – this poor woman. She was probably a well-known local character. In a village where everyone's life was public, people would know who she was and how long she'd been like this. Luke says she had 'a spirit of weakness', which probably means simply that nobody could explain medically why she had become bent double. Some today think that her disability had psychological causes; some people probably thought so then as well, though they might have said it differently. Maybe somebody had persistently abused her, verbally or physically, when she was smaller, until her twisted-up emotions communicated themselves to her body, and she found she couldn't get straight. Even after all the medical advances of the last few hundred years, we are very much aware that such things happen without any other apparent cause.

In the synagogue, though, you can see an unspoken power struggle going on. There is a synagogue president in charge of the meeting, but all eyes are on Jesus – which puts both of them in an awkward spot in terms of protocol. Jesus, however, doesn't wait. A word, a touch, and the woman is healed. The synagogue president, thoroughly upstaged, lets his anger take refuge in an official public rebuke, rather as if a policeman tried to arrest someone because their football team had just beaten his.

You, as the observer, understand all this. It's bound to be difficult for the local village hierarchy when someone like Jesus comes into town, and when he does extraordinary things in the synagogue it will inevitably cause a fuss. But listen to Jesus' answer. Think about what you've heard on the journey up to this point: the devastating analysis of what was wrong with Israel as a whole, the warnings of what lay ahead. Now hear what Jesus has to say, and ponder what it might mean.

'Double standards!' Jesus declares. 'You do one thing yourself and yet want to stop me doing something which is no different, and even more appropriate. This is just play-acting. You are quite happy (he must have known well enough what passed as legitimate sabbath practice and what didn't) to untie an animal that needs water; how much more should I untie this woman – Abraham's daughter, bound by **the satan**? And what better day than the sabbath?'

You get the point about untying the animal and untying the woman. But what is he saying about her? First, she's a daughter of Abraham; second, she has been tied up for 18 years by – the satan, the one who has Israel as a whole in his grip, the one against whom Jesus has won an initial victory! Suddenly new light dawns. What Jesus is doing for this poor woman is what he is longing to do for Israel as a whole. The enemy, the accuser, has had Israel in his power these many years, and Jesus' kingdom-message is the one thing that can free her. But Israel's insistence on tight boundaries, including the rigid application of the sabbath law, is preventing it happening. Unless the kingdom-message heals her, there is no hope.

Maybe, you think, Jesus is still hoping that there is time; that Israel, bent double and unable to stand upright, will be untied from her bondage in a great sabbath celebration, a great act of liberation. Maybe, you think, Jesus intends that by going to Jerusalem this will all come to pass . . .

And then there are the little sayings, which Luke at least regards as explanations of what has just happened. The **kingdom** is like a tiny seed producing a huge tree – which can then accommodate all the birds in the sky. One action in one synagogue on one sabbath; what can this achieve? But when Jesus sows the seed of the kingdom, nobody knows what will result. Or the kingdom as a small helping of leaven, hidden apparently in the flour. It seems insignificant and ineffectual; but before long the whole mixture is leavened. One healing of one woman – but every time you break the satanic chains that have tied people up, another victory is won which will go on having repercussions.

Ponder what you have seen and heard. Would you go up to Jerusalem following this man? It might be risky. It might be unpredictable. But where else would you go?

LUKE 13.22–30

Entering through the Narrow Door

²²Jesus went through the towns and villages, teaching as he went, making his way towards Jerusalem.

²³'Master,' somebody said to him, 'will there be only a few that are saved?'

²⁴'Struggle hard', Jesus replied, 'to get in by the narrow gate. Let me tell you: many will try to get in and won't be able to. ²⁵When the householder gets up and shuts the door – at that moment you will begin to stand outside and knock at the door and say, "Master, open the door for us." Then he will say in response, "I don't know where you've come from." ²⁶Then you will begin to say, "We ate with you and drank with you, and you taught in our streets!" ²⁷And he will say to you, "I don't know where you people are from. Be off with you, you wicked lot."

²⁸'That's where you'll find weeping and gnashing of teeth: when you see Abraham and Isaac and Jacob and all the prophets in God's kingdom, and you yourselves thrown out. ²⁹People will come from East and West, from North and South, and sit down to feast in God's kingdom. ³⁰And, listen to this: some who are last will be first, and some of the first will be last.'

I sat in the airport for two hours, waiting for my onward flight. I had come in to New York on a flight from England, and I was tired and eager to catch the connection to Washington, to get to where I was staying, and to rest for the night. Finally the small plane began to board. My seat had been confirmed, and I knew it was near the plane door; so I waited until almost everyone had got on.

As I approached the gate, to my horror the attendant shut it in my face. He apologized profusely, and said he hated this part of his job. Due to some obscure regulation, he said, this flight only allowed a certain number of people on board, and that number was already seated. What about my confirmed seat, I asked, showing him the ticket, which he himself had stamped as valid some while before. 'Yes,' he said, 'I know how you must feel. I am so sorry.'

He may have been sorry, but I was furious. I was too tired to make further protest, but wrote angry letters to the airline, and was eventually rewarded with US$100 free travel vouchers to use in the next couple of months – which was, of course, no good to someone living in another continent. I don't remember what time I got to bed that night, but I made a resolution never again to hang back when boarding a small aeroplane.

Jesus' warning in this passage sounds as though it's every bit as unreasonable as the airline regulation was that night. If you've got a confirmed place, surely you ought to be allowed on board no matter where you are in the line. It seems unfair for the householder to let people in up to a certain point and then, when he's shut the door in the faces of the next people, to protest that he never knew them. But a moment's thought about the whole sequence of teaching in Luke up to this point will reveal that the warning is very much needed.

The question about how many will be saved sends us to the question of ultimate and final salvation. Interestingly, Jesus refuses to answer this question directly; he will not give statistics and figures to satisfy mere human inquisitiveness. What he gives is a stern warning, not least because in the setting of his journey to Jerusalem 'being saved' is not simply a matter of ultimate destination after death, but the more immediate and pressing question of the crisis that hangs over the nation.

In this setting, his warning is both appropriate and necessary. As he goes about his mission, he is holding open the gate of the **kingdom** and urging people to enter it. The door isn't very wide, and it will take energy and commitment to get in; no question of strolling in by chance. One day, and not very long from now, the door will be shut, and it will be too late. God is giving Israel this last chance, through the work of Jesus, but he is the final messenger. If he is refused, there will be no further opportunity. The disciples in Acts urge people in his name to 'save themselves from this crooked generation' (Acts 2.40); if they do not respond to Jesus' call, they will pull down on themselves the judgment that 'this generation' has incurred. Those who wait to see what happens later, and who then presume that because they once shared a festive banquet with Jesus they will somehow be all right, will find that there are no promises for those who did not take the chance when it was offered.

The promise, and warning, of Jesus is that the very people his contemporaries were eager to fight – the **Gentiles** from east and west, north and south, who had over the centuries oppressed, bullied and harried them – might at this rate end up in God's kingdom ahead of them. The strange workings of God's grace, in which, though some are chosen for particular roles, none is assured of automatic privilege, mean that some who are first will be last, and vice versa.

We should be cautious about lifting this passage out and applying it directly to the larger question of eternal salvation. Jesus' urgent warnings to his own contemporaries were aimed at the particular emergency they then faced. But we should equally beware of assuming that it is irrelevant to such questions. Unless all human life is just a game; unless we are mistaken in our strong sense that our moral and spiritual choices matter; unless, after all, the New Testament as a whole has badly misled us – then it really is possible to stroll past the open gate to the kingdom of God, only to discover later the depth of our mistake.

LUKE 13.31-35

Jesus Grieves over Jerusalem

[31]Just then some Pharisees came up and spoke to Jesus.

'Get away from here,' they said, 'because Herod wants to kill you.'

[32]'Go and tell that fox,' replied Jesus, '"Look here: I'm casting out demons today and tomorrow, and completing my healings. I'll be finished by the third day. [33]But I have to continue my travels today, tomorrow and the day after that! It couldn't happen that a prophet would perish away from Jerusalem."

[34]'Jerusalem, Jerusalem! You kill the prophets, and stone the people sent to you! How many times did I want to collect your children, like a hen gathers her brood under her wings, and you would have none of it! [35]Look, your house has been abandoned. Let me tell you this: you will never see me until you are prepared to say, "Welcome with a blessing in the name of the Lord!"'

The house I live in was built after the Second World War. It replaced the much older one that stood here before, which was burnt to ashes one night in 1941, after a firebomb, dropped by an enemy aircraft, landed right on it. The people who lived in the house were helping to save another building nearby, and by the time they got water pumps to this house, and the one next door, it was too late.

In the ancient world fire was an ever-present danger. It was of course necessary for many aspects of life, but without modern precautions and fire-fighting equipment it could easily get out of control. Roman writers of the New Testament period speak graphically about fires in Rome's crowded streets and tenements; the summer of AD 64 saw a fire in Rome that lasted a week and destroyed half the city. Though the word 'fire' does not occur in this passage, the powerful image Jesus uses here has it in mind. It isn't, however, in a city, but in a farmyard.

Fire is as terrifying to trapped animals as to people, if not more so. When a farmyard catches fire, the animals try to escape; but, if they cannot, some species have developed ways of protecting their young. The picture here is of a hen, gathering her chicks under her wings to protect them. There are stories of exactly this: after a farmyard fire, those cleaning up have found a dead hen, scorched and blackened – with live chicks sheltering under her wings. She has quite literally given her **life** to save them. It is a vivid and violent image of what Jesus declared he longed to do for Jerusalem and, by implication, for all Israel. But, at the moment, all he could see was chicks scurrying off in the opposite direction, taking no notice of the smoke and flames indicating the approach of danger, nor of the urgent warnings of the one who alone could give them safety.

This picture of the hen and the chickens is the strongest statement so far in Luke of what Jesus thinks his death would be all about. But before we examine it further, we should go back to the earlier part of the passage. If chicks are in mind (at least for Luke; we cannot know whether verses 31–33, which do not occur in Matthew, were originally related to verses 34–35, which do), then the other great danger alongside fire was the predator, particularly the fox. And that's the image Jesus uses for Herod.

For most of the story, Herod has cast a dark shadow across the page, but he has not until now posed an explicit threat to Jesus. The **Pharisees** here, who warn Jesus of Herod's intentions, may have been among the many moderate Pharisees who, like Gamaliel in Acts 5, were happy to watch from the sidelines and see whether or not this new movement turned out to be from God. They may, of course, have been secretly hoping to get rid of Jesus, to get him off their territory; but Luke gives no hint of that if it was so. What is more important is Jesus' answer.

Jesus clearly indicates his contempt for Herod. Everyone knew, after all, that his only claim to royalty was because the Romans, recognizing his father as the most effective thug around, had promoted him from nowhere to keep order at the far end of their territories. Jesus also strongly affirms his own strange vocation: yes, he will eventually die at the hands of the authorities, but no, it won't be in Galilee. Herod will have an indirect hand in it (Luke 23.6–12), but he remains a minor player.

What matters is that Jesus has a destiny to fulfil, as he has already stated (9.22, 44; 12.50). It consists, in picture-language, of two days' work and one day's completion. Two days to cast out **demons** and cure illnesses; 'and I shall be finished on the third day'. No careful reader of Luke's gospel could miss the echoes, backwards and forwards: to the boy Jesus, found on the third day in the **Temple** (2.46); to the risen Jesus, alive again on the third day (24.21).

Jesus' destiny, then, is to go to Jerusalem and die, risking the threats of the fox, and adopting the role of the mother hen to the chickens faced with sudden danger. But will Jerusalem benefit from his offer? Jerusalem has a long history of rebelling against God, refusing the way of peace (that sentence, alas, seems to be as true in the modern as in the ancient world). As Ezekiel saw, rebellion meant that the holy presence of God had abandoned the Temple and the city, opening the way for devastating enemy attack (Ezekiel 10—11). The only way for the city and Temple to avoid the destruction which now threatened it was to welcome Jesus as God's peace-envoy; but all the signs were that they would not. When Luke brings us back to this point again, it will be too late.

What can we see from the vantage point of the end of chapter 13? We can see, with devastating clarity, what Jesus' journey to Jerusalem is going to mean. Israel's greatest crisis is coming upon her, and he is offering an urgent summons to repent, to come his **kingdom**-way, his way of peace. This is the only way of avoiding the disaster which will otherwise follow her persistent rebellion. Jesus' intention now, in obedience to his vocation, is to go to Jerusalem and, like the hen with the chickens, to take upon himself the full force of that disaster which he was predicting for the nation and the Temple. The one will give himself on behalf of the many.

LUKE 14.1–11

Jesus and the Pharisee

¹One sabbath, Jesus went to a meal in the house of a leading Pharisee. They were keeping a close eye on him.

²There was a man there in front of Jesus who suffered from dropsy. ³So Jesus asked the lawyers and Pharisees, 'Is it lawful to heal on the sabbath or not?' ⁴They remained silent. He took the man, healed him, and dismissed him.

⁵Then he said to them, 'Suppose one of you has a son – or an ox! – that falls into a well. Are you going to tell me you won't pull him out straight away on the sabbath day?' ⁶They had no answer for that.

⁷He noticed how the guests chose the best seats, and told them this parable.

⁸'When someone invites you to a wedding feast,' he said, 'don't go and sit in the best seat, in case some other guest more important is invited, ⁹and the person who invited you both comes and says to you, "Please move down for this man", and you will go to the end of the line covered with embarrassment. ¹⁰Instead, when someone invites you, go and sit down at the lowest place. Then, when your host arrives, he will say to you, "My dear fellow! Come on higher up!" Then all your fellow guests will show you respect. ¹¹All who push themselves forward, you see, will be humbled, and all who humble themselves will be honoured.'

Luke's **gospel** has more meal-time scenes than all the others. If his vision of the Christian life, from one point of view, is a journey, from another point of view it's a party. Several stories end with a festive meal – like, for instance, the **parable** of the prodigal son in the next chapter. These themes come together in the Last Supper and, finally, the story of the road to Emmaus in chapter 24.

In chapter 14 Luke has brought together two parables about feasting. The first, the one we have here in verses 7–11, is not always recognized as a parable, because it looks simply like a piece of social advice, of practical wisdom. You want to avoid embarrassment in front of your fellow guests? Then take this tip. But Jesus didn't come to offer good advice; and often his own conduct seems calculated to cause embarrassment. In any case, Luke tells us it's a parable (verse 7); in other words, we ought to expect it to have at least a double meaning. What is Jesus really talking about?

The rest of the chapter makes it clear that he's talking about the way in which people of his day were jostling for position in the eyes of God. They were, so it appeared to him, eager to push themselves forward, to show how well they were keeping the law, to maintain their own purity. They were precisely the sort of people he found himself with in the first section of the chapter (verses 1–6), people who would watch for any sign of irregularity, even at the cost of frowning upon actions, such as Jesus' healing of the man with dropsy, that made sense by their own actual standards. And Jesus, throughout this section of Luke, is turning things upside down. He is associating with the wrong kind of people. He is touching the untouchable and calling the nobodies.

The parable, then, isn't so much good advice for social occasions – though no doubt, within Jesus' world and beyond, there is practical human wisdom in the warning against pride and arrogance. The real meaning is to be found in the warning against pushing oneself forward in the sight of God. In Jesus' day it was all too easy for the well-off and the legally trained to imagine that they were superior in God's sight to the poor, to those without the opportunity to study, let alone practise, the law.

At the same time, in the world for which Luke was writing, there would be an obvious wider meaning. Within Luke's lifetime thousands of non-Jews had become Christians – had entered, that is, into the dinner party prepared by the God of Abraham, Isaac and Jacob. Many Jewish Christians, as we know from Acts, had found this difficult, if not impossible, to understand or approve. They were so eager to maintain their own places at the top table that they could not grasp God's great design to stand the world on its head. Pride, notoriously, is the great cloud which blots out the sun of God's generosity: if I reckon that

130

I deserve to be favoured by God, not only do I declare that I don't need his grace, mercy and love, but I imply that those who don't deserve it shouldn't have it.

Jesus spent his whole life breaking through that cloud and bringing the fresh, healing sunshine of God's love to those in its shadow. The **Pharisees** could watch him all they liked (verse 1), but the power both of his healings and of his explanations was too strong for them. The small-mindedness which pushes itself forward and leaves others behind is confronted with the large-hearted love of God. All Christians are called to the same healthy dependence on God's love and the same generosity in sharing it with those in need.

LUKE 14.12–24

The Parable of the Great Banquet

[12]He then turned to his host. 'When you give a lunch or a supper,' he said, 'don't invite your friends or your family or relatives, or your rich neighbours. They might ask you back again, and you'd be repaid. [13]When you give a feast, invite the poor, the crippled, the lame and the blind. [14]God will bless you, because they have no way to repay you! You will be repaid at the resurrection of the righteous.'

[15]One of the guests heard this, and commented, 'A blessing on those who eat food in God's kingdom!'

[16]Jesus said, 'Once a man made a great dinner, and invited lots of guests. [17]When the time for the meal arrived, he sent his servant to say to the guests, "Come now – everything's ready!" [18]But the whole pack of them began to make excuses. The first said, "I've just bought a field, and I really have to go and see it. Please accept my apologies." [19]Another one said, "I've just bought five yoke of oxen, and I've got to go and test them out – please accept my apologies." [20]And another one said, "I've just got married, so naturally I can't come." [21]So the servant went back and told his master all this. The householder was cross, and said to his servant, "Go out quickly into the streets and lanes of the town and bring in here the poor, the crippled, the lame and the blind." [22]"All right, Master," said the servant, "I've done that – but there's still room." [23]"Well then," said the master to the servant, "go out into the roads and hedgerows and make them come in, so that my house may be full! [24]Let me tell you this: none of those people who were invited will get to taste my dinner."'

Once, many years ago, I preached a sermon on this passage. I emphasized the extraordinary way in which Jesus tells his hearers to do something that must have been as puzzling then as it is now. Don't invite friends, relatives and neighbours to dinner – invite the poor and the disabled. The sermon had a strange effect. In the course of the next week my wife and I received dinner invitations from no fewer than three people who had been in church that day. Which category of guest we came into we were too polite – or anxious – to ask.

This time it looks as if the passage is real advice. The **parable** of the supper, which follows, is a parable all right, but Jesus really seems to have intended his hearers to take literally his radical suggestion about who to invite to dinner parties. Social conditions have changed, of course, and in many parts of the world, where people no longer live in small villages in which everyone knows everyone else's business, where meals are eaten with the doors open and people wander to and fro at will (see 7.36–50), it may seem harder to put it into practice. Many Christians would have to try quite hard to find poor and disabled people to invite to a party – though I know some who do just that. Nobody can use the difference in circumstances as an excuse for ignoring the sharp edge of Jesus' demand.

In particular, they cannot ignore it in the light of the parable. The story is, obviously, about people who very rudely snub the invitation to a splendid party. They make excuses of the usual kind. The householder, having gone to all the trouble of organizing and paying for a lavish feast, is determined to have guests at his table, even if he has to find them in unconventional locations. The original guests have ruled themselves out, and others have come in to take their place.

The first level of meaning of this parable should be clear. Jesus has been going around Galilee summoning people to God's great supper. This is the moment Israel has been waiting for! At last the time has arrived; those who were invited long ago must hurry up now and come! But most of them have refused, giving all kinds of reasons; we are reminded of the parable of the seeds and soils, in which various things caused most of the seeds to remain unfruitful. But some people have been delighted to be included: the poor, the disadvantaged, the disabled. They have come in and celebrated with Jesus.

The second level, as with the previous parable, is what this might mean for Luke in particular. Once again the expected guests are the Jews, waiting and waiting for the **kingdom**, only to find, when it arrived, that they had more pressing things to occupy them. Of course, in Luke's day many Jews had become Christians. The detail of the parable can't be forced at this point: it isn't true, at this level, that 'none of those who were invited shall taste my banquet', since clearly many Jews were part of Jesus' kingdom-movement from the beginning. But the majority of the nation, both in Palestine and in the scattered Jewish communities in the rest of the world, were not. Instead, as it must have seemed to those first Jewish Christians, God's messengers had gone out into the roads and hedgerows of the world, getting all kinds of unexpected people to join in the party – not just **Gentiles**, but people with every kind of moral and immoral background, people quite different from them culturally, socially, ethnically and ethically.

But there is a third twist to this parable, in which it bends back, as it were, on itself, returning to the challenge which Jesus gave in verses 12–14. The party to which the original guests were invited was Jesus' kingdom-movement, his remarkable welcome to all and sundry. If people wanted to be included in Jesus' movement, this is the sort of thing they were joining.

Once again, therefore, the challenge comes to us today. Christians, reading this anywhere in the world, must work out in their own churches and families what it would mean to celebrate God's kingdom so that the people at the bottom of the pile, at the end of the line, would find it to be **good news**. It isn't enough to say that we ourselves are the people dragged in from the country lanes, to our surprise, to enjoy God's party. That may be true; but party guests are then expected to become party hosts in their turn.

LUKE 14.25-35

The Cost of Discipleship

^{25}A large crowd was gathering around him. Jesus turned to face them. ^{26}'If any of you come to me,' he said to them, 'and don't hate your father and your mother, your wife and your children, your brothers and your sisters – yes, and even your own life! – you can't be my disciple. ^{27}If you don't pick up your own cross and come after me, you can't be my disciple.

^{28}'Don't you see? Supposing one of you wants to build a tower; what will you do? You will first of all sit down and work out how much it will cost, to see whether you have enough to finish it. ^{29}Otherwise, when you've laid the foundation and then can't finish it, everyone who sees it will begin to make fun of you. ^{30}"Here's a fellow", they'll say, "who began to build but couldn't finish!"

^{31}'Or think of a king, on the way to fight a war against another king. What will he do? He will first sit down and discuss with his advisers whether, with ten thousand troops, he is going to be a match for the other side who are coming with twenty thousand! ^{32}If they decide he isn't, he will send a delegation, while the other one is still a long way away, and sue for peace.

^{33}'In the same way, none of you can be my disciple unless you give up all your possessions.

³⁴'Salt is good; but if even the salt loses its savour, how can it be made salty again? ³⁵It's no good for soil and no good for manure. People throw it away. If you have ears, then listen!'

Imagine a politician standing on a soapbox addressing a crowd. 'If you're going to vote for me,' he says, 'you're voting to lose your homes and families; you're asking for higher taxes and lower wages; you're deciding in favour of losing all you love best! So come on – who's on my side?' The crowd wouldn't even bother heckling him, or throwing rotten tomatoes at him. They would just be puzzled. Why on earth would anyone try to advertise himself in that way?

But isn't that what Jesus is doing in this astonishing passage? 'Want to be my disciple, do you? Well, in that case you have to learn to hate your family, give up your possessions and get ready for a nasty death!' Hardly the way, as we say, to win friends and influence people.

But wait a minute. Supposing, instead of a politician, we think of the leader of a great expedition, forging a way through a high and dangerous mountain pass to bring urgent medical aid to villagers cut off from the rest of the world. 'If you want to come any further,' the leader says, 'you'll have to leave your packs behind. From here on the path is too steep to carry all that stuff. You probably won't find it again. And you'd better send your last postcards home; this is a dangerous route and it's very likely that several of us won't make it back.' We can understand that. We may not like the sound of it, but we can see why it would make sense.

And we can see, therefore, that Jesus is more like the second person than the first. Since Christianity has often, quite rightly, been associated with what are called 'family values', it comes as a shock to be told to 'hate' your parents, wife and children, and siblings; but when the instruction goes one step further, that one must hate one's own self, and be prepared for shameful death ('take up your cross' wasn't simply a figure of speech in Jesus' world!), then we begin to see what's going on. Jesus is not denying the importance of close family, and the propriety of living in supportive harmony with them. But when there is an urgent task to be done, as there now is, then everything else, including one's own **life**, must be put at risk for the sake of the **kingdom**.

The same is true of possessions. Many of Jesus' followers, then and now, have owned houses and lands, and have not felt compelled to abandon them. But being prepared to do so is the sign that one has understood the seriousness of the call to follow Jesus. Any of us, at any time, might be summoned to give up everything quite literally and respond to a new emergency situation. If we're not ready for that, we are like the tower-builder or warmonger who haven't thought through what they are really about.

These two pictures, the tower and the battle, themselves carried a cryptic warning in Jesus' day. The most important building project of his time was of course the **Temple** in Jerusalem: Herod the Great had begun a massive programme of rebuilding and beautifying it, and his sons and heirs were carrying on the work. But what was it all for? Would it ever be completed? Jesus has already warned that God had abandoned his house (13.35); Herod's Temple would shortly be left a smouldering ruin, its folly plain for all to see.

This is not unconnected to the second warning. If Jesus' contemporaries had fighting in mind, the chief enemy against whom they were longing to go to war was Rome. They probably only had a vague idea of who exactly the Romans were and what sort of forces they had at their command; otherwise, long before they came to blows, they would have taken the wise course and found a way to peace. But Jesus' warnings, and his urgings towards peace, were falling on deaf ears. His listeners, too concerned to hang on to their ancestral possessions, were eager for a war that would set them and their land free at last. Jesus was confronting them with a true emergency, and they were unable to see it and respond appropriately.

The last warning, therefore, comes with renewed force. Israel is supposed to be the salt of the earth, the people through whom God's world is kept wholesome and made tasty. But if Israel loses her particular ability and flavour, what is left? The warning backs up the cryptic sayings about the tower and the battle, and brings us back to the all-or-nothing challenge. Jesus is facing his contemporaries with a moment of crisis in which they must either be Israel indeed, through following him, or they must face the ruin of the tower and the devastation of the lost battle.

It is not difficult, and Luke may already have had this in mind, to reapply these hard sayings to the ongoing life of the church. At every stage of its life the church has faced the challenge, not only of living up to Jesus' demands, but of placing them before the world. Where are the towers, and where are the wars, that our world is hell-bent on building and fighting? How can we summon the human race once more to costly obedience?

LUKE 15.1-10

The Parables of the Lost Sheep and the Lost Coin

[1]All the tax-collectors and sinners were coming close to listen to Jesus. [2]The Pharisees and the legal experts were grumbling. 'This fellow welcomes sinners!' they said. 'He even eats with them!'

³So Jesus told them this parable. ⁴"Supposing one of you has a hundred sheep," he said, 'and you lose one of them. What will you do? Why, you'll leave the ninety-nine out in the countryside, and you'll go off looking for the lost one until you find it! ⁵And when you find it, you'll be so happy – you'll put it on your shoulders ⁶and come home, and you'll call your friends and neighbours in. "Come and have a party!" you'll say. "Celebrate with me! I've found my lost sheep!"

⁷'Well, let me tell you: that's how glad they will be in heaven over one sinner who repents – more than over ninety-nine righteous people who don't need repentance.

⁸'Or supposing a woman has ten drachmas and loses one of them. What will she do? Why, she'll light a lamp, and sweep the house, and hunt carefully until she finds it! ⁹And when she finds it she'll call her friends and neighbours in. "Come and have a party!" she'll say. "Celebrate with me! I've found my lost coin!"

¹⁰'Well, let me tell you: that's how glad God's angels feel when a single sinner repents.'

We had just moved house, to a dream location: quiet, secluded, at the end of a road near a lake. Everything seemed peaceful. Then, on the first Saturday night we were there, all chaos broke loose. Loud music, amplified voices making announcements, cheers, fireworks – all going on well into the small hours, keeping our young children awake. We were appalled. Was this going to happen every weekend? Where was the noise coming from? Why had nobody told us about this before we bought the house?

In the morning, the explanations came. No, it wasn't a regular occurrence. It would only happen once a year. It was the local Yacht Club's annual party, celebrating some great event in the sailing calendar. We returned to tranquillity. But it left me thinking about how one person's celebration can be really annoying for someone else, especially if they don't understand the reason for the party.

The three **parables** in Luke 15 are told because Jesus was making a habit of having celebration parties with all the 'wrong' people, and some others thought it was a nightmare. All three stories are ways of saying: 'This is why we're celebrating! Wouldn't you have a party if it was you? How could we not?' In and through them all we get a wide open window on what Jesus thought he was doing – and, perhaps, on what we ourselves should be doing.

At the heart of the trouble was the character of the people Jesus was eating with on a regular basis. The tax-collectors were disliked not just because they were tax-collectors – nobody much likes them in any culture – but because they were collecting money for either Herod or the Romans, or both, and nobody cared for them at all. And if they were in regular contact with **Gentiles**, some might have considered them unclean.

The 'sinners' are a more general category, and people disagree as to who precisely they were. They may just have been people who were too poor to know the law properly or to try to keep it (see John 7.49). Certainly they were people who were regarded by the self-appointed experts as hopelessly irreligious, out of touch with the demands that God had made on Israel through the law.

Throughout the chapter Jesus is *not* saying that such people were simply to be accepted as they stand. Sinners must repent. The lost sheep and lost coin are found. The prodigal son comes to his senses and returns home. But Jesus has a different idea to his critics of what '**repentance**' means. For them, nothing short of adopting their standards of purity and law-observance would do. For Jesus, when people follow him and his way, that is the true repentance. And – he doesn't say so in so many words, but I think it's there by implication – the **Pharisees** and **legal experts** themselves need to repent in that way. 'Righteous persons who don't need to repent' indeed (verse 7)! Try saying the sentence with a smile and a question mark in your voice and you will, I think, hear what Jesus intended.

The point of the parables is then clear. This is why there's a party going on: all **heaven** is having a party, the angels are joining in, and if we don't have one as well we'll be out of tune with God's reality.

In the stories of the sheep and the coin, the punch line in each case depends on the Jewish belief that the two halves of God's creation, heaven and earth, were meant to fit together and be in harmony with each other. If you discover what's going on in heaven, you'll discover how things were meant to be on earth. That, after all, is the point of praying that God's **kingdom** will come 'on earth as in heaven'. As far as the legal experts and Pharisees were concerned, the closest you could get to heaven was in the **Temple**; the Temple required strict purity from the **priests**; and the closest that non-priests could get to copying heaven was to maintain a similarly strict purity in every aspect of life. But now Jesus was declaring that heaven was having a great, noisy party every time a single sinner saw the light and began to follow God's way. If earth-dwellers wanted to copy the life of heaven, they'd have a party, too. That's what Jesus was doing.

The particular sheep, and the particular coin, weren't themselves special. (The coins, by the way, may well have been the woman's savings, possibly her dowry. Losing one would be a personal as well as a financial disaster.) In one of the late, corrupt versions of Jesus' teaching which were circulated in subsequent centuries, Jesus is made to say to the lost sheep, 'I love you more than the others'. But the whole point of the parable is that the *only* thing different about this sheep is that it was lost. Imagine the impact of this on the repentant sinners who heard the stories. They didn't have to earn God's love or Jesus' respect. He loved coming looking for them, and celebrated finding them.

And what Jesus did – this is the deepest point of these parables, and the ultimate reason why the Pharisees objected to them – was what God was doing. Jesus' actions on earth corresponded exactly to God's love in the heavenly realm.

The real challenge of these parables for today's church is: what would we have to do, in the visible, public world, if we were to make people ask the questions to which stories like these are the answer? What might today's Christians do that would make people ask, 'Why are you doing something like that?', and give us the chance to tell stories about finding something that was lost?

LUKE 15.11–24

The Parable of the Prodigal: The Father and the Younger Son

[11]Jesus went on: 'Once there was a man who had two sons. [12]The younger son said to the father, "Father, give me my share in the property." So he divided up his livelihood between them. [13]Not many days later the younger son turned his share into cash, and set off for a country far away, where he spent his share in having a riotous good time.

[14]'When he had spent it all, a severe famine came on that country, and he found himself destitute. [15]So he went and attached himself to one of the citizens of that country, who sent him into the fields to feed his pigs. [16]He longed to satisfy his hunger with the pods that the pigs were eating, and nobody gave him anything.

[17]'He came to his senses. "Just think!" he said to himself. "There are all my father's hired hands with plenty to eat – and here am I, starving to death! [18]I shall get up and go to my father, and I'll say to him: 'Father; I have sinned against heaven and before you; [19]I don't deserve to be called your son any longer. Make me like one of your hired hands.'" [20]And he got up and went to his father.

'While he was still a long way off, his father saw him and his heart was stirred with love and pity. He ran to him, hugged him tight, and kissed him. [21]"Father," the son began, "I have sinned against heaven and before you; I don't deserve to be called your son any longer." [22]But the father said to his servants, "Hurry! Bring the best clothes and put them on him! Put a ring on his hand, and shoes on his feet! [23]And bring the calf that we've fattened up, kill it, and let's eat and have a party! [24]This son of mine was dead, and is alive again! He was lost, and now he's found!" And they began to celebrate.'

We might think that the **parable** of the prodigal son, as it's usually known, hardly needs an introduction. It has inspired artists and writers down the years. Rembrandt's famous painting, with the younger son on his knees before the loving and welcoming father, has become for many almost as much of an inspiration as the story itself. Phrases from the story – the 'fatted calf', for instance, in the King James Version of the Bible – have become almost proverbial.

And yet. People often assume that the story is simply about the wonderful love and forgiving grace of God, ready to welcome back sinners at the first sign of **repentance**. That is indeed its greatest theme, which is to be enjoyed and celebrated. But the story itself goes deeper than we often assume.

Let's be sure we've understood how families like this worked. When the father divided the property between the two sons, and the younger son turned his share into cash, this must have meant that the land the father owned had been split into two, with the younger boy selling off his share to someone else. The shame that this would bring on the family would be added to the shame the son had already brought on the father by asking for his share before the father's death; it was the equivalent of saying 'I wish you were dead'. The father bears these two blows without recrimination.

To this day, there are people in traditional cultures, like that of Jesus' day, who find the story at this point quite incredible. Fathers just don't behave like that; he should (they think) have beaten him, or thrown him out. There is a depth of mystery already built in to the story before the son even leaves home. Again, in modern Western culture children routinely leave homes in the country to pursue their future and their fortune in big cities, or even abroad; but in Jesus' culture this would likewise be seen as shameful, with the younger son abandoning his obligation to care for his father in his old age. When the son reaches the foreign country, runs through the money, and finds himself in trouble, his degradation reaches a further low point. For a Jew to have anything to do with pigs is bad enough; for him to be feeding them, and hungry enough to share their food, is worse.

But of course the most remarkable character in the story is the father himself. One might even call this 'the parable of the Running Father': in a culture where senior figures are far too dignified to run anywhere, this man takes to his heels as soon as he sees his young son dragging himself home. His lavish welcome is of course the point of the story: Jesus is explaining why there is a party, why it's something to celebrate when people turn from going their own way and begin to go God's way. Because the young man's degradation is more or less complete, there can be no question of anything in him commending him to his father, or to any other onlookers; but the father's closing line says it all. 'This my son was dead and is alive; he was lost and now is found.' How could this not be a cause of celebration?

Inside this story there is another dimension which we shouldn't miss. One of the great stories of Israel's past was of course the **Exodus**, when Israel was brought out of Egypt and came home to the promised land. Many years later, after long rebellion, Israel was sent into **exile** in Babylon; and, though many of the exiles returned, most of Jesus' contemporaries reckoned that they were still living in virtual exile, in evil and dark days, with pagans ruling over them. They were still waiting for God to produce a new Exodus, a liberation which would bring them out of their spiritual and social exile and restore their fortunes once and for all. For Jesus to tell a story about a wicked son, lost in a foreign land, who was welcomed back with a lavish party – this was bound to be heard as a reference to the hope of Israel. 'This my son was dead, and is alive'; ever since Ezekiel 37 the idea of **resurrection** had been used as picture-language for the true return from exile.

Yes, says Jesus, and it's happening right here. When people repent and turn back to God – which, as we've seen, meant for Jesus that they responded positively to his **gospel** message – then and there the 'return from exile' is happening, whether or not it looks like what people expected. His answer to the **Pharisees** and other critics is simple: if God is fulfilling his promises before your very eyes, you can't object if I throw a party to celebrate. It's only right and proper.

There is a danger in splitting the story into two, as we've done. The second half is vital, and closely interwoven with the first. But in this first section the emphasis is on the father's costly love. From the moment he generously gives the younger son what he wanted, through to the wonderful homecoming welcome, we have as vivid a picture as anywhere in Jesus' teaching of what God's love is like, and of what Jesus himself took as the model for his own ministry of welcome to the outcast and the sinner.

LUKE 15.25–32

The Parable of the Prodigal: The Father and the Older Son

25'The older son was out in the fields. When he came home, and got near to the house, he heard music and dancing. 26He called one of the servants and asked what was going on.

27'"Your brother's come home!" he said. "And your father has thrown a great party – he's killed the fattened calf! – because he's got him back safe and well!"

28'He flew into a rage, and wouldn't go in.

'Then his father came out and pleaded with him. [29]"Look here!" he said to his father, "I've been slaving for you all these years! I've never disobeyed a single commandment of yours. And you never even gave me a young goat so I could have a party with my friends. [30]But when this son of yours comes home, once he's finished gobbling up your livelihood with his whores, you kill the fattened calf for him!"

[31]"My son," he replied, "you're always with me. Everything I have belongs to you. [32]But we had to celebrate and be happy! This brother of yours was dead and is alive again! He was lost, and now he's found!"'

A vivid phrase from a schoolboy poem, written by a classmate of mine over thirty years ago, remains with me to this day. He described a park-keeper whose job was to pick up litter on a spiked pole. Surrounded by the glorious beauty of flowers and trees, with the sun sparkling through the leaves, he only had eyes for the garbage he had to collect, and the damage it did. The lines I remember sum up his plight:

'Destroys the nature in this park, litter,' he said, without
Lifting his head.
He could only see the bad, and was blind to the beauty.

That sums up the older brother in the story. And it's the older brother who provides the real punchline of the **parable**. This is Jesus' response to his critics. They were so focused on the wickedness of the tax-collectors and sinners, and of Jesus himself for daring to eat with them despite claiming to be a prophet of God's **kingdom**, that they couldn't see the sunlight sparkling through the fresh spring leaves of God's love. Here were all these people being changed, being healed, having their lives transformed physically, emotionally, morally and spiritually; and the grumblers could only see litter, the human garbage that they normally despised and avoided.

The portrait of the older brother is brilliantly drawn, with tell-tale little shifts of phrase and meaning. 'Your brother', says the servant, 'has come home'; but he won't think of him like this. 'This son of yours', he says angrily to his father. 'This brother of yours', says the father, reminding him gently of the truth of the matter. 'I've been slaving for you', he says to his father, whereas in fact they had been working as partners, since the father had already divided his assets between them (verse 12). Everything the father has belongs to him, since the younger brother has spent his share; and that, presumably, is part of the problem, since the older brother sees all too clearly that anything now spent on his brother will be coming out of his own inheritance.

The phrase which ties the story to Jesus' opponents comes out tellingly: 'I've never disobeyed a single commandment of yours.' That was the **Pharisees'** boast (compare Philippians 3.6); but the moral superiority which it appears to give melts like snow before the sunshine of God's love. Where **resurrection** is occurring – where new **life** is bursting out all around – it is not only appropriate, it is *necessary* to celebrate (verse 32). Not to do so is to fail to meet generosity with gratitude. It is to pretend that God has not after all been at work. It is to look only at the garbage and to refuse to smell the flowers.

In terms of what God was doing in Israel through Jesus, we can see once more that the new kingdom-work which was going forward was indeed like a return from **exile**. Sinners and outcasts were finding themselves welcomed into fellowship with Jesus, and so with God, in a way they would have thought impossible. But whenever a work of God goes powerfully forwards, there is always someone muttering in the background that things aren't that easy, that God's got no right to be generous, that people who've done nothing wrong are being overlooked. That happened at the time when the exiles returned from Babylon; several people, not least the Samaritans, didn't want them back.

This story reveals above all the sheer self-centredness of the grumbler. The older brother shows, in his bad temper, that he has had no more real respect for his father than his brother had had. He lectures him in front of his guests, and refuses his plea to come in. Once more the father is generous, this time to his self-righteous older son. At this point we sense that Jesus is not content simply to tell the grumblers that they're out of line; he, too, wants to reason with the Pharisees and the lawyers, to point out that, though God's generosity is indeed reaching out to people they didn't expect, this doesn't mean there isn't any left for them. If they insist on staying out of the party because it isn't the sort of thing they like, that's up to them; but it won't be because God doesn't love them as well.

This parable, like some of the others, points, for Luke, beyond the immediate situation of Jesus' ministry and into the early church. There, **Gentiles** were coming into the church, and Jews and Jewish Christians often found it very difficult to celebrate the fact. Equally, as Paul realized when writing Romans, it was vital that the new communities never gave the impression to their older brother that God had finished with him. Somehow the balance must be kept.

The story is, of course, unfinished. We naturally want to know what happened next. How will the younger brother behave from now on? What arrangements will they make? Will the two sons be reconciled? Sometimes when a storyteller leaves us on the edge of our seats like this it's because we are supposed to think it through, to ask ourselves where we fit within the story, and to learn more about ourselves and our churches as a result. Which role in the story do you and your church find comes most naturally to you? How can we move towards becoming people through whom 'resurrection' happens to others? How can we celebrate the party of God's love in such a way as to welcome not only the younger brothers who have come back from the dead, but also the older brothers who thought there was nothing wrong with them?

LUKE 16.1–9

The Parable of the Shrewd Manager

¹Jesus said to his disciples, 'Once there was a rich man who had a steward, and charges were laid against him that he was squandering his property. ²So he called him and said to him, "What's all this I hear about you? Present an account of your stewardship; I'm not going to have you as my steward any more!"

³'At this, the steward said to himself, "What shall I do? My master is taking away my stewardship from me! I can't do manual work, and I'd be ashamed to beg . . .

⁴"'I have an idea what to do! – so that people will welcome me into their households when I am fired from being steward."

⁵'So he called his master's debtors to him, one by one. "How much", he asked the first, "do you owe my master?"

⁶'"A hundred measures of olive oil", he replied.

'"Take your bill," he said to him, "sit down quickly, and make it fifty."

⁷'To another he said, "And how much do you owe?"

'"A hundred measures of wheat", he replied.

'"Take your bill," he said, "and make it eighty."

⁸'And the master praised the dishonest steward because he had acted wisely. The children of this world, you see, are wiser than the children of light when it comes to dealing with their own generation.

⁹'So let me tell you this: use that dishonest stuff called money to make yourselves friends! Then, when it gives out, they will welcome you into homes that will last.'

She came up to me after the service and demanded to know what it meant. This passage had been read as the second lesson, while the first had been a prophetic denunciation (from Ezekiel 18, I think) of all kinds of sins, including the making of money by lending at interest. She had obviously been listening to the readings, and couldn't make head or tail of what was going on. Was the Bible against making money out of other money, or was it – was Jesus, indeed – telling us we should use any sharp financial practices we could to get ourselves out of difficulties?

The problem is made worse in some of the usual translations of verse 9, which seem to say that you can buy your way into **heaven**; and by the puzzle of verse 8, where it isn't clear whether 'the master' who is commending the dishonest steward is the master in the story, or whether this is Luke's reporting of what 'the master', Jesus, said about it all. How can we sort all this out?

The first thing to do is to understand how the story works. It looks as though the master in the story had himself been acting in a somewhat underhand manner. Jews were forbidden to lend money at interest, but many people got round this by lending in kind, with oil and wheat being easy commodities to use for this purpose. It is likely that what the steward deducted from the bill was the interest that the master had been charging, with a higher rate on oil than on wheat. If he reduced the bill in each case to the principal, the simple amount that had been lent, the debtors would be delighted, but the master couldn't lay a charge against the steward without owning up to his own shady business practices. Thus, when the master heard about it (I think 'the master' in verse 9 is certainly the master in the story, not Jesus), he could only admire the man's clever approach.

But the second thing is to realize, as the whole setting in Luke helps us to do, what the **parable** is really about. It is, after all, a *parable*, not a piece of moral teaching about money and how (not) to use it – though, as with the sayings about feasts in chapter 14, we find some moral teaching on the subject placed alongside, which does rather confuse the issue, at least to begin with.

If we were faced with a first-century Jewish story we'd never seen before, about a master and a steward, we should know at once what it was most likely about. The master is God; the steward is Israel. Israel is supposed to be God's property manager, the light of God's world, responsible to God and set over his possessions. But Israel – as we've seen in so much of this **gospel** – has failed in the task, and is under threat of imminent dismissal. What then ought Israel to do?

The **Pharisees'** answer was to pull the regulations of the law even tighter, to try to make Israel more holy. This, as we've seen, had the effect that they were excluding the very people that Jesus was reaching out to. Jesus, in this parable, indicates that if Israel is facing a major crisis the answer is rather to throw caution to the winds, to forget the extra bits and pieces of law which the Pharisees have heaped up, and to make friends as and where they can. That's what 'the children of this world' would do, and 'the children of light' – that is, the Israelites – ought to do so as well, learning from the cunning people of the world how to cope in the crisis that was coming upon their generation.

Thus, instead of hoarding money and land, Jesus' advice was to use it, as far as one could, to make friends. A crisis was coming, in which alternative homes, homes that would last (not 'eternal habitations' in the sense of a heavenly dwelling after death), would be needed.

This parable thus appears to be directed very specifically to the situation of Jesus' own hearers. How can it be reused in our own day?

Obviously it has nothing to do with commending sharp practice in business or personal finance. Rather, it advises us to sit light to the extra regulations which we impose on one another, not least in the church, which are over and above the gospel itself. The church passes through turbulent times, and frequently needs to reassess what matters and what doesn't. The twentieth century saw the so-called 'mainline' churches in many parts of the world – the traditional denominations – in decline, with newer churches, not least in the Third World, growing and spreading. What should traditional churches do when faced with their own mortality? Perhaps they should learn to think unconventionally, to be prepared to make new friends across traditional barriers, to throw caution to the winds and discover again, in the true fellowship of the gospel, a home that will last.

LUKE 16.10-18

Teachings on Stewardship

[10]'Someone who is faithful in a small matter', Jesus continued, 'will also be faithful in a large one. Someone who is dishonest in a small matter will also be dishonest in a large one. [11]If you haven't been faithful with that wicked thing called money, who is going to entrust you with true wealth? [12]And if you haven't been faithful in looking after what belongs to someone else, who is going to give you what is your own?

[13]'Nobody can serve two masters. You will end up hating one and loving the other, or going along with the first and despising the other. You can't serve God and money.'

[14]The Pharisees, who loved money, heard all this, and mocked Jesus. [15]So he said to them, 'You people let everyone else know that you're in the right – but God knows your hearts. What people call honourable, God calls abominable!

[16]'The law and the prophets lasted until John. From now on, God's kingdom is announced, and everyone is trying to attack it. [17]But it's easier for heaven and earth to pass away than for one dot of an "i" to drop out of the law.

[18]'Anyone who divorces his wife and marries another commits adultery, and a person who marries a divorced woman commits adultery.'

Wealth is a killer. About half the stories in the newspapers seem to be about money in one way or another – the glamour and glitz it seems to provide, the shock and the horror when it runs out, the never-ending scandals about people getting it, embezzling it, losing it and getting it again. The lines between legitimate business and sharp practice are notoriously blurred. When does a gift become a bribe? When is it right to use other people's money to make money for yourself, and when is it wrong? And then there are the robberies, burglaries, and the numerous other obvious ways in which money is at the centre of simple, old-fashioned wrongdoing.

From a **parable** about money, Luke moves us to actual teaching about money; the chapter will end with another parable in which money is both part of the story and part of the point. This passage contains some of Jesus' strongest and most explicit warnings about the dangers of wealth, and experience suggests that neither the church nor the world has taken these warnings sufficiently to heart. Somewhere along the line serious **repentance**, and a renewed determination to hear and obey Jesus' clear teaching, seems called for.

The key to it all is in the opening verses: it's about *faithfulness*. Money is not a possession, it's a trust: God entrusts property to people and expects it to be used to his glory and the welfare of his children, not for private glory or glamour. Money also, according to this passage, points beyond itself, to the true riches which await us in the **life** to come. What they are, we can hardly guess; but there are 'true riches' which really will belong to us, in a way that money doesn't, if we learn faithfulness here and now.

If we don't, we shall find ourselves torn between two masters. This situation was particularly acute in Jesus' day. As in most peasant societies, there was a very small number of extremely rich people and a very large number of the very poor. The rich included the chief **priests** (some of their opulent houses in Jerusalem have been discovered by archaeologists), so any attack on the rich would include an attack on them. The **Pharisees** were more of a populist movement; but the danger they faced, with the land as a key part of their religion, was that they would equate possession of land, and the wealth it brought, with God's blessing. The stern warnings at the end of chapter 14 had already made it clear that this was not the way. Here Jesus insists starkly that God's standards are not just subtly different from human ones, but are the exact opposite.

Is Jesus saying something new in all this? The Pharisees might well have answered him by pointing out that there was much in the Jewish **law** which encouraged people to think that possessions were a sign of God's favour. Jesus, of course, takes the opposite view, with a good deal

146

of the prophetic writings obviously on his side; and the law itself commanded Israel to care for the poor and needy. His relationship to the Jewish law, though, is not exactly straightforward, and verses 16–17 need examining with some care.

He sees the law and the prophets (meaning the books we call 'the Old Testament') as taking their place in a sequence of events within God's plan. They are not God's last word; they hold sway until the time of **John the Baptist**, after which God's **kingdom** has been coming in a new way. Something fresh is happening here, where Jesus is; but this doesn't mean that the law and the prophets were wrong, or are now irrelevant. They remain fixed and unalterable. They are a true signpost to what God is going to do, even though they cannot themselves bring about the new day, the new world, that God is creating through Jesus. When, therefore, God does what he intends to do through Jesus, the law and the prophets will look on in approval, even though they couldn't have done it by themselves. That is part of the point of the next parable in the chapter.

The saying about divorce seems to be included here as an example of a commandment which many within Judaism were quietly setting aside. Only the strictest of Jewish teachers at this time supported the complete ban on divorce which is implied by such Old Testament passages as, for instance, Malachi 2.14–16. How this is worked out in today's pastoral practice is another question, which will need the fuller teaching of Matthew (5.32; 19.9) and Paul (1 Corinthians 7) as well as great care and sensitivity.

Putting the passage together, we find the underlying challenge to be faithful: faithful in our use of money, faithful to God rather than money, faithful in our hearts not just in our outward appearances, faithful to the kingdom which has now begun with Jesus, faithful to our marriages. As soon as we begin to think of money, or land, or other people, as commodities we might own or exploit, we take a step away from our vocation to be truly human beings, God's true children, and towards the other master, who is always ready to accept new servants.

LUKE 16.19–31

The Parable of the Rich Man and Lazarus

[19]"There was once a rich man,' said Jesus, 'who was dressed in purple and fine linen, and feasted in splendour every day. [20]A poor man named Lazarus, who was covered with sores, lay outside his gate. [21]He longed to feed himself with the scraps that fell from the rich man's table. Even the dogs came and licked his sores.

147

²²'In due course the poor man died, and was carried by the angels into Abraham's bosom. The rich man also died, and was buried. ²³As he was being tormented in Hades, he looked up and saw Abraham far away, and Lazarus in his bosom.

²⁴'"Father Abraham!" he called out. "Have pity on me! Send Lazarus to dip the tip of his finger in water and cool my tongue! I'm in agony in this fire!"

²⁵'"My child," replied Abraham, "remember that in your life you received good things, and in the same way Lazarus received evil. Now he is comforted here, and you are tormented. ²⁶Besides that, there is a great chasm standing between us. People who want to cross over from here to you can't do so, nor can anyone get across from the far side to us."

²⁷'"Please, then, father," he said, "send him to my father's house. ²⁸I've got five brothers. Let him tell them about it, so that they don't come into this torture-chamber."

²⁹'"They've got Moses and the prophets", replied Abraham. "Let them listen to them."

³⁰'"No, father Abraham," he replied, "but if someone went to them from the dead, they would repent!"

³¹'"If they don't listen to Moses and the prophets," came the reply, "neither would they be convinced, even if someone rose from the dead."'

We have all seen him. He lies on a pile of newspapers outside a shop doorway, covered with a rough blanket. Perhaps he has a dog with him for safety. People walk past him, or even step over him. He occasionally rattles a few coins in a tin or cup, asking for more. He wasn't there when I was a boy, but he's there now, in all our cities, east, west, north and south.

As I see him, I hear voices. It's his own fault, they say. He's chosen it. There are agencies to help him. He should go and get a job. If we give him money he'll only spend it on drink. Stay away – he might be violent. Sometimes, in some places, the police will move him on, exporting the problem somewhere else. But he'll be back. And even if he isn't, there are whole societies like that. They camp in tin shacks on the edges of large, rich cities. From the door of their tiny makeshift shelters you can see the high-rise hotels and office blocks where, if they're very lucky, one member of the family might work as a cleaner. They have been born into debt, and in debt they will stay, through the fault of someone rich and powerful who signed away their rights, their lives in effect, a generation or two ago, in return for arms, a new presidential palace, a fat Swiss bank account. And even if rich and poor don't always live side by side so blatantly, the television brings us together.

So we all know Lazarus. He is our neighbour. Some of us may be rich, well dressed and well fed, and walk past him without even noticing; others of us may not be so rich, or so finely clothed and fed, but compared with Lazarus we're well off. He would be glad to change places with us, and we would be horrified to share his life, even for a day.

Jesus' story about Lazarus and the unnamed rich man (he's often called 'Dives', because that's the Latin word for 'rich', but in the story he remains anonymous) works at several levels. It is very like a well-known folk tale in the ancient world; Jesus was by no means the first to tell of how wealth and poverty might be reversed in the future life. In fact, stories like this were so well known that we can see how Jesus has changed the pattern that people would expect. In the usual story, when someone asks permission to send a message back to the people who are still alive on earth, the permission is granted. Here, it isn't; and the sharp ending of the story points beyond itself to all sorts of questions that Jesus' hearers, and Luke's readers, were urged to face.

The **parable** is not primarily a moral tale about riches and poverty – though, in this chapter, it should be heard in that way as well. If that's all it was, some might say that it was better to let the poor stay poor, since they will have a good time in the future life. That sort of argument has been used too often by the careless rich for us to want anything to do with it. No; there is something more going on here. The story, after all, doesn't add anything new to the general folk belief about fortunes being reversed in a future life. If it's a *parable*, that means once again that we should take it as picture-language about something that was going on in Jesus' own work.

The ending gives us a clue, picking up where, a chapter earlier, the story of the father and his two sons had ended. 'Neither will they be convinced, even if someone were to rise from the dead'; 'this your brother was dead, and is alive again'. The older brother in the earlier story is very like the rich man in this: both want to keep the poor, ragged brother or neighbour out of sight and out of mind. Jesus, we recall, has been criticized for welcoming outcasts and sinners; now it appears that what he's doing is putting into practice *in the present world* what, it was widely believed, would happen in the future one. 'On earth as it is in **heaven**' remains his watchword. The **age to come** must be anticipated in the present.

The point is then that the **Pharisees**, being themselves lovers of money, were behaving to the people Jesus was welcoming exactly like the rich man was behaving to Lazarus. And, just as the steward was to be put out of his stewardship, and was commended for taking action in the nick of time to prevent total disaster, so the Pharisees, and anyone else tempted to take a similar line, are now urged to change their ways while there is still time. All Jesus is asking them, in fact, is to do what Moses and the prophets would have said. As Luke makes clear throughout, his **kingdom**-mission is the fulfilment of the whole story of Israel. Anyone who understands the law and the prophets must therefore see that Jesus is bringing them to completion.

If they do not, then not even someone rising from the dead will bring them to their senses. The last sentence of the parable, like a great crashing chord on an organ, contains several different notes. It speaks of the whole hope of Israel for restoration and renewal. It speaks, as does the story of the prodigal son, of the poor and outcast being welcomed by Jesus. And it speaks, for Luke's readers from that day to this, most powerfully of Jesus himself. One day soon, the reader knows, the law and the prophets will all come true in a new way, as Jesus himself rises again, opening the door to God's new age in which all wrongs will be put right.

LUKE 17.1–10

Forgiveness, Faith and Obedience

[1]Jesus said to his disciples, 'There are bound to be things that trip people up; but woe betide the person who brings them about! [2]It would be better to have a millstone hung around your neck, and be thrown into the sea, than to trip up one of these little ones. [3]So watch out for yourselves.

'If your brother sins against you, rebuke him; and if he apologizes, forgive him. [4]Even if he sins against you seven times, and turns round seven times and says "sorry" to you, you must forgive him.'

[5]The apostles said to the master, 'Give us greater faith!'

[6]'If you had faith', replied the master, 'as a grain of mustard seed, you would say to this mulberry tree, "Be uprooted and be planted in the sea", and it would obey you.

[7]'Supposing one of you has a slave ploughing or keeping sheep out in the field. When he comes in, what will you say? "Come here at once, and sit down for a meal?" [8]No; you will be far more likely to say, "Get something ready for me to eat! Get properly dressed, and wait on me while I eat and drink! After that you can have something to eat and drink yourself." [9]Will you thank the slave because he did what you told him?

[10]'That's how it is with you. When you've done everything you're told, say this: "We're just ordinary slaves. All we've done is what we were supposed to do."'

There is a famous story about a man who wrote a book with the title, *Humility and How I Achieved It*. The title is almost as self-contradictory as, in Jesus' world, the phrase 'the good Samaritan' would have been.

150

One of the paradoxes of humility is that, unlike the other virtues, those who really possess it usually don't have the slightest idea that they do.

The various short sayings which Luke has collected here have this as their common thread. They all point towards the humility which true servants of Jesus must learn. That seems, at least, to be one connecting link, and it's worth exploring further.

Think first about the warnings of people tripping each other up. This may have some reference to the previous two chapters, in which 'the little ones' would refer to the outcasts welcomed by Jesus, whom the **Pharisees** and others wanted to stop from entering into the **kingdom** on Jesus' terms. But the point seems to be wider. The way the world now is, until God's final victory over the enemy, there are bound to be times when people will find their **faith** tested, and tested sometimes beyond what they can bear. There is no way of avoiding that altogether. But that doesn't excuse anyone who inflicts such a test on someone else. In one of the most graphic descriptions of punishment anywhere in the **gospels**, Jesus warns that it would be better for a millstone, which is shaped around a central hole, to become a collar to drag you to the bottom of the ocean, rather than to suffer the punishment in store for people who upset the faith of those who trust in him.

Christian leaders and teachers need this warning on a regular basis. It is possible for them to do and say things which make others think, 'Well, if that's how God's representatives behave, I suppose the whole thing's a waste of time!' How can you avoid putting someone in that situation? Humility.

Or what about the call for repeated forgiveness? How easy to take the moral high ground: I haven't done anything wrong, so if I choose to forgive you that makes me superior to you. Then, once I've enjoyed exercising that position once or twice, it's time to draw back a bit. Why should I go on giving you all that freedom?

Jesus' approach is utterly different. When you forgive someone, you are making yourself their servant, not their master. Forgiving someone again and again ought not to get harder and harder; it shouldn't be a matter of restraining anger for a longer and longer time, like someone trying to hold their breath under water for ten seconds, then for twenty, then for thirty, and so on. If that's what it's like, you've missed the meaning altogether. The point is that you're not scoring moral points at all. You are to be humble, to take no advantage of the situation, to give to the other person the generous and welcoming forgiveness that (as Jesus indicates on numerous other occasions) God has shown you in the first place. That, after all, is the real source of humility. If in doubt, meditate on God's grace.

Perhaps not surprisingly, the **disciples** realize in verse 5 that all this will require more faith than they think they have. Jesus is quick to respond. It's not great faith you need; it is faith in a great God. Faith is like a window through which you can see something. What matters is not whether the window is six inches or six feet high; what matters is the God that your faith is looking out on. If it's the creator God, the God active in Jesus and the **spirit**, then the tiniest little peephole of a window will give you access to power like you never dreamed of. Of course, this cannot be used for your own whim or pleasure; as soon as you tried, it would show that you'd forgotten, once more, who this God really was. Humility once again.

Finally, the shocking lesson that all we do, even the hard work we do for God, never for a moment puts God in our debt. How often do we hear it said (and how many more times is it thought): I've done all this, I've given all that money, I've worked so hard – surely God will be satisfied with that? The answer is that all genuine service to God is done from gratitude, not to earn anything at all. Saying 'We're not worth anything at all' doesn't mean that we lack a proper sense of self-worth and self-love. It just means that we must constantly remind ourselves of the great truth: we can never put God in our debt.

LUKE 17.11–19

Ten Men Healed

[11]As Jesus was on his way to Jerusalem, he passed along the border-lands between Samaria and Galilee. [12]As he was going into one particular village he was met by ten men with virulent skin diseases who stayed at some distance from him.

[13]'Jesus, Master!' they called out loudly. 'Have pity on us!'

[14]When Jesus saw them he said to them, 'Go and show yourselves to the priests.' And as they went, they were healed.

[15]One of them, seeing that he had been healed, turned back and gave glory to God at the top of his voice. [16]He fell on his face in front of Jesus' feet and thanked him. He was a Samaritan.

[17]'There were ten of you healed, weren't there?' responded Jesus. 'Where are the nine? [18]Is it really the case that the only one who had the decency to give God the glory was this foreigner?

[19]'Get up, and be on your way', he said to him. 'Your faith has saved you.'

What would make you shout for joy at the top of your voice? What would make you fall on the ground – yes, flat on your face! – in front of someone?

Two explorers were lost in the South American jungle not long ago. For nine months they wandered about, not knowing where they were or how to get out. Finally, after many adventures and often giving up hope, they were found and rescued. They probably didn't have enough energy to shout, but they will have felt like it. Certainly their relatives back home did.

You might shout for joy when the doctor told you that someone you loved very dearly had come safely through the operation, and was going to be all right after all. You might do it when suddenly all your debts were rolled away and you were given a new start in life.

Which, then, is the more surprising: the fact that one person came back, shouted for joy, and fell down at Jesus' feet? Or the fact that nine didn't?

Luke, once again, focuses on Jesus' attitude to the outsider, the foreigner. Like the Samaritan in one of his own stories, this man put to shame the Jews who had been healed but who didn't say 'thank you'. Perhaps, once they'd seen the **priest** (the priest who lived locally had the responsibility to declare when people were healed from such diseases), they were afraid to go back and identify themselves with Jesus, who by now was a marked man. Perhaps, having realized they had been healed, they were so eager to get back to their families, whom they hadn't been able to live with all the time the disease had affected them, that they simply didn't think to go back and look for Jesus.

Luke doesn't say that they were any less cured, but he does imply that they were less grateful. After the lesson in humility comes the lesson in gratitude. Humility, of course, is still built in: only the outsider, only the foreigner, gives God the glory, showing up the Jews whose very name reminded them to praise God (the word 'Judah' in Hebrew means 'praise').

It is not only the nine ex-lepers who are shown up. It is all of us who fail to thank God 'always and for everything', as Paul puts it (Ephesians 5.20). We know with our heads, if we have any Christian **faith** at all, that our God is the giver of all things: every mouthful of food we take, every breath of air we inhale, every note of music we hear, every smile on the face of a friend, a child, a spouse – all that, and a million things more, are good gifts from his generosity. The world didn't need to be like this. It could have been far more drab (of course, we have often made it dull and lifeless, but even there God can spring surprises). There is an old spiritual discipline of listing one's blessings, naming them before God, and giving thanks. It's a healthy thing to do, especially in a world where we too often assume we have an absolute right to health, happiness and every possible creature comfort.

153

Jesus' closing words to the Samaritan invite a closer look. The word for 'get up' is a word early Christians would have recognized as having to do with '**resurrection**'. Like the prodigal son, this man 'was dead, and is alive again'. New **life**, the life which Israel was longing for as part of the **age to come**, had arrived in his village that day, and it had called out of him a faith he didn't know he had. Once again (compare 5.20; 8.48; 8.50), faith and healing go hand in hand. Once again, 'faith' here means not just any old belief, any generally religious attitude to life, but the belief that the God of life and death is at work in and through Jesus, and the trust that this is not just a vague general truth but that it will hold good in *this* case, here and now. This rhythm of faith and gratitude simply is what being a Christian, in the first or the twenty-first century, is all about.

LUKE 17.20–37

The Coming of the Kingdom

²⁰The Pharisees asked Jesus when the kingdom of God was coming.

'God's kingdom', replied Jesus, 'isn't the sort of thing you can watch for and see coming. ²¹People won't say "Look, here it is", or "Look, over there!" No: God's kingdom is within your grasp.'

²²Then Jesus said to the disciples, 'The days are coming when you will long to see one of the days of the son of man, and you won't see it. ²³They will say to you, "Look, there!" or "Look, here!" Don't go off or follow them. ²⁴The son of man in his day will be like lightning that shines from one end of the sky to the other. ²⁵But first he must suffer many things and be rejected by this generation.

²⁶'What will it be like in the days of the son of man? It will be like the days of Noah. ²⁷People were eating and drinking, they were getting married and giving wedding parties, until the day when Noah went into the ark. And on that day the flood came and swept them all away. ²⁸And it will be like the days of Lot. They were eating and drinking, they were buying and selling, they were planting and building. ²⁹But on the day when Lot left Sodom, it rained fire and sulphur from the sky and they were all destroyed. ³⁰That's what it will be like on the day when the son of man is revealed.

³¹'On that day anyone up on the roof, with all their possessions in the house, shouldn't go down to get them. Anyone out in the field shouldn't go back to get anything. ³²Remember Lot's wife. ³³If you try to save your life you'll lose it, but anyone who loses it will keep it.

³⁴'Let me tell you, in that night there will be two people sleeping side by side: one will be taken, and the other left behind. ³⁵There will be two women working side by side grinding corn: one will be taken, and the other left behind.'

> [37]'Where will this be, master?' they asked him.
> 'Where the body is,' replied Jesus, 'there the vultures will gather.'

What does the word 'apocalypse' conjure up to you? Hollywood fantasies? Stars falling from the sky, volcanoes and earthquakes? People in terror, panicking and rushing this way and that?

The Bible has plenty of apocalypses, and sometimes they sound like that. This passage is one of them: Noah's flood sweeping everybody away, and fire and sulphur raining on Sodom as Lot and his family escape. That's exactly the sort of thing many people think of when they hear the word 'apocalypse'.

But did Jesus think it would be like that? What does this passage mean?

There has been a growth industry in writing books based on passages like this. 'One will be taken, and the other left'; some have assumed that being 'taken' in this sense means being snatched up to **heaven** to be with God, leaving the others behind to survive in a frightening world from which all the true believers have been removed. That's not what the passage means, though; it's actually the other way round. The people who are 'taken' are the ones in danger; they are being taken away by hostile forces, taken away to their doom.

But what are these hostile forces? What are the vultures that will gather around the 'body', and what will they do? And what has all this got to do with 'the days of the **son of man**', which the **disciples** will long for but won't see?

The rest of Luke's **gospel** makes it clear how he thought we should understand it. The passage does not refer to an event in which natural or supernatural forces will devastate a town, a region or the known world; rather, like so many of Jesus' warnings in Luke, it refers to the time when enemy armies will invade and wreak sudden destruction. The word that means 'vultures' is the same word as 'eagles' (ancient writers thought vultures were a kind of eagle), and there may be a cryptic reference here to the Roman legions, with the eagle as their imperial badge.

This makes sense of the warnings. When the legions arrive, the best thing to do is to get out and run; don't even think about collecting belongings. Normal life will be going on one moment, the next there will be a panic, and the wisest advice is not to think about the necessities of life itself until you're well out of the way. People who are found either asleep or working indoors at a mill, and thus taken unawares, will find that the invaders will snatch one here and one there. And there won't be any doubt that it's happening. It won't be a 'spiritual' event that would need special discernment. It will be like lightning, suddenly lighting up a dark sky.

What has this got to do, then, with the son of man? 'The days of the son of man' seems to refer to the days when, as in the prophecy of Daniel (chapter 7), the 'one like a son of man' will be vindicated by God after suffering. The sign of this will be the destruction of the oppressor, the power that has opposed God's people and God's purpose. In Daniel, this power is the fourth 'beast', the greatest of the pagan armies. For Jesus, in one of the most dramatic twists of thinking, the force that has most directly opposed his teaching and his **kingdom**-ministry is official Israel itself, focused on the **Temple** and its hierarchy, and the **Pharisees** whose thinking and practice derived from the Temple.

We have seen again and again in Luke that Jesus warns of awful destruction coming upon his contemporaries for their failure to heed his message. Now he uses the 'apocalyptic' language of some Jewish prophecy to ram the same warnings home. 'The days of the son of man' are the days in which this figure, representing God's true people, is finally vindicated after his suffering. And that vindication will take the form of the destruction of the city, and the Temple, that have set their face against his gospel of peace.

Why then does Jesus say, at the start of this passage, that God's kingdom isn't the sort of thing for which there are advance signs?

The question from the Pharisees implies that Jesus has a timetable in mind, in which certain things would happen in a particular order so that one could tick them off and get ready for the final drama. Part of Jesus' answer, as we have seen, is that it won't be like that. Life will go on as normal until the last moment; but there is something else to be said as well. God's kingdom, he says, is *within your grasp*.

The phrase he uses in verse 21 is sometimes translated 'within you', and people have often thought it meant that the kingdom is purely spiritual, a private, interior relationship with God. But Jesus never uses 'God's kingdom' in that sense. It always refers to things that happen in the public world, not to private experience. Others have suggested that the phrase means 'in your midst'; God's kingdom, in other words, is present but secret, hidden, waiting for them to discover it. That is closer, but still not quite there. The phrase is more active. It doesn't just tell you where the kingdom is; it tells you that you've got to do something about it. It is 'within your grasp'; it is confronting you with a decision, the decision to believe, trust and follow Jesus. It isn't the sort of thing that's just going to happen, so that you can sit back and watch. God's sovereign plan to put the world to rights *is waiting for you to sign on*. That is the force of what Jesus is saying.

The warnings of Jesus came true in AD 70. But the promise of the kingdom remains. It may well be that, at the still-future time when God finally overcomes sin and death for good and remakes the heavens

156

and the earth, there will once more be a moment when, in the midst of normal life, ruin breaks in on those who have not heeded God's call. But that isn't what this passage is about. The passage holds out an invitation, to this day, to those who are anxious about the future: God's sovereign rule of the world, his healing love, are not only yours for the grasping, but are waiting for your help.

LUKE 18.1–14

The Parables of the Persistent Widow and the Tax-Collector

¹Jesus told them a parable, about how they should always pray and not give up.

²'There was once a judge in a certain town,' he said, 'who didn't fear God, and didn't have any respect for people. ³There was a widow in that town, and she came to him and said, "Judge my case! Vindicate me against my enemy!"

⁴'For a long time he refused. But, in the end, he said to himself, "It's true that I don't fear God, and don't have any respect for people. ⁵But because this widow is causing me a lot of trouble, I will put her case right and vindicate her, so that she doesn't end up coming and giving me a black eye."

⁶'Well,' said the master, 'did you hear what this unjust judge says? ⁷And don't you think that God will see justice done for his chosen ones, who shout out to him day and night? Do you suppose he is deliberately delaying? ⁸Let me tell you, he will vindicate them very quickly. But – when the son of man comes, will he find faith on the earth?'

⁹He told this next parable against those who trusted in their own righteous standing and despised others.

¹⁰'Two men,' he said, 'went up to the Temple to pray. One was a Pharisee, the other was a tax-collector. ¹¹The Pharisee stood and prayed in this way to himself: "God, I thank you that I am not like the other people – greedy, unjust, immoral, or even like this tax-collector. ¹²I fast twice in the week; I give tithes of all that I get."

¹³'But the tax-collector stood a long way off, and didn't even want to raise his eyes to heaven. He beat his breast and said, "God, be merciful to me, sinner that I am." ¹⁴Let me tell you, he was the one who went back to his house in the right before God, not the other. Don't you see? People who exalt themselves will be humbled, and people who humble themselves will be exalted.'

Come with me into a court of law, where a civil case is being tried. I haven't often been in a court, but we see them on the television and in the newspapers, and from time to time legal cases are widely reported and make history.

If it wasn't so serious, it would be like a sporting contest. Here is the plaintiff, claiming eagerly that he has been wronged by the person opposing him. He has his team of lawyers, and they are arguing the case, producing witnesses, trying to persuade the judge that he is in the right. Here, opposite, is the defendant, the man the plaintiff is accusing. He and his team are trying to persuade the judge that *he* is in the right. Though experts who are watching may have a sense of which way the verdict is going to go, the result isn't known until the judge, like a referee, finally sums up and announces the result.

In the ancient Jewish lawcourt, all cases were like that, not just civil ones. If someone had stolen from you, you had to bring a charge against them; you couldn't get the police to do it for you. If someone had murdered a relative of yours, the same would be true. So every legal case in Jesus' day was a matter of a judge deciding to vindicate one party or the other: 'vindication' or 'justification' here means upholding their side of the story, deciding in their favour. This word '**justification**', which we meet a lot in Paul but hardly ever in the **gospels**, means exactly this: that the judge finds in one's favour at the end of the case. (See, e.g., Romans 2.1–16; 3.21–31; Galatians 2.16–21.)

These two **parables**, very different though they are in some ways, are both about vindication. The first is more obviously so, since it is actually set in a lawcourt; but here we are puzzled at first glance, since, though Jesus clearly intends the judge to stand for God, this judge is about as unlike God as possible. He has no respect for God himself, and he doesn't care whether he does the right thing for people or not. The point of the parable is then to say: if even a rotten judge like that can be persuaded to do the right thing by someone who pesters him day and night until it happens, then of course God, who is Justice in person, and who cares passionately about people, will vindicate them, will see that justice is done.

The parable assumes that God's people are like litigants in a lawsuit, waiting for God's verdict. What is the lawsuit about? It seems to be about Israel, or rather now the renewed Israel gathered around Jesus, awaiting from God the vindication that will come when those who have opposed his message are finally routed. It is, in other words, about the same scenario as described in the previous chapter: the time when, through the final destruction of the city and **Temple** that have opposed him, Jesus' followers will know that God has vindicated Jesus himself, and them as his followers. Though this moment will itself be terrifying, it will function as the liberating, vindicating judgment that God's people have been waiting and praying for. And if this is true of that final moment, it is also true of all such lesser moments, with which Christian living is filled.

The second parable looks at first as though it is describing a religious occasion, but it, too, turns out to be another lawsuit. Or perhaps we should say that the **Pharisee** in the Temple has already turned it into a contest: his 'prayer', which consists simply of telling God all about his own good points, ends up exalting himself by the simple expedient of denouncing the tax-collector. The tax-collector, however, is the one whose small **faith** sees through to the great heart of God (see 17.6), and he casts himself on the divine mercy. Jesus reveals what the divine judge would say about this: the tax-collector, not the Pharisee, returned home vindicated.

These two parables together make a powerful statement about what, in Paul's language, is called 'justification by faith'. The wider context is the final lawcourt, in which God's chosen people will be vindicated after their life of suffering, holiness and service. Though enemies outside and inside may denounce and attack them, God will act and show that they truly are his people. But this doesn't mean that one can tell in the present who God's elect are, simply by the outward badges of virtue, and in particular the observance of the minutiae of the Jewish **law**. If you want to see where this final vindication is anticipated in the present, look for where there is genuine penitence, genuine casting of oneself on the mercies of God. 'This one went home vindicated'; those are among the most comforting words in the whole gospel.

LUKE 18.15–30

The Rich Young Ruler

[15]People were bringing even tiny babies to Jesus for him to touch them. When the disciples saw it, they forbade them sternly. [16]But Jesus called them. 'Let the children come to me,' he said, 'and don't stop them! God's kingdom belongs to the likes of these. [17]I'm telling you the truth: anyone who doesn't receive God's kingdom like a child will never get into it.'

[18]There was a ruler who asked him, 'Good teacher, what must I do to inherit the life of the age to come?'

[19]'Why call me good?' said Jesus to him. 'No one is good except God alone. [20]You know the commandments: Don't commit adultery, don't kill, don't steal, don't swear falsely, honour your father and mother.'

[21]'I've kept them all', he said, 'since I was a boy.'

[22]When Jesus heard that, he said to him, 'There's just one thing you're short of. Sell everything you own, and distribute it to the poor, and you will have treasure in heaven. Then come and follow me.'

[23]When he heard that he became very sad. He was extremely wealthy.

159

²⁴Jesus saw that he had become sad, and said, 'How hard it is for those with possessions to enter God's kingdom! ²⁵Yes: it's easier for a camel to go through the eye of a needle than for a rich man to enter God's kingdom.'

²⁶The people who heard it said, 'So who can be saved?'

²⁷'What's impossible for humans', said Jesus, 'is possible for God.'

²⁸'Look here', said Peter, 'we've left everything and followed you.'

²⁹'I'm telling you the truth', said Jesus, 'everyone who has left house or wife or brothers or parents or children, because of God's kingdom, ³⁰will receive far more in return in the present time – and in the age to come they will receive the life that belongs to that age.'

Luke, ever the artist, is building up his great picture with colour after colour, layer after layer of paint, until he draws the eye towards the great scene he has in mind when Jesus arrives in Jerusalem. He has given us Jesus' lessons on humility and gratitude. He has given us two **parables** about God's vindication of his people, both in the future and also, for those with humble and penitent **faith**, in the present. He now builds on both of these, still leading us towards Jerusalem, and speaks here of the extraordinary challenge of entering God's **kingdom**, of sharing the life of the **age to come**.

Luke emphasizes how young the babies were that people were bringing to Jesus. Jesus' rebuke to the **disciples** rings out still today in a world where thousands of children are treated as subhuman, as disposable commodities. These are the ones, he says, who most truly show us what it means to accept and enter God's kingdom. There is something about the helplessness of children, and their complete trust of those who love and care for them, which perfectly demonstrates the humble trust he has been speaking of all along. Jesus doesn't offer a romantic or sentimental view of children; he must have known, in the daily life of a village, and through growing up as the oldest of several children, just how demanding and annoying they can be. But he sees to the heart of what it means to receive God's kingdom; it is like drinking in one's mother's milk, like learning to see – and to smile! – by looking at one's mother's eyes and face.

By contrast, the rich ruler who appears so confident, so well organized, so determined, looks into the face of the one he calls 'good' and turns away sad. He had hoped to impress Jesus with his piety and devotion; unlike the 'sinners' of whom we have heard so much in the previous chapters, he had a clean moral record in keeping the well-known commandments. His question, Jesus' answer, and the subsequent conversation with the crowd and the disciples, enable us to see to the heart of what is going on as Jesus approaches Jerusalem.

Jesus was putting into operation that for which most Jews had longed: God's kingdom, God's sovereign saving power operating in a new way for the benefit of the whole world. This meant that already, in the **present**, the period of time they spoke of as 'the age to come' was breaking in. It would come fully in the future, when all evil had been done away with, and then those who belonged to it would share 'the life of the coming age'. Because the word for 'age' here is often translated 'eternal', the phrase 'eternal life' has regularly been used to describe this life. For many today, this simply means an existence going on and on for ever. This may or may not be desirable; opinions will differ. But in any case it doesn't catch the flavour, the sheer excitement, carried by the original.

In God's new age, so the Jews believed, everything will be new, fresh, and free from corruption, decay, evil, bitterness, pain, fear and death. And that's just the beginning. There will be new possibilities and opportunities, new joys and delights. **Heaven** and earth will be joined together, God and his children will live with each other. That's the state of things people were longing for. It would come about when God finally ruled the world with his saving power.

And this is what Jesus was bringing in the present. Evil and death, to be sure, were still going on all around. Jesus himself had yet to face the full force of the powers of the old age. But where he was, and where people with humble and penitent trust accepted that God's kingdom was active in and through him, there the life of the new age began to be seen.

That was why the rich ruler became sad. In order to inherit the life of the new age, he had to abandon the values of the old and trust himself totally to the new, like a diver throwing himself forwards into the water. He couldn't seriously be seeking for the new age if he couldn't abandon the symbols of the old. The commandments were good and important; but if he was wedded to possessions – which, as we've seen, formed an important symbol of identity for the Jews to whom the land had been promised – then he would never be able to accept God's kingdom like a child, with the humble trust that allowed God to be God. The true wealth is to be found in the heavenly dimension: 'treasure in heaven' doesn't simply mean the sort of treasure you possess after you die, but treasure that's kept safe in God's storehouse until the time when heaven and earth are brought into their intended unity.

Already, even in the present time, this new age breaks in to our sad old world. Within the life of Christian fellowship there are new homes, new families, new possibilities that open up for those who leave behind the old ways. The church is called in every age to be that sort of community, a living example of the age to come. In that sort of selfless and trusting common life, church members themselves, and the world around, can glimpse what God's new world is like, and learn to live that way more and more.

LUKE 18.31–43

Jesus Heals a Blind Beggar

³¹Jesus took the Twelve aside.

'Look,' he said, 'we're going up to Jerusalem. Everything that's written in the prophets about the son of man will be fulfilled. ³²Yes: he will be handed over to the pagans; he'll be mocked, abused and spat upon. ³³They will beat him and kill him; and on the third day he'll be raised.'

³⁴They didn't understand any of this. The word was hidden from them, and they didn't know what he meant.

³⁵As they were getting near Jericho there was a blind man sitting by the road, begging. ³⁶When he heard a crowd passing through the town he asked what was going on.

³⁷'Jesus of Nazareth is coming by,' people said to him.

³⁸So he shouted out, 'Jesus – David's son! Have pity on me!'

³⁹The people who were at the front of the group firmly told him to be silent. But he yelled out all the more, 'David's son! Have pity on me!'

⁴⁰Jesus stopped, and told them to bring the man to him. When he came up, he asked him, ⁴¹'What d'you want me to do for you?'

'Master,' he said, 'I want to see again.'

⁴²'Then see again,' said Jesus. 'Your faith has saved you.'

⁴³At once he received his sight again, and followed him, glorifying God. And when all the people saw it, they gave praise to God.

Sometimes when you listen to a fine piece of music you discover that the composer is leading you into greater and greater tension, until something inside you is longing for it to be resolved into a final great chord or tune. One strand of music is building up in one direction, and another in another. The notes seem to be clashing against each other. Sometimes, in a concerto, the solo instrument seems to be struggling against the orchestra, each determined to take over from the other. Sometimes it's the different instruments of a quartet striving for mastery among themselves. Sometimes the tension is within the single solo part of a great song or piano piece. Music thrives on tension, and pulls the listener forwards until it's resolved.

Luke, in this passage, builds up the tension between two strands which will finally come together, and find their resolution, in the crucifixion and **resurrection** of Jesus. On the one hand, Jesus tells the **disciples** again that the reason for their journey to Jerusalem is so that 'the **son of man**' – now clearly identified as himself – may be treated brutally by the pagan occupying forces, and killed, and be raised on the third day. This is so totally outside anything that they have imagined, wanted, dreamed of, or pondered that they simply can't understand it. They assume he must be speaking in riddles, but they don't know what the riddle means. They certainly don't think he means it literally. They do, however, go on following him.

On the other hand, we find a blind beggar who trusts Jesus so completely that, when offered the chance to scale down his great request (how easy it would have been to ask for money or food instead), he goes for the chance of a lifetime and asks for his sight back again. Once more Jesus can tell someone that their **faith** has been the means of their rescue, their salvation. The man joins the crowd, following and praising God.

The disciples can't see; the beggar now can. The journey is at once puzzling and dark, and joyful and bright. We have almost arrived in Jerusalem, and all the themes which Luke has built into the journey are coming together at the great moment of arrival. On the one hand, this is the place where the forces of darkness are gathering, and will wreak their worst fury on Jesus himself. Behind that awful event, as we know well by now, there stands the warning on the city and the **Temple**: if they do not accept Jesus' offer, his message of peace, then the fate he is about to enact will be theirs as well. And the disciples, walking into this darkness, still don't understand it.

On the other hand, the powers of the new age are already at work. Wherever Jesus is, people are not only welcomed into the **kingdom**; they are healed, given a new life which truly anticipates the total healing and joy that are due to appear in God's final new day. There is excitement, heartfelt praise, celebration of God's kingdom.

How do these things fit together? At the moment they don't. The warnings fall on puzzled, incomprehending ears. The crowds, praising God, expect that the final kingdom is about to appear, not that their leader is to be arrested and executed. But in the middle of the scene Luke places the strand of teaching which, having run through the whole ministry of Jesus to this point, continues now until everything is complete. All this is happening, says Jesus, because what was spoken by the prophets must be fulfilled (verse 31). This is how the plan of God, communicated to the prophets of old, must be fulfilled. Indeed, it is because Jesus is drawing on to himself the dark powers of the old age, and ultimately death itself, that there is new **life** welling up elsewhere. As the music builds up to its climax, the great chords of cross and resurrection, we discover that this is what those events will mean: Luke once again is telling us, in advance, what Jesus will accomplish in his death. As we listen, we learn how this music can become the theme song of our lives as well.

In his death, Jesus will take on himself the blindness and despair of the world. There is so much, still, that we do not understand; so much in the world, and indeed in scripture, that remains hidden from us, as Jesus' words were to the disciples. There is much that, if we understood it fully, might make us turn back, and no longer wish to follow Jesus on the road. But Luke is telling us that if we go with him Jesus will take the full weight of that evil on to himself – indeed, that he has already done so on the cross, so that the things we still face need hold no terrors for us. Equally, there is much already given to us, when we believe and trust in God's power to heal and restore, that should make us praise him even as we go forward into the unknown.

All of this, for us as for them, involves trusting the God who has revealed his plan in scripture and supremely in Jesus. We are not stumbling forwards without a guide. We are not praising God in a superficial, flippant way. We follow, and we worship, with the humility and hope that Luke has been holding out as the central characteristics of Christian living. When we arrive with Jesus at the destination, we will find ourselves celebrating with him in the kingdom he has already achieved, and now longs to bring to full completion.

LUKE 19.1–10

The Calling of Zacchaeus

[1]They went into Jericho and passed through. [2]There was a man named Zacchaeus, a chief tax-collector, who was very rich. [3]He was trying to see who Jesus was, but, being a small man, he couldn't, because of the crowd. [4]So he ran on ahead, along the route Jesus was going to take, and climbed up into a sycamore tree to see him.

[5]When Jesus came to the place, he looked up.

'Zacchaeus,' he said to him, 'hurry up and come down. I have to stay at your house today.' [6]So he hurried up, came down, and welcomed him with joy.

[7]Everybody began to murmur when they saw it. 'He's gone in to spend time with a proper old sinner!' they were saying.

[8]But Zacchaeus stood there and addressed the master.

'Look, Master,' he said, 'I'm giving half my property to the poor. And if I have defrauded anyone of anything, I'm giving it back to them four times over.'

[9]'Today,' said Jesus, 'salvation has come to this house, because he too is a son of Abraham. [10]You see, the son of man came to seek and to save the lost.'

Sunday schools love Zacchaeus. At least, they love to act out his story and sing about him. The little man who climbs up a tree to see Jesus provides one of the most vivid short stories in the whole Bible. Children can identify with Zacchaeus; they often find themselves at the back of a crowd and can't see what's going on. Many adults, too, can identify with him; they might like to get closer to Jesus, but find it embarrassing to do so, and potentially costly.

Luke, of course, makes Zacchaeus one of his minor heroes. Luke's is the only **gospel** that tells of him and his sudden moment of glory, and the hardened old tax-collector fits in to three of Luke's regular themes: the problem of riches and what to do about it, the identification of Jesus with 'sinners', and the **faith** which recognizes Jesus as Lord and discovers new **life** as a result. Luke tells this story as a kind of balance to the sad tale of the rich young ruler in the previous chapter, and uses it as the final piece of framing before Jesus approaches Jerusalem. This kind of healing, this kind of new life, he seems to be saying, is what Jesus has come to bring. If only people in Jerusalem could see the point and make a similar response!

Nobody in Jericho liked Zacchaeus. They would have been horrified to think that, of all the inhabitants of the town, he would be the one known by name to millions of people two thousand years later. He was exactly the kind of man everybody despised. Not only a tax-collector but a chief tax-collector; that is, not only did he make money on the side, in addition to his legitimate collections, but he almost certainly made more money from the tax-collectors working under him. Wherever money changes hands, whether across a grubby table in a tin shack in a dusty small town or across a sparkling computer screen in a shiny office on the ninety-ninth floor of a Wall Street skyscraper, the hands all too easily get dirty. Whenever money starts to talk, it shouts louder than the claims of honesty, respect and human dignity. One can only imagine the reaction of neighbours, and even of friends and relatives, as Zacchaeus's house became more lavishly decorated, as more slaves ran about at his bidding, as his clothes became finer and his food richer. Everyone knew that this was their money and that he had no right to it; everyone knew that there was nothing they could do about it.

Until Jesus came through the town. The moment when the eyes of the two men met is worthy of an operatic aria. Inquisitiveness had got the better of the little rich man, an unspoken question emerging from behind his hard, crafty look. Jesus saw straight through the layers of graft and greed, of callous contempt for his fellow-citizens. He had met enough tax-collectors already to know exactly what life was like for them, and how, even though they couldn't resist the chance to make

165

more for themselves than they should, there was a sickness at the heart for which he had the remedy.

So once again Jesus finds himself relaxing in the company of the wrong sort of people. And once again the crowd outside grumble. But this time, instead of Jesus telling a **parable** – Luke no doubt wants us to think of the prodigal son and the other similar stories he's already given us – the tax-collector himself speaks to Jesus in public, and gives evidence of his extravagant **repentance**. Repentance here isn't just a change of heart; as in Judaism in general, repentance involves restoration, making amends. Zacchaeus is determined to do so lavishly. He doesn't offer to sell all his property, nor does Jesus demand it. But by the time he'd given half of it away, and made fourfold restitution where necessary, we can imagine that he would find himself in seriously reduced circumstances.

He doesn't care. He has found something more valuable. 'Today I have to stay at your house' becomes 'Today salvation has come to this house'; where Jesus is, there salvation is to be found, for those who accept him as master and reorder their lives accordingly. Once more Jesus links a former outcast back into the true family of Abraham (compare 13.16). Zacchaeus isn't going to follow Jesus on the road to Jerusalem, escaping the puzzled and probably still angry looks of the neighbours. He is going to live out his new life and re-establish himself as part of the renewed Israel right where he is.

The final comment points ahead once more, up the steep and dusty road to Jerusalem. We are almost there. The prophets have spoken of the fate that awaits the **son of man**; but his mission is not just to suffer and die, but rather, through that fate, to search out and rescue the lost sheep. 'He has gone in to spend time with a sinner' will soon change to 'He has gone out to die with the brigands'; and the same reason will underlie both. The son of man has come to seek and save the lost.

LUKE 19.11–27

The King, the Servants and the Money

> [11]While people were listening to this, Jesus went on to tell a parable. They were, after all, getting close to Jerusalem, and they thought that the kingdom of God was going to appear at any moment.
>
> [12]'There was once a nobleman,' he said, 'who went into a country far away to be given royal authority and then return. [13]He summoned ten of his slaves and gave them ten silver coins. "Do business with these", he said, "until I come back." [14]His subjects, though, hated him, and sent a delegation after him to say, "We don't want this man to be our king."

¹⁵"So it happened that when he received the kingship and came back again, he gave orders to summon the slaves who had received the money, so that he could find out how they had got on with their business efforts. ¹⁶The first came forward and said, "Master, your money has made ten times its value!"

¹⁷"'Well done, you splendid servant!" he said. "You've been trustworthy with something small; now you can take command of ten cities."

¹⁸"The second came and said, "Master, your money has made five times its value!"

¹⁹"'You too – you can take charge of five cities."

²⁰"The other came and said, "Master, here is your money. I kept it wrapped in this handkerchief. ²¹You see, I was afraid of you, because you are a hard man: you profit where you made no investment, and you harvest what you didn't sow."

²²"'I'll condemn you out of your own mouth, you wicked scoundrel of a servant!" he replied. "So: you knew that I was a hard man, profiting where I didn't invest and harvesting where I didn't sow? ²³So why didn't you put my money with the bankers? Then I'd have had the interest when I got back!"

²⁴"'Take the money from him," he said to the bystanders, "and give it to the man who's made ten of them!" ²⁵("Master," they said to him, "he's got ten coins already!")

²⁶"Let me tell you: everyone who has will be given more; but if someone has nothing, even what he has will be taken away from him. ²⁷But as for these enemies of mine, who didn't want me to be king over them – bring them here and slaughter them in front of me."

King Richard I reigned over England from 1189 to 1199. For most of the first half of his reign he was abroad, fighting in the Crusades; then, as he made his way home, he was captured and imprisoned. During his absence, his brother John gained support for his rival claim to the throne from various powerful persons, including the Bishop of Lichfield. When Richard finally returned in 1194, he pardoned the bishop for his disloyalty, on condition that he rebuild his cathedral. Thus, through the return and judgment of an unexpected king, there arose the glorious church which stands to this day.

Jesus' story of the returning king, and of those who had not wanted him to rule over them, is all the more terrifying because there is no pardon. We cannot flatten the story out, or creep nervously round its sharp edges, because Luke has made sure in the rest of the chapter that the meaning will stay with us. Jesus' tears over the city, and his stern action in the **Temple**, indicate well enough that the judgment at the end of the **parable** was meant to be taken seriously.

Who then is the king? Who are the servants? When is the judgment taking place?

For most of church history, this parable has been taken as a picture of the last judgment, the time when, at the final end of history, Jesus returns as king to reward his faithful followers and punish the disloyal. But we can be sure that Luke didn't think of it like that. Luke believes, of course, in Jesus' second coming (see Acts 1.11), but he does not intend us to read this story as a reference to it. The parable is about something happening much closer to Jesus' own day.

Jesus is telling a story about the king who comes back to see what his servants have been doing, and he tells it for the same reason as he told almost all his parables: to explain what he himself was doing, and what it meant. He was coming to Jerusalem, the end and goal of his long journey. And he was challenging his hearers to see and understand this event as the long-awaited return of Israel's God, the sovereign one, the rightful king. This was the hidden meaning of his journey all along. This was what it would look like when the true God finally returned to Zion.

The prophets had spoken of this day. Long after the exiles had returned geographically to Jerusalem, Malachi had spoken of 'the Lord, whom you seek' coming suddenly to the Temple, bringing fiery judgment. Zechariah also spoke of God coming at last, and all the holy ones (angels?) with him. Clearly many Jews of the time believed that, though the Temple had long since been rebuilt (and was now being beautified and extended by Herod), the living God had still not returned to live in it. Now, Jesus is saying, this is happening at last. But who will be able to stand before him?

Within the world of first-century Judaism, as we have seen before, a story about a king and his servants would naturally be read as a story about God and Israel. How should one then interpret the period of time between God's leaving Israel at the time of the **exile** and his eventual return? The answer of this parable is: as the time in which Israel has been given tasks to perform, which God on his return will investigate. Jesus has been warning, throughout the previous ten chapters, that judgment will fall on the nation, the city and the Temple itself if they do not finally heed his call. Now God himself is coming, and the servant who has hidden his master's money in a handkerchief will be found out.

The darkest strand in the story concerns the citizens who don't want this man to be their king. This almost certainly echoes the story of Archelaus, the older brother of Herod Antipas. After the death of their father, Herod the Great, in 4 BC, Archelaus went to Rome to be

168

confirmed as king, followed by a delegation of Judaeans who didn't want him. (Ten years later, after much misrule, he went again, only to find another delegation of Jews and Samaritans opposing his appointment – this time successfully.) But now, Jesus is implying, the unwanted King is coming back in power: not another wicked Herod, but the true King, the King who comes with a message of grace and peace, the King who was rejected because his people wanted to keep the kingdom for themselves.

The story therefore says three things to Jesus' hearers. First, to the people who supposed God's **kingdom** was coming immediately, it declares that it is indeed coming, but that it is coming with judgment as well as with mercy. Second, it indicates that as Jesus arrives in Jerusalem, the city that is already rejecting his message, God's judgment is being prepared. If they will not receive his kingdom-announcement, there is no more that can be done. Third, it brings together dramatically Jesus' own journey and the return of God himself, and thus unveils the hidden secret inside so much of the **gospel** story. Jesus is not just speaking about God, God's kingdom, God's return to Zion. Jesus is embodying it. Concealed within his own **messianic**, royal mission is the ultimate, and more fateful, mission: Israel's God himself, in human form, is returning at last to the city and Temple dedicated to his honour, to put to rights, at every level, that which has gone wrong. We who still await the final day of God's judgment, the final 'coming' of Jesus to our world, do well to ponder this 'coming' to Jerusalem as its sign and foretaste.

LUKE 19.28–40

The Triumphal Entry

[28]With these words, Jesus went on ahead, going up to Jerusalem.

[29]As they came close, as near as Bethany and Bethphage, at the place called the Mount of Olives, he sent two of the disciples on ahead. [30]'Go into the village over there,' he said, 'and as you arrive you'll find a colt tied up, one that nobody has ever ridden. Untie it and bring it here. [31]If anyone says to you, "Why are you untying it?" you should say, "Because the master needs it."'

[32]The two who were sent went off and found it just as Jesus had said to them. [33]They untied the colt, and its owners said to them, 'Why are you untying the colt?'

[34]'Because the master needs it', they replied.

[35]They brought it to Jesus, threw their cloaks on the colt, and mounted Jesus on it. [36]As he was going along, people kept spreading their cloaks on the road.

³⁷When he came to the descent of the Mount of Olives, the whole crowd of disciples began to celebrate and praise God at the tops of their voices for all the powerful deeds they had seen.

³⁸'Welcome, welcome, welcome with a blessing', they sang. 'Welcome to the king in the name of the Lord! 'Peace in heaven, and glory on high!'

³⁹Some of the Pharisees from the crowd said to Jesus, 'Teacher, tell your disciples to stop that.'

⁴⁰'Let me tell you,' replied Jesus, 'if they stayed silent, the stones would be shouting out!'

Mile after uphill mile, it seems a long way even today in a car. You wind up through the sandy hills from Jericho, the lowest point on the face of the earth, through the Judaean desert, climbing all the way. Halfway up, you reach sea level; you've already climbed a long way from the Jordan valley, and you still have to ascend a fair-sized mountain. It is almost always hot; since it seldom if ever rains, it's almost always dusty as well.

That was the way the pilgrims came, with Jesus going on ahead, as he had planned all along. This was to be the climax of his story, of his public career, of his vocation. He knew well enough what lay ahead, and had set his face to go and meet it head on. He couldn't stop announcing the **kingdom**, but that announcement could only come true if he now embodied in himself the things he'd been talking about. The living God was at work to heal and save, and the forces of evil and death were massed to oppose him, like Pharaoh and the armies of Egypt trying to prevent the Israelites from leaving. But this was to be the moment of God's new **Exodus**, God's great Passover, and nothing could stop Jesus going ahead to celebrate it.

Even when you drive, rather than walk, from Jericho to the top of the Mount of Olives, the sense of relief and excitement when you reach the summit is intense. At last you exchange barren, dusty desert for lush green growth, particularly at Passover time, at the height of spring. At last you stop climbing, you crest the summit, and there before you, glistening in the sun, is the holy city, Jerusalem itself, on its own slightly smaller hill across a narrow but deep valley. Bethany and Bethphage nestle on the Jericho side of the Mount of Olives. Once you pass them, Jerusalem comes into view almost at once. The end of the journey; the pilgrimage to end all pilgrimages; Passover time in the city of God.

For Jesus it's a royal occasion, to be carefully planned and staged so as to make exactly the right point. The animal he chose – presumably by prearrangement with the owners; this wasn't the first time Jesus had been to Bethany! – was a young foal, almost certainly a donkey's colt.

(The word Luke uses would more normally mean a young horse or pony; but he knew Zechariah 9.9, the prophecy of the **Messiah** riding on a young donkey, and he uses the word that occurs there.) Like the tomb in which Jesus would lie a week later (23.52), it had never been used before. The **disciples** pick up the theme, and in a kind of instant royal celebration they spread cloaks along the road for him. Down they go, down the steep path to the Kidron valley, and the crowd starts to sing part of the great psalm of praise (Psalm 118) that pilgrims always sang on the way to Jerusalem: a song of victory, a hymn of praise to the God who defeats all his foes and establishes his kingdom. Jesus will himself quote from the psalm in one of his debates in Jerusalem (20.17). He comes himself as the fulfilment of the nation's hopes, answering their longings for a king who would bring peace to earth from **heaven** itself.

And yet . . . the grumblers are still there; some **Pharisees**, going along with the crowd, suddenly become anxious about what will happen if the authorities in Jerusalem think for a minute that there's a messianic demonstration going on. Jesus knows, and Luke knows, and we as his readers know, what awaits the Master when he gets to the city. From Jesus' point of view, this is why there is such a celebration in the first place: it is appropriate precisely because he is coming to bring God's salvation, God's great Exodus, through his own Passover action on the cross. Had the crowds known this, they would have been puzzled and distressed, as indeed they soon will be.

As we arrive at Jerusalem with Jesus, the question presses upon us. Are we going along for the trip in the hope that Jesus will fulfil some of our hopes and desires? Are we ready to sing a psalm of praise, but only as long as Jesus seems to be doing what we want? The long and dusty pilgrim way of our lives gives most of us plenty of time to sort out our motives for following Jesus in the first place. Are we ready not only to spread our cloaks on the road in front of him, to do the showy and flamboyant thing, but also now to follow him into trouble, controversy, trial and death?

LUKE 19.41–48

Jesus Cleanses the Temple

[41]When he came near and saw the city, he wept over it.

[42]'If only you'd known,' he said, 'on this day – even you! – what peace meant. But now it's hidden, and you can't see it. [43]Yes, the days are coming upon you when your enemies will build up earthworks all round you, and encircle you, and squeeze you in from every direction. [44]They will bring you crashing to the ground, you and your

children within you. They won't leave one single stone on another, because you didn't know the moment when God was visiting you.' ⁴⁵He went into the Temple and began to throw out the traders. ⁴⁶'It's written,' he said, 'my house shall be a house of prayer; but you've made it a brigands' cave.'

⁴⁷He was teaching every day in the Temple. But the chief priests, the scribes and the leading men of the people were trying to destroy him. ⁴⁸They couldn't find any way to do it, because all the people were hanging on his every word.

At last it is Jesus' turn to cry. Earlier in the **gospel** we find other people in tears: the widow at Nain, Jairus's family, and others in distress coming to him for healing and new **life**. The women of Jerusalem will shortly be weeping for Jesus himself (23. 27). But Jesus is not immune to tears. In John's gospel, Jesus weeps at the tomb of his friend Lazarus (John 11.35). Now here he weeps over the city, and there is no one to console him.

Jesus' tears are at the core of the Christian gospel. This was not a moment of regrettable weakness, something a real **Messiah** ought to have avoided. Again and again during his long journey he had warned of God's impending judgment on the city and **Temple**, because they, like the towns of Galilee, had resisted his call for peace, for the gospel of God's grace which would reach out in love to the **Gentile** world. Unless you repent, he said, you will all likewise perish (13.3, 5); now here he was, face to face with the city where Pilate had killed Galileans and would shortly kill one more, face to face with the city where the tower of Siloam had fallen and where, before too long, towers and walls and the Temple itself would come crashing down.

It is an essential part of Jesus' message of warning and judgment that it is uttered, finally, through sobs and tears. Luke's writing of the scene is vivid, conveying the sense of Jesus sobbing out a few phrases, until he finally controls himself sufficiently to utter the solemn warning upon the city that has chosen to ignore the moment when God was coming in solemn 'visitation' (compare 1.68; 7.16).

If we had taken a few of the judgment sayings at random from the earlier chapters, they might have been made to sound as if Jesus was gloating over the city; it had rejected him, and would be destroyed. But now the moment has come, and there is no sense of 'I told you so' or 'It serves you right'; only the shaking sobs of the prophet like Jeremiah, the weeping of great David's greater son as he reverses the sorrowful route of his ancestor, fleeing from his rebel son Absalom (2 Samuel 15). The terrible judgment that has been pronounced, and will shortly be executed, proceeds not from a stern and cold justice but from a heart of love, that wants the best for, and from, the people, and so must now oppose, with sorrow and tears, the rebellion that had set its own interests and agendas before those of the God who had established them there in the first place.

The tears and the Temple action, then, go together. Jesus is not simply mounting an angry protest about the commercialization of Temple business. His action is a solemn prophetic warning, echoing those of Jeremiah and others, that if the Temple becomes a hideout for brigands, literally or metaphorically, it will come under God's judgment. Now, it appears, the brigands are indeed running the show. Jesus is not so much concerned with the traders; they, to be sure, are doubtless making a few extra shekels on the side, but that's trivial compared with what the **high priests** and their entourage have been doing.

The Temple had become the focal point of the national ideology. As in Isaiah's day, it stood in the public imagination for the unshakeable promise of Israel's God to keep Israel safe, come what may. And, as in Isaiah's day, Israel had to face the challenge that unless the promise was met with **faith** and obedience it would count for nothing, and indeed worse than nothing; it would turn into a curse. If you're in **covenant** with the holy God, disobedience doesn't simply prevent blessings, bringing you back, as it were, to square one. It calls down the judgment that a sorrowful God will pour out on his people when they reject him and his purposes.

Not surprisingly, the message was unpopular with the ruling group, clerical and lay. Jesus' action in the Temple was the immediate cause of his arrest. But behind what he did, and how the rulers reacted, was the whole weight of his previous ministry, not least the warnings that occupy a significant part of the middle section of Luke's gospel. As the storm clouds gather, we sense the inevitability which Luke in any case highlights frequently: this was how it 'must' be. This is how God's plan of salvation must be accomplished.

When you reflect on Jesus' words and deeds of judgment, don't forget the tears. And remember, with awe, that if Luke 19.11–27 is indeed about Jesus embodying the long-awaited return of God to Zion, those tears are not just the human reaction to a sad and frustrating situation. They are the tears of the God of love.

LUKE 20.1–8

The Question about Jesus' Authority

¹On one of those days, while Jesus was teaching the people in the Temple, and announcing the good news, the chief priests and the scribes came up with the elders, and said to him, ²'Tell us: by

what authority are you doing these things? Or who gave you this authority?'

³'I've got a question for you, too,' said Jesus, 'so tell me this: ⁴was John's baptism from God, or was it merely human?'

⁵'If we say it was from God,' they said among themselves, 'he'll say, So why didn't you believe him? ⁶But if we say "merely human", all the people will stone us, since they're convinced that John was a prophet.'

⁷So they replied that they didn't know where John and his baptism came from.

⁸'Very well, then', said Jesus. 'Neither will I tell you by what authority I do these things.'

There is a debate today in Britain about how loud soldiers should shout while on parade. The army is anxious, it seems, that sooner or later a soldier will suffer damaged hearing because a sergeant major has bellowed an order at high volume and at close range. The newspapers, naturally, think this is ridiculous. Orders have to be heard. It's no use whispering on the field of battle.

At the same time, the sergeant major receives orders from more senior officers, and they do not normally shout. In fact, the further up the ranks you go, the less likely are the orders to make any noise: the commanding officer may simply write down his instructions, or speak them in a quiet voice to his next in command. So if someone were to come to a parade ground or army barracks and try to discover who was in command, and where they got their authority from, it wouldn't be much good assuming that the loudest voice meant the most important authority.

We might have forgotten **John the Baptist** by this stage of the **gospel** story, but Luke hasn't, because Jesus hasn't. When Jesus came into Jerusalem and threw the traders out of the **Temple**, he was acting like someone who thinks he's in charge. But there already was an authority structure in the Temple, a pyramid with guards at the bottom and the chief **priests** at the top, with the high priest himself as the most senior figure. Who does Jesus think he is to come in, without any accreditation, and start throwing his weight about? That is the natural question to ask.

But Jesus' answer, which seems to take them by surprise, must not have seemed natural at all. What has John got to do with Jesus? Is this just (as their whispered debate among themselves seems to suggest they think) a trick question to catch them out and make them look foolish in the eyes of the people?

Not at all. The reason Jesus asks the question is because the authority he has over the Temple is precisely his royal, **messianic** authority;

and his royal status and authority was conferred on him publicly at the time of John's **baptism**, with the descent of the dove and the voice from **heaven**. If John was a true prophet, then Jesus is indeed the true **Messiah**, with authority over the Temple, because he was marked out as such as he came up out of the water. If, of course, John was not a true prophet – if he was simply a dangerous dreamer, leading people astray – then Jesus, too, may be acting out of line (as the authorities obviously think, but dare not say). By making John so important in the early parts of the story, Luke has already explained what is happening.

Authority is therefore passing, quietly and without many people noticing, from the old system to the new. For Luke, writing with half an eye at least on the Roman Empire, this is enormously important. Jesus, for him, is the Lord of the world, the one before whom Caesar himself ought to shiver in his shoes; how much more is he Lord of the Temple and all that is in it? The high priest may make the loudest noise in Jerusalem, with his henchmen and his court, his access to the Roman governor, and the prestige that comes with his ceremonial and political role. But now his power is challenged by one who speaks more quietly, one who comes with prophetic and royal authority that challenges the old regime and introduces the new. From now on – even as he hangs on the cross that marked Caesar's rule, mocked by the same chief priests! – Jesus will exercise that authority, the powerful authority of saving and healing love, until all acknowledge it.

We today, living out beyond the rule of Caesar and the chief priests, may find it quite a complex business to come to terms with the authority of Jesus. We should of course, as Christians, acknowledge him as sovereign of our lives, our thoughts and actions, and seek to live under that authority, even when it comes (as it often does) in whispers rather than in a loud voice. But if Jesus is Master or Lord of the whole world, as Luke certainly believed, we have the task of making that lordship known. Normally it won't be appropriate to overturn tables and expel people from buildings; what symbolic actions will be appropriate in our world, to make the point that Jesus possesses all authority in heaven and on earth?

LUKE 20.9–19

The Parable of the Tenants

⁹Jesus began to tell the people this parable. 'There was a man who planted a vineyard, let it out to tenant farmers, and went abroad for a long while. ¹⁰When the time came, he sent a slave to the farmers to collect from them some of the produce of the vineyard. But the

farmers beat him and sent him away empty-handed. [11]He then sent a further slave, and they beat him, abused him, and sent him back empty-handed. [12]Then he sent yet a third, and they beat him up and threw him out.

[13]'So the master of the vineyard said, "What shall I do? I'll send my beloved son. They will certainly respect him!" [14]But when the farmers saw him they said to each other, "This is the heir! Let's kill him, and then the inheritance will belong to us!" [15]And they threw him out of the vineyard and killed him.

'So what will the master of the vineyard do? [16]He will come and wipe out those farmers, and give the vineyard to others.'

When they heard this, they said, 'God forbid!' [17]But Jesus looked round at them and said, 'What then does it mean in the Bible when it says,

'"The very stone the builders refused
now for the corner's top is used"?

[18]'Everyone who falls on that stone will be smashed to smithereens; but if it falls on anyone, it will crush them.'

[19]The scribes and the chief priests tried to lay hands on him then and there. But they were afraid of the people, because they knew that Jesus had told this parable against them.

One of the most dramatic scenes ever to take place in the British House of Commons occurred in January 1642. King Charles I went in person to the House to try to arrest five Members of Parliament who had opposed him. The Speaker of the House himself stood in his way, and prevented the king coming any further into the chamber where the Commons met. A painting of the incident hangs in the lobby of the Palace of Westminster to this day. It was something of a turning-point: another step on the road to civil war, and to the king's eventual execution.

No self-respecting first-century monarch would ever have allowed himself to get in that position; and no landowner would tolerate for very long the kind of behaviour described in this **parable**. But there are striking parallels between this story and the one Jesus told, his last explanation (in parable form) of what was going on in his coming to Jerusalem. The vineyard owner has sent messengers to the tenant farmers, to no effect. (No first-century Jew would have needed to be told that the owner stood for God, the farmers for Israel, and the messengers for the prophets.) Finally, having no one left to send, he sent his own beloved son. In Jesus' own understanding, he came as the rightful King to his Father's tenants; and they were barring his way, determined to keep the vineyard for themselves. Eventually they threw him out and killed him.

So far, the meaning of the story is obvious – and fits like a glove with the whole of Luke's **gospel** so far. Jesus is the rightful heir to the ancient prophets, and has come to complete their work, challenging Israel one more time to give to the **covenant** God the honour and obedience that is his due. Israel was charged with bearing the fruit of justice in her own life, and showing God's grace to the world around. But Israel has insisted on keeping the grace for itself, practising injustice in its own life, and seeking to repel and resist the world around by whatever violence might be necessary. Israel has rejected the way of peace, and will now reject its final messenger (19.41–44).

But the story doesn't stop there. The vineyard owner will return at last (Luke has long prepared us for this, too), and, when he does, the judgment Israel longed to see on the pagan nations will be meted out on her. He will destroy the tenants, and give the vineyard to others. The present regime in Jerusalem, and the self-appointed guardians of Israel's laws and heritage, are signing their own death warrants. Their rejection of Jesus will be taken up by God into the rebuilding plans for his people: 'the stone the builders refused', in this case the **Messiah** sent to Israel but rejected, 'has become the head cornerstone'.

This quotation from Psalm 118.22 (the same psalm echoed by the crowds in 19.38; it was, after all, a psalm of pilgrimage) uses a quite different image from that of the vineyard. Imagine a builders' yard, full of stone ready for the great task. The workers are sorting out the lumps of marble and granite into different sizes and shapes, so they can haul them up to their places on the wall. There is one stone that doesn't belong in any of the groups; they put it over by itself, expecting to throw it out when the job is done. But when they have almost finished, they discover that they need a stone of a particular shape for the very last piece, to round off the top of the corner. There is the stone they rejected earlier. It wouldn't fit anywhere else, but it will fit here.

To quote this verse at this point rams the message home. The workers may reject Jesus now, but they will find that he will be vindicated. He will be seen as the true Messiah. He will build the true **Temple**, and will himself be its chief feature, the standard by which everything and everyone else is to be judged (that is probably the meaning of the otherwise puzzling verse 18).

If this was what happened when Jesus came to Jerusalem, what should we expect to happen when his followers go today to the places of power and injustice? What sort of reaction will the gospel receive when it is announced in places where people use religion – including

Christianity! – as a means of reinforcing their own security instead of shining God's light into the world? It may well mean rejection and violence; the history of Christian martyrdom, not least in the last century, bears stark witness to that.

But the vineyard owner will have the last word. Not only is the blood of the martyrs always the seed of the church. What happened to Jesus was not just an example of what always happens under these circumstances. It was the decisive victory. Ever since then, his followers have gone on their mission, not in order to try yet one more time to persuade the rich, the powerful and even the religious to accept God's way of peace and love, but in order to declare, by their life and their words, that this way has already triumphed in Jesus, that the renewed vineyard is bearing fruit, that the new Temple is being built, with its cornerstone already in place.

LUKE 20.20–26

On Paying Taxes to Caesar

²⁰So the authorities watched Jesus, and sent people to lie in wait for him. They pretended to be upright folk, but were trying to trap him in something he said, so that they could hand him over to the rule and authority of the governor. ²¹So they asked him this question.

'Teacher,' they said, 'we know that you speak and teach with integrity. You are completely impartial, and you teach God's way and God's truth. ²²So: is it right for us to give tribute to Caesar, or not?'

²³Jesus knew they were playing a trick.

²⁴"Show me a tribute-coin', he said. 'This image . . . and this inscription . . . who do they belong to?'

'Caesar', they said.

²⁵"Well, then', replied Jesus, 'you'd better give Caesar back what belongs to him! And give *God* back what belongs to *him.*'

²⁶They couldn't catch him in anything he said in front of the people. They were amazed at his answer, and had nothing more to say.

We went a few weeks ago to see the longest-running stage play in history. Agatha Christie's play *The Mousetrap* has now been performed continuously for almost my entire lifetime. At the time of writing it has had over 20,000 performances. And it's still pulling in the crowds.

The plot turns, as with so many murder mysteries, on the audience's expectation that one character, or perhaps another, is in fact the real culprit. Almost everyone on stage, it seems, might just possibly have been the murderer, and everybody is waiting eagerly to find out the answer. Then, near the end, it turns out after all to be . . . but I don't want to spoil the story. The main thing is the cleverness of the writer, producer and actors in making you think one thing is going to happen, only then to discover something completely different.

That is how this story of Jesus and the coin must have seemed, both when it first happened and when the story was then eagerly told, again and again, by enthusiastic listeners. The long build-up sets the scene, just like a stage play. The authorities are eager to find a way of framing a charge against Jesus, before his teaching inflames the crowds so much that they cause a riot. So they send people to him who appear to be good, devout Jews, wrestling with a question which was after all very difficult for many at the time. If they were observing God's law, how could they possibly agree to pay taxes to a pagan overlord? Especially when the coins they had to use flouted Jewish **law** by using a picture of a human being (Caesar himself, of course) and by describing him in words that a Jew would regard as blasphemous. On the other hand, did they have a choice? Not to pay would be to court disaster.

'They pretended to be righteous', says Luke, echoing chapter 18: there, Jesus tells the **parable** of the tax-collector, directed against those who 'trusted in themselves that they were righteous'. Actually, what they had in mind was what Jesus himself had predicted long ago, that they would hand him over to the Roman governor. The trick question they had prepared looked as if it would do this job very well. It would either expose him as a revolutionary (by making him oppose the tribute), or it would show the crowds that he really wasn't the kind of leader they wanted after all (by making him say that the **kingdom** was a purely spiritual thing, with no purchase on everyday reality – something the Lord's Prayer itself would deny). How, the audience thinks, can Jesus possibly get out of that one?

The heavy-handed introduction to the question, laying on the flattery as though with a trowel, serves to heighten the expectation that the questioners are leading Jesus right into their trap. Surely he won't now be able to avoid their cunning? In terms of the drama, the audience now supposes that Jesus is on the spot, about to be found out, when suddenly everything is reversed, and the accusers (which is what they really are) become the accused. He puts them on the defensive right away by asking them to produce one of the coins: what are they doing possessing such blasphemous objects? His key question, more probing than theirs in its implications, gets them to admit that it is indeed Caesar's coinage they have about their persons, with its haughty image of Tiberius Caesar himself, and the inscription that proclaims him son of God and much more besides.

Jesus' double-edged command, which finishes the conversation, not only answers their own question, but throws back such a strong

179

challenge that the whole drama is stood on its head. The accusers are not just accused, but convicted. On the one hand, there is a dark appropriateness about giving Caesar back his blasphemous coinage. Better get rid of the stuff. The theme of 'giving the Romans back what they deserve' might itself have been heard as a sign that the revolutionaries, though wrong in their methods, were right in their belief that God's people should not be crushed under pagan rule. But, on the other hand, the challenge to Jerusalem, the **Temple**, its rulers, and their hypocritical underlings, are all concentrated in the second half of the command: give *God* back what belongs to *him*. Jesus' own accusation against his contemporaries is that they have consistently failed to worship their true and living God, and to live as his people before the world. The very Temple itself, the place where Israel was supposed to come and give to God what was his own, in worship, prayer, holiness and **sacrifice** – the Temple had become a brigands' lair. Put that right, and the question of Caesar will in the long run sort itself out.

Underneath the debate stands a darker theme. The accusers have failed this time; but Jesus knows, and Luke's readers know, that they will soon succeed (the moment comes in 23.2, when they accuse him of saying what he has here refused to say). The leading Jews are going to hand over to Caesar not only the coin that bears his image, and his false title 'son of God', but the human being who truly bears God's image, and who truly bears that title. But, in that act, they are unwittingly offering to God the one stamped with the mark of self-giving love. The cross itself is taken up into both Caesar's purposes and God's: Caesar's favourite weapon, the cross, becomes God's chosen instrument of salvation.

It is impossible to read out of this exchange a theory of 'church and state' or 'Christianity and politics'. It is too brief, dense and specific. However, every thoughtful Christian must sooner or later face those questions, and when that happens we should at least get the priorities right. What does it mean today to give to God what belongs to him?

LUKE 20.27–40

Marriage and the Resurrection

²⁷Some of the Sadducees came to Jesus to put their question. (The Sadducees deny that there is any resurrection.)
²⁸'Teacher,' they said, 'Moses wrote for us that "If a man's brother dies, leaving a widow but no children, the man should marry the widow and raise up a family for his brother." ²⁹Well, now: there were

seven brothers; the eldest married a wife, and died without children. [30]The second [31]and the third married her, and then each of the seven, and they died without children. [32]Finally the woman died as well. [33]So, in the resurrection, whose wife will the woman be? The seven all had her as their wife.'

[34]'The children of this age', replied Jesus, 'marry and are given in marriage. [35]But those who are counted worthy of a place in the age to come, and of the resurrection of the dead, don't marry, and they are not given in marriage. [36]This is because they can no longer die; they are the equivalent of angels. They are children of God, since they are children of the resurrection.

[37]'But when it comes to the dead being raised, Moses too declares it, in the passage about the burning bush, where scripture describes the Lord as "the God of Abraham, the God of Isaac, and the God of Jacob". [38]God is God, not of the dead, but of the living. They are all alive to him.'

[39]'That was well said, teacher', commented some of the scribes, [40]since they no longer dared ask him anything else.

Many churches possess a sequence of pictures that, together, tell a complete story. Sometimes these are in the windows, in stained glass. Sometimes they are painted on the walls or the ceiling. Sometimes they form a frieze, a decorated band along a wall or above the altar. What look like distinct pictures, when you 'read' them one after the other, in fact tell a complete story.

The debates in Luke 20 are just like that, and it will help us to understand this one if we see where it comes in the sequence (which Luke has, most likely, drawn from Mark, though he has made his own editorial changes on the way).

We began with the question about authority, which was raised by Jesus' dramatic entrance into Jerusalem and his action in the **Temple**. His reply was to go back to **John the Baptist** and ask whether he was or was not a true prophet sent from God. This then led to the **parable** of the tenant farmers, which highlighted Jesus' coming to Jerusalem as the son of the vineyard owner, last in the sequence of prophets but himself greater than all. This indicated that, as a result, he would be rejected and killed. We have then heard the question and answer about tribute to Caesar, which Luke has told us was intended to lead to Jesus' handing over to the Romans for execution. We now have the question about **resurrection**; and this will be followed at once by Jesus' own question about how David's son can also be David's Lord. Each of these is important in its own right; but put them together like a frieze, or like a sequence of stained-glass windows, and what do they say?

They tell, in miniature, the whole story of Jesus. They are a summary of the **gospel**. Jesus emerges from John's prophetic movement; he is anointed as **Messiah**. He comes to Israel, to the towns of Galilee, and ultimately to Jerusalem, with a message of warning and pleading, the final message from the vineyard owner. They reject him, thereby calling down judgment on themselves. He is handed over to Caesar's men for execution; and on the third day he is raised. As a result, his followers discover that he is not only David's son, the Messiah (as they had already come to believe); he is also David's Lord. This sequence can hardly be accidental.

But what does it say about our present passage, the debate on resurrection? It is interesting that this, and its equivalents in Matthew and Mark, is the only discussion of this vital topic anywhere in the gospels. Jesus raises people from the dead, as we have seen, but, though this is wonderful, it is not yet 'the resurrection' in the full sense. We know, of course, what Luke thought the resurrection of Jesus was like; we have remarkable stories of it at the end of this gospel, and these stories must remain as the guide to Luke's own view. They match well, in any case, with first-century Jewish views of 'the resurrection'.

When Jews thought of 'the resurrection', they had in mind a particular story, a set of pictures: the story of Israel, from Abraham (or even Adam) to their own time, and on into the future when God would raise all Israel, perhaps even all humans, from the dead, and create a new world for them to live in. This hope was not about what we think of as 'life after death', a non-bodily state in which people simply went on existing in some form or other. It was about a future event that had not yet happened, as a result of which the dead would be alive again in a way they weren't at present, and all the wrongs of the world would be put to rights.

This was what the **Sadducees** denied. They may have denied it because they supposed it a new, modern heresy; it was easier to prove it from comparatively recent books like Daniel (12.1–3) than from the older ones, especially the five books of Moses. Or they may have denied it because they realized how revolutionary it was (people who believe God is going to do that sort of thing are more likely to take drastic political action without fearing the consequences), and the Sadducees were the aristocrats, anxious for their own power. Or it may have been both. So they told stories to illustrate just how stupid such a belief seemed; there are other puzzles like this one in Jewish writings of the time. How can the dead be raised, they say, if they will then not be able to tell who is married to whom?

In reply, Jesus makes two basic points. First, resurrection life will not be exactly the same as the present one. Death will have been abolished, and so sexual relations, and especially the need to continue a particular family line, will be irrelevant. Those who are raised will therefore be 'equal to angels': not in the sense that they will *become* angels (as folk-religion belief sometimes suggests), but in the sense that they will live in a deathless, immortal state. Jesus is not here suggesting that the resurrection will not be bodily; merely that the bodies of the raised will be, in significant ways, quite unlike our present ones. Those whom God counts worthy of 'the age to come', as opposed to 'the **present age**' (verses 34–35), will have bodies appropriate for the new world in which death will be no more.

Second, Jesus proposes that the book of Exodus, one of those the Sadducees acknowledged as authoritative, does indeed teach the resurrection, when it describes God as 'the God of Abraham, Isaac and Jacob'. The patriarchs are still 'alive to God'. This doesn't mean they are already 'raised from the dead'. Any first-century Jew would have known that was not the case. It means that they are alive in God's presence, awaiting their final resurrection. The Sadducees denied that, while the **Pharisees** believed it (see Acts 23.6–9). Jesus is here firmly on the side of the Pharisees.

The resurrection of Jesus, of course, gave a huge boost to his followers' belief both about Jesus himself and about their own future life. But they went on telling this story about his debate with the Sadducees, not just because it indicated his own teaching on the subject, but because Easter had shown that the aristocracy, the guardians of the Temple, had been proved wrong. God could and did act decisively to reverse even a sentence of death. God could and would act decisively to overturn the Sadducees' power and vindicate his true people.

LUKE 20.41—21.4

David's Son and the Widow's Mite

⁴¹Jesus said to them, 'How can people say that the Messiah is the son of David? ⁴²David himself says, in the book of Psalms,

"The Lord says to the Lord of mine
sit here at my right hand;
⁴³until I place those foes of thine
right underneath thy feet."

⁴⁴'David, you see, calls him "Lord"; so how can he be his son?'
⁴⁵As all the people listened to him, he said to the disciples, ⁴⁶'Watch out for the scribes who like to go about in long robes, and enjoy being greeted in the marketplace, sitting in the best seats in the synagogues,

and taking the top table at dinners. ⁴⁷They devour widows' houses, and make long prayers without meaning them. Their judgment will be all the more severe.'

²¹·¹He looked up and saw rich people putting their contributions into the Temple treasury. ²He also saw an impoverished widow putting in two tiny copper coins.

³'I'm telling you the truth', he said. 'This poor widow has put in more than all of them. ⁴They all contributed to the collection out of their plenty, but she contributed out of her poverty, and gave her whole livelihood.'

'Can you get this balloon into that box?' I asked the little children at the party. The balloon was big, and the box was small. They tried squeezing it in but it wouldn't fit. It kept oozing out through their fingers. One little boy suggested sticking a pin into it, but the others agreed that that was cheating.

Then a little girl, with small, nimble fingers, took the balloon, and undid the knot that was keeping the air inside it. Very carefully she let about half the air out, and quickly tied it up again. Then, with a smile of triumph, she placed the balloon in the box, where it fitted exactly.

That wasn't quite what I'd had in mind, but I had to admit it was clever. Meanwhile, another child had seen the answer. The box was made of cardboard, folded double in places. She unglued two of its sides, and opened it up to its full dimensions. Now the full-size balloon went in perfectly.

Some people, faced with questions like the one Jesus asks about David's Lord and David's son, try to solve it by letting the air out of the balloon. They imagine that God, in order to become human, either stopped being God altogether (the equivalent of a pin in the balloon), or at least shrank his divinity quite severely. The whole New Testament, including Luke, would disagree. For the early Christians, part of the point about Jesus was that the living God was fully and personally present in him, not half present or partly present. What happened in Jesus, and supremely in his death, was the personal action of God himself, not some deputy or demi-god.

The real answer in this case is that the meaning of '**Messiah**' is bigger than the Jews of Jesus' day had realized. They were thinking simply of a human king like other human kings, who would fight their battles, rebuild their **Temple**, and rule with justice. The hints in the prophets and psalms, that when the true king appeared he would be the embodiment of God himself, don't seem to have been picked up at the time. How could they be? The box appeared too small. The balloon wouldn't fit.

Of course, the illustration isn't perfect. Nobody in their right mind would try to get serious theology out of a children's party game. But the question Jesus asked – one of the very few questions he asked, as opposed to the questions other people asked him – went to the heart of explaining what he was doing in Jerusalem, and what his mission was all about.

Much of Luke's gospel has been warning of what will happen if Israel doesn't obey Jesus' kingdom-announcement. Now the psalm Jesus quotes (Psalm 110) speaks of the Messiah as one who will be enthroned until victory is attained over those who have opposed him. The Messiah will be exalted, and judgment will be meted out on those who have chosen the way of violence and injustice. And this Messiah will be one whom David himself, the supposed author of the psalm, does not merely see as a son (and therefore inferior), but as 'my Lord'. The box labelled 'messiahship' is bigger than anyone had realized. It is designed to contain one who will share the very throne of God.

From that point of view, we shouldn't be surprised that the regular human measures of size look misleading and irrelevant. The **scribes** measure their own value by the length of their robes, the flattering greetings in public, and the places of honour at worship or at dinner. They are living by one scale, but God will measure them by the true one. Privately, they are using their legal skills to acquire legacies from widows who have nobody to speak up for them. Their religion is a sham, and God sees it.

By contrast – another time when the scale of measurement works the opposite way to what people would expect – the poor widow who gave all she had into God's treasury had given more than the rich people who gave what they could easily afford. Back to balloons again: when a small balloon is full of air, the air it releases may only be a small amount, but it leaves the balloon totally flat. Release the same amount of air from a large balloon, and you'll hardly notice the difference.

Putting together these very different stories – Jesus' question about a matter of high theology, and his comment on the scribes and on a poor widow – may seem odd. But the same principle applies to both, and indeed because of that same principle we must insist on holding them together. Because God's way of measuring reality is not our way – because it was always his intention that David's Lord should become David's son – it is also his desire that the same attention be given to the questions of human behaviour and integrity, on large and small scales, as we give to the questions of defining and defending the faith.

LUKE 21.5–19

Signs of the End

[5]Some people were talking about the Temple, saying how wonderfully it was decorated, with its beautiful stones and dedicated gifts.

'Yes,' said Jesus; [6]'but the days will come when everything you see will be torn down. Not one stone will be left standing on another.'

[7]'Teacher,' they asked him, 'when will these things happen? What will be the sign that it's all about to take place?'

[8]'Watch out that nobody deceives you,' said Jesus. 'Yes: lots of people will come using my name, saying "I'm the one!" and "The time has come!" Don't go following them. [9]When you hear about wars and rebellions, don't be alarmed. These things have to happen first, but the end won't come at once.

[10]'One nation will rise against another,' he went on, 'and one kingdom against another. [11]There will be huge earthquakes, famines and plagues in various places, terrifying omens, and great signs from heaven.

[12]'Before all this happens they will lay hands on you and persecute you. They will hand you over to the synagogues and prisons. They will drag you before kings and governors because of my name. [13]That will become an opportunity for you to tell your story. [14]So settle it in your hearts not to work out beforehand what tale to tell; [15]I'll give you a mouth and wisdom, which none of your opponents will be able to resist or contradict.

[16]'You will be betrayed by parents, brothers and sisters, relatives and friends, and they will kill some of you. [17]You will be hated by everyone because of my name. [18]But no hair of your head will be lost. [19]The way to keep your lives is to be patient.'

A news reader announces that an asteroid passed close to the earth. When they say 'close', they mean about half a million miles; but in terms of the solar system, that's quite near at hand. It shows, as one commentator said, that the planet Earth is in a bit of a shooting gallery. If I had lived in ancient Greece, or Rome or Egypt, instead of being in the modern world, with efficient telescopes watching, and well-trained scientists ready to explain everything they see, the sight of a strange, moving light in part of the sky where there hadn't been anything before would at once have been seized upon as a sign. Something dramatic was going to happen.

These near misses happen about once a century. Of course, if the asteroid had hit the earth, something dramatic would have happened all right; not only would it make a hole nearly a mile across, but the energy released as it did so would be the equivalent of several atom bombs. No question of the significance of that.

But in Jesus' day dramatic and unexpected happenings in the night sky were often thought to signify more than just physical disaster as large objects crashed to earth. People looked at them carefully because they believed they would tell them about the imminent rise and fall of kings and empires. And when Jesus' **disciples** asked him how they would know when the frightening events he was talking about would take place, that's probably the sort of thing they had in mind. Surely Jesus would want them to know, and so would give them signs to watch out for?

Jesus will give them signs of a sort (we'll come to that in the next section), but actually the main thing he wants them to learn is that there will be a period of waiting, when they will have to be patient through dangerous and testing times.

But what great event will they be waiting for? Luke, more than all the other **gospels**, has prepared us for the answer. His alert readers will not be surprised at Jesus' prediction; it has been anticipated in many sayings over the last ten chapters or so, and Jesus' dramatic action in the **Temple** was a prophetic sign, warning of what was to come. The Temple, the most beautiful building one could imagine, adorned and decorated by the skill and love of hundreds of years, and occupying the central place in the national life, religion and imagination – the Temple itself would be torn down. It had come to stand for the perversion of Israel's call that Jesus had opposed throughout his public career. If he was right, the present Temple was wrong; if God was to vindicate him, that would have to include the Temple's destruction. This was as unthinkable for a devout Jew as it would be for an American to imagine the destruction of the White House, the Washington Memorial and the Statue of Liberty; only much more so, because the Temple signified a thousand years of God's dealings with Israel.

Jesus' warnings about what the disciples will face in the days to come clearly indicate that he will no longer be with them, but that they will still be marked out as his followers. Others will come pretending to be him, or to be his spokesperson (I had a letter this morning, as it happens, from someone claiming to be the reincarnation of Jesus). The world will be convulsed with wars and revolutions, all the more alarming because, without radio, television, telephones or newspapers, people would hear of such things by rumour from travellers, and would pass on the news with additional speculation until a border skirmish had been inflated, in the telling, to become an all-out war, and the Emperor's occasional sneeze had been exaggerated into a fatal illness.

Jesus clearly expects that amid these turbulent times his followers will be marked out as undesirables. People would retain a memory of

Jesus as someone leading Israel astray, deflecting people from keeping the **law**, and from defending the national interest, with his dangerous talk of God's **kingdom**, of peace and grace for all. When the going got tough, in Israel and in Jewish communities around the world, those who were known as Jesus' people would be in the firing line; and, quite soon, non-Jewish communities would follow their example. Families would be split; sometimes it would seem that the Christians were the ones blamed for everything, the ones everybody loved to hate. If ever they needed patience, they would need it then.

Jesus promises, though, that he will give them what they need during this time of waiting: 'a mouth and wisdom'. This promise should not, of course, be taken as licence to ignore the hard work required for regular Christian teaching. It refers to the times when people are on trial for their lives because of their allegiance to Jesus. The story of the first generation of Christianity – the time between the **resurrection** of Jesus and the fall of the Temple in AD 70 – bears out these prophecies. And many early Christians would testify that Jesus had indeed been with them and given them words to say.

But this passage, though vital in its specific reference to that first generation, has a good deal to say to the subsequent church as well. Wherever Christians are persecuted for their **faith** – and, sadly but not surprisingly, this is still common in many parts of the world – they need not only the prayers and support of their fellow-believers in more fortunate places, but also the comfort and encouragement of these words: 'Don't let anyone deceive you'; 'a chance to tell your story'; 'I'll give you wisdom'; 'you'll keep your lives through patience'. These are still precious promises, to be learnt ahead of time and clung to in the moment of need.

LUKE 21.20-33

The Distress of Jerusalem Predicted

[20]'But,' continued Jesus, 'when you see Jerusalem surrounded by armies, then you will know that her time of desolation has arrived. [21]Then people in Judaea should run off to the hills, people in Jerusalem itself should get out as fast as they can, and people in the countryside shouldn't go back into the city. [22]Those will be the days of severe judgment, which will fulfil all the biblical warnings. [23]Woe betide pregnant women, and nursing mothers, in those days! There is going to be huge distress on the earth, and divine anger against this people. [24]The hungry sword will eat them up. They will be taken as prisoners to every nation; and Jerusalem will be trampled by the pagans, until the times of the pagans are done.

²⁵'There will be signs in the sun, the moon and the stars. On earth the nations will be in distress and confusion because of the roaring and swelling of the sea and its waves. ²⁶People will faint from fear, and from imagining all that's going to happen to the world. The powers of the heavens will be shaken. ²⁷Then they will see "the son of man coming on a cloud" with power and great majesty. ²⁸When all these things start to happen, stand up and lift up your heads, because the time has come for you to be redeemed.'

²⁹He told them this parable. 'Look at the fig tree and all the trees. ³⁰When they are well into leaf, you can see for yourselves and know that summer is upon you. ³¹In the same way, when you see all these things happening, you will know that God's kingdom is upon you. ³²I'm telling you the truth; this generation won't be gone before all of this happens. ³³Heaven and earth may disappear, but these words of mine won't disappear.'

At school we were sometimes made to write stories which included several very different characters and objects. 'Write a story', the teacher might say, 'including a rabbit, a telescope, a cathedral and a man with a wooden leg.' Often this would involve huge leaps of the imagination, as young minds struggled to come up with something that met the requirements and yet made sense in itself.

Many people have felt, reading Luke 21, as though Jesus is setting us a puzzle rather like that. How can we make sense of an event which involves armies round a city, the roaring of the sea, the coming of the **son of man** on a cloud, and the arrival of the **kingdom** of God? And how can whatever-it-is be said to happen within a generation of when Jesus was speaking?

The best place to begin is on safe ground – safe for us in terms of our understanding of the text, but decidely unsafe for anyone there at the time. Verses 20–24 are clear, and fit with everything Luke has reported Jesus as saying up to this point. A time of great crisis is coming, in which the failure of Israel in general and Jerusalem in particular to repent and follow the kingdom-way advocated by Jesus would have its disastrous result. The Romans would come (they are not mentioned by name, but if anyone was likely to surround Jerusalem with armies it was surely them) and would lay siege to the city. The result would not be in doubt.

When that happened, those who were able to get out and run while there was time should do so. Jesus' instructions at this point are quite specific; his followers were not to imagine, out of false national loyalty, that they had a duty to stay in Jerusalem and go down with the ship. Just as the Israelites were commanded to leave Babylon in a hurry before

God's judgment fell on her (Isaiah 48.20; Jeremiah 50.8; 51.6, 45), so Jesus' followers are to leave Jerusalem while there is still time. Violent death and enforced deportation will await those who are caught there. Instead of the Jews making Jerusalem a delight, the pagans will flatten it and have it all to themselves. These warnings, of course, came true in and after AD 70.

But how does this square with the rest of the passage? The answer is that we must learn, again, how to understand the picture language that was common at the time. 'Signs in the sun, moon and stars' might well be taken literally, but such a phrase could easily mean that the great nations and kingdoms of the earth would be, as we say in our own picture language, 'going through convulsions'. Those who have lived through the fall of the apartheid regime in South Africa, and of the Berlin Wall, will know how quickly, and how unexpectedly, great changes can sweep through large systems, with huge and unpredictable consequences. Anyone living in the Roman Empire during the years AD 60-70 might well feel the same, particularly during the last two or three years of that period. After Nero's suicide in 68, four emperors followed in quick succession, each one at the head of an army. The much-vaunted 'Roman peace' that Augustus and his successors claimed to have brought to the world was shattered from the inside. A convulsive shudder went through the whole known world. That fits verses 25-26 exactly.

The 'coming of the son of man' must then be understood, as first-century Jews would certainly have understood it, as the fulfilment of the prophecy of Daniel 7. One of the most popular prophecies of the day, this passage was believed to speak about the time when God's true people would be vindicated after their suffering at the hands of the 'beasts', the pagan nations who had oppressed them. This prophecy imagines a great lawcourt scene, in which God, the judge, finds in favour of his people, 'the son of man', and against the oppressive 'beast'. The judgment that falls on the pagan nations is the same judgment that vindicates 'the son of man', who is then brought on a cloud to share the throne of God himself.

The best way of understanding this passage in Luke is then to see it as the promise that, when the Jerusalem that had opposed his message is finally overthrown, this will be the vindication of Jesus and his people, the sign that he has indeed been enthroned at his Father's side in **heaven** (see 20.42-43). Luke does, of course, believe in the 'second coming' of Jesus (Acts 1.11), but this passage is not about that. It is about the vindication of Jesus and the rescue of his people from the system that has oppressed them.

Here, then, are the signs that the **disciples** are to look for. God's kingdom has come near, and God's city has rejected it; the fulfilment of the kingdom will involve the destruction of the city. All must take place within a generation, because Jesus is after all the last prophet; once the vineyard owner has sent the son, he has no other messenger left (20.13).

Christian readers, puzzling over this passage nearly two thousand years later, are often at a loss to know what it can say to them. For us, the destruction of Jerusalem, an act of great pagan brutality, is far away in the past, and we know of so many other subsequent crises that the church has faced that we are inclined to think of it as comparatively insignificant. We, however, live and preach the **gospel** in a world which, as Jerusalem did to Jesus, often refuses the summons to peace. We have at least a duty to warn our contemporaries that to reject God's invitation may well lead to disaster. And in the meantime we must continue to practise patience. We never know when we shall need it.

LUKE 21.34–38

Watching for the Son of Man

[34]'So watch out for yourselves', said Jesus. Don't let your hearts grow heavy with dissipation and drunkenness and the cares of this life, letting that day come upon you suddenly, [35]like a trap. It will come, you see, on everyone who lives on the face of the earth. [36]Keep awake at all times, praying that you may have strength to escape all these things that will happen, and to stand before the son of man.'

[37]Jesus was teaching in the Temple by day, but at night he went out and stayed in the place called the Mount of Olives. [38]From early morning all the people flocked to him in the Temple, to hear him.

Travel with me, back in time, to Jerusalem. The year is AD 58, nearly thirty years after Jesus' crucifixion and **resurrection**. Many people in the holy city came to believe in Jesus in the heady days nearly a generation ago, and many of them are still here, older and more puzzled perhaps, but still waiting and hoping and praying.

Things have been difficult, on and off. Once Pontius Pilate stopped being governor people hoped life might improve, but there was then a huge crisis over the Emperor's plan to place a vast statue of himself in the **Temple**. The threat, fortunately, was seen off; Gaius, the Emperor in question, had died soon after; and when one of Herod's grandsons, Agrippa, was made king of the Jews in 41 everyone in Jerusalem stood up and cheered. To be ruled by one of your own might be better than having governors from far away who didn't understand local customs. That didn't last, though. He too had died, struck down (said some) by

God for blasphemously claiming the sort of divine honours that his pagan masters had given themselves. Now there had been a string of new Roman governors, each one (it seemed) worse than the last. But in 54, when Nero became Emperor, many people hoped again that peace and justice would triumph.

All along, though, people in Jerusalem were aware of the political tensions building up. Revolutionary movements arose, had their moment of glory, and were brutally crushed. Some said the **priests** were secretly involved. Some said it was all the wicked brigands, refusing to let ordinary people go about their business in peace. Some wanted an easy-going peace with Rome, others were all for driving hard bargains, others again wished the **Messiah** would come. Daily life went on: buying and selling, growing crops, tending herds, woodwork, leatherwork, moneychanging, pottery, with the daily round of Temple **sacrifices**, music, celebrations and the seasonal feasts as the constant backdrop. The Temple itself was almost complete: the programme of rebuilding begun by Herod the Great seventy years earlier was finally drawing to a close.

And in the middle of all this, those who named the name of Jesus, who still met to break bread and worship in his name, and to teach one another the stories of what he'd done and said, were pulled and pushed this way and that. Some of them were friends of the ex-**Pharisee** Saul of Tarsus, now known as Paul. He had been here not long ago, and had caused a riot (his friends said his opponents had caused it, but the word on the street was that riots tended to happen wherever Paul went). Now he'd gone, sent to Rome for trial, and he wouldn't be back. Peter, too, had gone on his travels and hadn't been seen for years. Others were sceptical of Paul; he had compromised God's law, they said, allowing **Gentiles** to worship God through Jesus without demanding **circumcision**. The leader of the Jerusalem Christians, the wise and devout James, the brother of Jesus himself, was getting older, and his prayers for the redemption of his people didn't seem to be answered.

How easy it was for Jerusalem Christians to become weary! If the **gospel** was producing exciting results, it was doing so across the sea, and they only heard about it every once in a while, and didn't always like what they heard (Gentiles claiming to worship Jesus but not keeping the law of Moses – that sort of thing). Their lives dragged on day by day. Friends asked them, sometimes unkindly, when this Messiah of theirs was going to reappear, and could he please hurry up because much more of these Romans banging around would bring on a world war, and anyway look what's happened to the price of bread, and if

Jesus had really been the Messiah why has nothing much happened since? Not much use to say that when you met for worship the sense of Jesus' presence and love was so real you could almost reach out and touch him. Not much of an answer to say that you had been told to be patient. Thirty years is a long time. All you could do would be to retell the stories, including the sayings of Jesus such as you find in this passage. Hang on. Be alert. Prop your eyes open – physically, perhaps, spiritually for sure. Pray for strength to meet whatever comes. The **son of man** will be vindicated, and when he is you want to be on your feet.

Now travel with me to San Francisco, or Sydney, or Bujumbura, or San Salvador, in the twenty-first century. You emerge from the church on Sunday morning – the Pentecostal celebration, the Anglican Matins, the Spanish mass – and there is the world going about its business, or as it may be its pleasure. Your friends think you're odd still going to church. Everybody knows Christianity is outdated, disproved, boring and irrelevant. What you need is more sex; more parties; more money-making; more revolution. Anyway, hasn't the church done some pretty bad things in its time? What about the Inquisition? (They always say that.) What about the Crusades? Who needs Christianity now that we have computers and space travel? (They said it before about electricity and modern medicine.)

And anyway, they say, if your Jesus is so special, why is the world still in such a mess? They don't want to know about the freeing of the slaves, the rise of education and the building of hospitals; they certainly don't want to know about the lives that are changed every day by the gospel. They want to load you with the cares of this life; and, as Jesus warned, with dissipation and drunkenness, literal and metaphorical. They want to wear you down, to make you think you're odd and stupid. Why study an old book, they say, that's never done anyone any good?

The answer is the same for us as it was for the Jerusalem Christians nearly a generation after Jesus. Keep alert. This is what you were told to expect. Patience is the key. Pray for strength to keep on your feet. There are times when your eyes will be shutting with tiredness, spiritual, mental, emotional and physical, and when you will have to prop them open. This is what it's about: not an exciting battle, with adrenalin flowing and banners flying, but the steady tread, of prayer and hope and scripture and sacrament and witness, day by day and week by week. This is what counts; this is why patience is a fruit of the **spirit**. Read the story again. Remind one another of what Jesus said. And keep awake.

LUKE 22.1–23

The Last Supper

¹The time came for the festival of unleavened bread, known as Passover. ²The chief priests and the scribes looked for a way to assassinate Jesus, a difficult task because of the crowds.

³The satan entered into Judas, whose surname was Iscariot, who was one of the company of the Twelve. ⁴He went and held a meeting with the chief priests and officers, to discuss how he might hand Jesus over. ⁵They were delighted, and promised to pay him. ⁶He agreed, and started to look for an opportunity to hand him over to them when the crowds weren't around.

⁷The day of unleavened bread arrived, the day when people had to kill the Passover lamb. ⁸Jesus dispatched Peter and John.

'Off you go,' he said, 'and get the Passover ready for us to eat.'

⁹'Where d'you want us to prepare it?' they asked him.

¹⁰'Listen carefully', said Jesus. 'As you go into the city a man will meet you carrying a jar of water. Follow him, and when he goes into a house, go after him. ¹¹Then say to the householder there, "The teacher says, 'Where is the living-room where I can eat the Passover with my disciples?' " ¹²And he will show you a large upstairs room, laid out and ready. Make the preparations there.'

¹³So they went and found it as he had said to them, and they prepared the Passover.

¹⁴When the time came, Jesus sat down at table with the apostles. ¹⁵'I have been so much looking forward to eating this Passover with you before I have to suffer', he said to them. ¹⁶'For – let me tell you – I won't eat it again until it's fulfilled in the kingdom of God.'

¹⁷Then he took a cup, and gave thanks, and said, 'Take this and share it among yourselves. ¹⁸Let me tell you, from now on I won't drink from the fruit of the vine until the kingdom of God comes.'

¹⁹Then he took some bread. He gave thanks, broke it and gave it to them.

'This is my body', he said, 'which is given for you. Do this in memory of me.'

²⁰So too, after supper, with the cup: 'This cup', he said, 'is the new covenant, in my blood which is shed for you.

²¹'But look here! Someone here is going to betray me. His hand is with mine at this table. ²²The son of man is indeed going, as it is marked out for him; but woe betide that man by whom he is betrayed!'

²³They began to ask each other which of them was going to do this.

When Jesus wanted to give his followers – then and now – a way of understanding what was about to happen to him, he didn't teach them a theory.

Theories about how Jesus' death dealt with our sins have come and gone throughout church history. Many of them are profoundly moving, drawing together deep spiritual insight, remarkable theological understanding, and a commitment to bring God's saving love to the needy world. Many of them have inspired Christian people with a new view of God's grace and mercy. Theories have their proper place. But they weren't the main thing that Jesus gave his followers.

He gave them an act to perform. Specifically, he gave them a meal to share. It is a meal that speaks more volumes than any theory. The best way of finding out what it says is of course to do it, not to talk or write about it; but since this is a book, and my readers are not with me at the Lord's table, let me suggest some of the things that Jesus seems to have intended – and some of the things that Luke, in writing about it, seems to have wanted to draw out.

It was, first and foremost, a *Passover* meal. Luke has told us all along that Jesus was going to Jerusalem to 'accomplish his **Exodus**' (9.31). He has come to do for Israel and the whole world what God did through Moses and Aaron in the first Exodus. When the powers of evil that were enslaving God's people were at their worst, God acted to judge Egypt and save Israel. And the sign and means of both judgment and rescue was the Passover: the angel of death struck down the firstborn of all Egypt, but spared Israel as the firstborn of God, 'passing over' their houses because of the blood of the lamb on the doorposts (Exodus 12). Now the judgment that had hung over Israel and Jerusalem, the judgment Jesus had spoken of so often, was to be meted out; and Jesus would deliver his people *by taking its force upon himself*. His own death would enable his people to escape.

Escape from what? From the powers of evil. A little later Jesus spoke of the dark powers having their moment of glory (22.53). We still don't understand the nature and power of evil much better than people did in Jesus' day, but if we believe that in any sense God's plan of salvation for the world was reaching its climax in Jesus it isn't surprising that the forces of evil were doing their best to thwart it. Jesus has been going through a lifetime of 'trials' (verse 28), and the supreme one is now upon him. He will go through it so that his followers need not. They must 'eat his body' and 'drink his blood', finding their **life** through his death.

Jesus had been passionately looking forward to this meal. It was, for him, the moment above all when he would explain to his followers, in deeds and words rich and heavy with meaning, what he was about to do and how they could profit from it. It's no accident, therefore, that the story of the meal is interwoven with the story of betrayal. John's **gospel** speaks of a period after Judas has left the room, in which Jesus could instruct the eleven in peace – though even then much of that instruction centred upon the coming persecution (John 13.31—17.26). In Luke's scene, Judas is there throughout, presumably slipping away unnoticed as the meal draws to a close.

At the small-scale level, Judas provided what the chief **priests** needed: an opportunity to arrest Jesus when there were no crowds around. (It was to avoid this danger that Jesus made secret plans for the Passover celebration.) But in Luke's understanding – and this is vital to what he sees going on at the supper itself – 'the satan' is using Judas for a purpose. The satan's purpose is always to accuse. Jesus is to be accused of being a deceiver, a rebel, a false prophet, a fake **Messiah**: in other words, a liar who is endangering Israel. Judas's betrayal is the first step in this process of accusation.

But Luke will tell us in a hundred ways, between now and the end of his gospel, that Jesus is in fact innocent of the charges laid against him, and that it is Israel itself that is guilty. The blend of celebration and betrayal in the scene at supper is preparing us for the blend of triumph and tragedy in the crucifixion itself. Jesus accomplishes his true mission by being falsely accused. He achieves his divine vocation by submitting to the punishment that others had deserved. As God took the arrogant opposition of Pharaoh in Egypt and made it serve his own ends in the spectacular rescue of his people, so now, through this one man at supper with his friends, we see God doing the same thing. When the powers of evil do their worst, and crucify the one who brings God's salvation, God uses that very event to defeat those powers.

We who, daily, weekly or however often, come together to obey Jesus' command, to break bread and drink wine in his memory, find ourselves drawn into that salvation, that healing life. The powers may still rage, like Pharaoh and his army pursuing the Egyptians after Passover. But they have been defeated, and rescue is secure.

LUKE 22.24–38

Prediction of Peter's Denial

[24]A quarrel began among them: which of them would be seen as the most important?

[25]'Pagan kings lord it over their subjects,' said Jesus to them, 'and people in power get themselves called "Benefactors". [26]That's not how it's to be with you. The most important among you ought to be like the youngest. The leader should be like the servant. [27]After all, who is the more important, the one who sits at table or the one who waits on him? The one at table, obviously! But I am with you here like a servant.

196

²⁸'You are the ones who have stuck it out with me through the trials I've had to endure. ²⁹This is my bequest to you: the kingdom my father bequeathed to me! ³⁰What does this mean? You will eat and drink at my table, in my kingdom, and you will sit on thrones, judging the twelve tribes of Israel.

³¹'Simon, Simon, listen to this. The satan demanded to have you. He wanted to shake you into bits like wheat. ³²But I prayed for you; I prayed that you wouldn't run out of faith. And, when you turn back again, you must give strength to your brothers.'

³³'Master,' replied Simon, 'I'm ready to go with you to prison – or to death!'

³⁴'Let me tell you, Peter,' replied Jesus, 'before the cock crows today, you will three times deny that you know me.

³⁵'When I sent you out', Jesus said to them, 'without purse or bag or sandals, were you short of anything?'

'Nothing', they replied.

³⁶'But now', he said, 'anyone who has a purse should take it, and the same with a bag. And anyone who doesn't have a sword should sell his cloak and buy one. ³⁷Let me tell you this: when the Bible says, "He was reckoned with the lawless", it must find its fulfilment in me. Yes; everything about me must reach its goal.'

³⁸'Look, Master,' they said, 'we've got a couple of swords here.'

'That's enough!' he said to them.

Imagine a football manager trying to prepare his squad for the match of their lives. They are facing their greatest opponents, with a major trophy at stake. He needs them to be totally focused on the task in hand. He has just outlined to them the strategy they must follow if they are to have a chance of winning. He has warned them that their opponents are cunning and will exploit any weaknesses they show.

But the minute he stops talking they start to squabble about who is the best player among them. They boast of how many goals they've scored, and argue about who did best in different games. They quarrel about who should really be playing in which position. They bicker about who should hold the trophy for the photographs after the match. Anything less like a team ready for a big game it would be hard to imagine.

So the manager tries again. He explains to them that they've come a long way together; he has moulded them into a splendid outfit, and has great plans for where they'll go from here. He warns the captain that he's going to have a particularly difficult game, but assures him that it will be all right in the end. The captain protests that he's going to play superbly, but the manager tells him that before half-time he will have given away two penalties and will have risked getting sent off.

Then he tries another tack. This game is going to be so hard, he tells them. He won't be there on the field with them. They'll have to think for themselves. It's going to be a fight. 'That's all right', says one of them brightly. 'I just can't wait for a chance to punch them on the nose.' The manager gives up. 'That's enough', he says. 'We'll call a halt right there.'

A great football manager, Bill Shankly, denied that football was a matter of life and death. 'It's much more important than that', he said. But the issue that the **disciples** faced that night at the supper, if Jesus was right and if Luke is right, was the most important of all time. This was to be the turning-point of history, and they simply weren't ready for it. They dispute about which of them is going to be regarded as the greatest; Jesus answers by standing the notion of greatness itself on its head. When he does imply that Peter has a leadership role among them he makes it clear that this is only because he, Jesus, has given him protection in advance for a trial that would otherwise have proved fatal. As if to prove the point, Peter will this very night deny he even knows Jesus.

But the strangest of Jesus' warnings comes in the last section. They are now going to face a time of testing in which the power and protection they had when Jesus sent them ahead of him on the road (9.1–6; 10.1–20) won't be available any longer. At that earlier stage, Jesus had won an initial victory over the forces of evil; now, however, he faces the greatest battle of all, which will involve him being hunted down as though he were a lawless brigand. And if Jesus himself is to go unprotected in the face of the last enemy, his followers need to watch out for themselves. They don't understand that he's talking in pictures, and seem to think he means them to get ready for an actual fight. When Jesus says 'That's enough!' he isn't suggesting that two swords would be sufficient for the job in hand (what could that possibly mean?); he is wearily putting a stop to the entire conversation, in which at every point they seem determined to misunderstand him.

What emerges from this whole picture is the sheer loneliness of Jesus, both at the supper for which he had longed, and as he goes off to wait for betrayal, arrest and all that would follow. There are times when all Christian work carries this element: when the one entrusted with a vision, a vocation, a particular ministry finds that he or she has to carry it forwards despite misunderstanding, opposition, doubt and denial, even from close friends and associates. Those who want to be bearers of the promise must be prepared for this puzzle. It seems to be built in to the fabric of how the **kingdom** has come and will come. Part of Jesus' own vocation, that he would bear the weight of Israel's and the world's sin and shame, was that he should do so alone; and the word 'alone' seems to gain new depths as we read this story.

Through it all, though, there shine out three principles and promises that none of this gathering gloom can quench. First, Jesus is among his followers like a servant waiting at table. This standing on its head of the world's idea of greatness is central not only to all Christian work and ministry; it is the key to what Jesus was about. It points to the second feature: Jesus was fulfilling, and knew he was fulfilling, the scriptural prophecies about the Servant, that strange figure, Israel in person, whom we find in Isaiah 40—55, in particular in the decisive passage Isaiah 52.13—53.12. 'He was reckoned with the lawless'; at the very moment when Jesus seems abandoned and defeated, exactly then he is completing what scripture had foretold.

Held between these two is the promise of the kingdom coming true at last. In a passage that sounds almost Johannine, Jesus assures his followers that, just as the Father has bequeathed the kingdom to him, so he now bequeaths it to them. They don't understand yet what the kingdom is, or how it is to come. But that doesn't make the promise invalid. Part of the sheer grace of the **gospel**, seen to good advantage in a passage like this, is precisely the way in which God's work goes ahead despite the human failure all around. And that is strangely comforting, whether in the first or the twenty-first century.

LUKE 22.39–53

Jesus Is Arrested

³⁹So off they went. Jesus headed, as usual, for the Mount of Olives, and his disciples followed him.

⁴⁰When he came to the place, he said to them, 'Pray that you won't come into the trial.'

⁴¹He then withdrew from them about a stone's throw, and knelt down to pray.

⁴²'Father,' he said, 'if you wish it – please take this cup away from me! But it must be your will, not mine.' ⁴³An angel appeared to him from heaven, strengthening him. ⁴⁴By now he was in agony, and he prayed very fervently. And his sweat became like clots of blood, falling on the ground. ⁴⁵Then he got up from praying, and came to the disciples and found them asleep because of sorrow.

⁴⁶'Why are you sleeping?' he said to them. 'Get up and pray, so that you won't come into the trial.'

⁴⁷While he was still speaking, a crowd appeared. The man named Judas, one of the Twelve, was leading them. He approached Jesus to kiss him, ⁴⁸but Jesus said to him, 'Judas! Are you going to betray the son of man with a kiss?'

⁴⁹Jesus' followers saw what was about to happen.

'Master!' they said. 'Shall we go in with the swords?' ⁵⁰And one of them struck the high priest's servant, and cut off his right ear.

⁵¹'Enough of that!' said Jesus, and healed the ear with a touch.

⁵²Then Jesus spoke to the arresting party – the chief priests, the Temple guards, and the elders.

'Anyone would think I was a brigand,' he said, 'seeing you coming out like this with swords and clubs! ⁵³Every day I've been in the Temple with you and you never laid hands on me. But your moment has come at last, and so has the power of darkness.'

One of the most noticeable changes in my life in the last thirty years – apart from increasing baldness – has been my changing attitude to one of the sports that I loved as a young man. I learned to rock climb when I was at school, and for ten or more years I did as much of it as I could, never with great skill but always with huge enjoyment. But now, though I love walking in the hills, I have no desire whatever to find myself with my toes wobbling on tiny ledges and my heels suspended over a few hundred feet of fresh air.

Apart from anything else, there is a peculiarly tragic aspect to many mountaineering accidents. The rope that's supposed to save, by joining the climbers together, can also kill. However well prepared the climbers may be, it sometimes happens that when one person falls he or she pulls the other climbers off the rock as well. One person's downfall can take the others with them.

That is what Jesus was most anxious to avoid in this passage. The **disciples** didn't understand what he was doing or saying, but with hindsight we can see it. He knew not only that he would be arrested, tried and killed, but that it was his God-given vocation that this should be so. But he also knew that he must go alone into the hour and power of darkness. When rebel leaders were rounded up, their associates were frequently captured, tortured and killed along with them; it was vital that this shouldn't happen to Peter and the rest. Jesus would fall, but he mustn't drag them down with him; his vocation was to give his life for the sheep, not to have them killed as well. In any case, they were the ones who would carry his mission forward in the days to come; he had prayed for Peter particularly (22.32), and it was vital that he and the others should stay out of the process that would shortly engulf him.

That's why he tells them to pray 'that they may escape the trial'. What 'trial' is he talking about? At one level, it's the trial that Jesus knows will await him once he's arrested. But this trial will be only the human and earthly version of the greater 'trial' that is coming on Jesus, on Israel, on the whole world. 'Your moment has come,' he said to the arresting party, 'and so has the power of darkness.' Like many Jews of his day,

Jesus believed that Israel's history, and with it world history, would pass into a moment of great terror and darkness, unspeakable suffering and sorrow, and that God's redemption, the coming **kingdom** and all that it meant, would emerge on the other side. This would be the 'trial', the 'test', the 'great tribulation'. Unlike any other leaders of the day, Jesus believed that it was his appointed task to go into that darkness, that terror, all by himself, to carry the fate of Israel and the world through to the other side. He would face The Trial, in both senses, alone.

Only this explains the horror that Jesus faced in the garden. Others (Socrates, famously; thousands of martyrs, Christian and non-Christian alike, in fame or obscurity) have gone to their deaths, including horrific and agonizing ones, with apparent equanimity. Jesus had just celebrated the meal at which he had not only foretold his own death but given his own key to what it would mean. Why did he now shrink?

The best answer is that he knew this death would carry with it the full horror of darkness, of God-forsakenness. He was going to the place where the evil powers of the world could and would do their worst at every level. And part of the torture was precisely the mental agony, the insistent questioning: perhaps there would be another way, maybe he'd misread God's signals, maybe, as with Abraham when he was about to **sacrifice** Isaac, now that he'd come this far perhaps God would do something new which would mean he didn't have to go through with it. Luke's addition of the medical detail about Jesus' sweating drops of blood has been confirmed by modern research; under conditions of extreme stress and horror, this can and does happen.

And in the middle of it, the disciples still didn't understand what Jesus' kingdom, his message of peace, was all about. Their attempts at defending him missed the point just as much as the swords and clubs of the guardsmen. He was neither a revolutionary fighter nor a military **Messiah**. But the time for explanations had passed. The hour of darkness had come, and nobody would see clearly again until the new dawn three days later.

LUKE 22.54-71

Peter Denies Jesus

[54]So they arrested Jesus, took him off, and brought him into the high priest's house. Peter followed at a distance. [55]They lit a fire in the middle of the courtyard and sat around it, and Peter sat in among them.

[56]A servant-girl saw him sitting by the fire. She stared hard at him. 'This fellow was with him!' she said.

[57]Peter denied it. 'I don't know him, woman', he said.

⁵⁸After a little while another man saw him and said, 'You're one of them!'

'No, my friend, I'm not', replied Peter.

⁵⁹After the space of about an hour, another man insisted, 'It's true! This man was with him; he's a Galilean too!'

⁶⁰'My good fellow', said Peter, 'I don't know what you're talking about.' And at once, while he was still speaking, the cock crowed. ⁶¹The master turned and looked at Peter, and Peter called to mind the words the master had spoken to him: 'Before the cock crows, this very day, you will deny me three times.' ⁶²And he went outside and wept bitterly.

⁶³The men who were holding Jesus began to make fun of him and knock him about. ⁶⁴They blindfolded him.

'Prophesy!' they told him. 'Who is it that's hitting you?' ⁶⁵And they said many other scandalous things to him.

⁶⁶When the day broke, the official assembly of the people, the chief priests and the scribes came together, and they took him off to their council.

⁶⁷'If you are the Messiah', they said, 'tell us!'

'If I tell you', he said to them, 'you won't believe me. ⁶⁸And if I ask you a question, you won't answer me. ⁶⁹But from now on the son of man will be seated at the right hand of God's power.'

⁷⁰'So you're the son of God, are you?' they said.

'You say that I am', he said to them.

⁷¹'Why do we need any more witnesses?' they said. 'We've heard it ourselves, from his own mouth!'

I was fortunate enough to be involved in a service commemorating the life and witness of Wang Zhiming. He was a Chinese pastor who, after maintaining a clear Christian witness in the days of Mao's cultural revolution, was executed in front of a large crowd. He is one of hundreds of martyrs who, in recent memory, have given their life for the Christian faith.

Among the things people saw in him, the things that made the authorities angry, was that he went on telling the truth even when it became first costly, then dangerous, and finally almost suicidal, to do so. **Faith** and truth, expressed with grace and dignity, are unconquerable. That's why Wang Zhiming is portrayed in a statue on the west front of Westminster Abbey, while nobody today remembers his accusers or executioners.

Luke highlights Jesus' faith and truth as he tells what happened the night Jesus was arrested. Peter denies he even knows Jesus. The soldiers play games, mocking Jesus as a false prophet at the very moment his prediction about Peter comes true. The council quiz him, not to know what he really believes but to find a way of framing a charge they can take to the Roman governor in the morning. And in the middle of it all stands the Master, sorrowing over Peter, wounded by the soldiers, shaking his head over the self-serving Jewish leadership, and continuing to tell the truth.

It's a scene worth stepping into for a few moments, as we ponder what is at stake and what it all meant. Think of the fireside, that chilly April night. Loyalty has taken Peter this far, but as the night wears on tiredness has sapped his resolve. It's a familiar problem, which sometimes strikes in the middle of the night but more often strikes in the middle of someone's life, or of some great project. We sign on to follow Jesus, and we really mean it. We start work on our vocation, and we have every intention of accomplishing it. Beginnings are always exciting, if daunting; the midday heat, or the midnight weariness, can drain away our intentions, our energy, our enthusiasm. Few if any Christians will look down on Peter and despise him. Most, if not all, of us will think: yes, that's what it's like. That's what happens. Perhaps it's only when we've been there that, like Peter, we can start to live and work in a new way, no longer out of our own energy but out of a fresh, and humbling, call of God.

Now see the guardroom where Jesus is blindfolded. Some of the guards are brutal and rough, ready for any sport that comes along. Others are simply doing a job, but are unable to stand back when an ugly mood takes over. Their colleagues would think them weak, and might make them the next target for their fun. One of the things that makes a bully all the more violent is the sight of weakness; he covers up his own inner fears by mocking others.

This doesn't only happen in guardrooms with soldiers. It also happens in offices and boardrooms, in school playgrounds and restaurant kitchens. It happens wherever people forget that every single other person they deal with is a beautiful, fragile reflection of the creator God, to be respected and cherished – and that they themselves are commanded, too, to reflect this God in the world. It happens, in other words, whenever people decide to make themselves feel good by making other people feel bad. Once again, we have all known what that's like.

Finally and tragically, step into the courtroom. The council members have real power, if only as puppets of Rome. They have inherited a thousand-year tradition of believing in the God of justice, and they boast of how their nation can bring that justice to God's world. But their overmastering aim here is to get rid of Jesus at all costs. For the moment everything else is on hold. One statement from him will do, however cryptic it may be, as long as they can twist it and spin it to frame a charge. This is a familiar tactic to politicians, journalists and lawyers. Anyone with a quick mind, a ready tongue and a flexible conscience can practise it. And it creates innocent victims wherever it happens.

Someone asked me today what it means to say that Jesus died for the sins of the world. I gave a rather rambling, but I hope adequate answer. But Luke is answering that question all through this passage. Peter's weakness, the guards' bullying, the court's perversion of justice; all this and much more put Jesus on the cross. It wasn't just a theological transaction; it was real sin, real human folly and rebellion, the dehumanized humanity that has lost its way and spat in God's face. 'They said many other scandalous things to him'; yes, and we've all done so. As Luke leads our eyes to the foot of the cross he means us to feel not just sorrow and pity, but shame.

LUKE 23.1–12

Jesus Before Pilate and Herod

[1]The whole crowd of them got up and took Jesus to Pilate.

[2]They began to accuse him. 'We found this fellow', they said, 'deceiving our nation! He was forbidding people to give tribute to Caesar, and saying that he is the Messiah – a king!'

[3]So Pilate asked Jesus, 'You are the king of the Jews?'

'You said it', replied Jesus.

[4]'I find no fault in this man', said Pilate to the chief priests and the crowds. [5]But they became insistent.

'He's stirring up the people,' they said, 'teaching them throughout the whole of Judaea. He began in Galilee, and now he's come here.'

[6]When Pilate heard that, he asked if the man was indeed a Galilean. [7]When he learned that he was from Herod's jurisdiction he sent him to Herod, who happened also to be in Jerusalem at that time.

[8]When Herod saw Jesus he was delighted. He had been wanting to see him for quite some time now, since he'd heard about him, and had hoped to see him perform some sign or other. [9]He questioned him this way and that, but Jesus gave no answer at all. [10]The chief priests and the scribes stood by, accusing him vehemently. [11]Herod and his soldiers treated Jesus with contempt; they ridiculed him by dressing him up in a splendid robe, and sent him back to Pilate. [12]And so it happened, that very day, that Herod and Pilate became friends with each other. Up until then, they had been enemies.

Many plays, many novels and many real-life episodes reach a climax when two people, long separated, come together at last, for good or ill. 'We meet at last, Mr Bond!' declares the villain with an ugly smile, believing he finally has the secret agent in his power. Characters in plays from Aeschylus to Shakespeare and beyond stare at one another: 'Can it really be you?' they exclaim. 'It's so good to see you at last!' we declare as a pen-friend or distant cousin steps off the plane.

We will not understand Luke's scene between Jesus and Herod unless we sense that quality in it. Herod has been in the background throughout the gospel. Only Luke tells us that he had wanted to hunt Jesus down and kill him much earlier, during Jesus' Galilean ministry (13.31); only Luke now gives us this scene where they meet at last, the present and precarious 'king of the Jews' face to face with the real and coming King. Herod had longed for this moment. He saw Jesus as a combination of **John the Baptist**, who had fascinated him with his talk but frightened him with his warnings, and the kind of circus artiste who can do magic stunts to order.

Jesus disappoints him. He says nothing, and does no **miracles**. We might have expected that, like Moses at the court of Pharaoh, the leader of the new Exodus would either threaten Herod with God's judgment or perform remarkable feats to demonstrate his claims, but Jesus does neither. He isn't that sort of prophet, and he isn't that sort of king. Luke, for whom Jesus is certainly both a true prophet and the true king of the Jews, places this meeting in a sequence of scenes designed to reveal the truth of this kingship and the falsehood of all other types. At this moment, the truth is more eloquently stated by silence.

Why then did Pilate say that Jesus was innocent of the charges laid against him? Why did Herod noticeably not accede to the chief **priests'** accusations? Partly, it seems, because it was obvious that Jesus was not leading the sort of revolution normally spearheaded by would-be 'kings of the Jews'. His few close followers were only lightly armed, and had in any case run away. Jesus made no threats, offered no resistance, and said hardly anything. They could see that the main reason he was before them was because the chief priests and their associates wanted to get rid of him – and both Herod and Pilate disliked them and tried to do them down, as part of the power struggles that dribbled on throughout this period. Once again, Jesus was caught at the point where competing interests and agendas met. Not only the sins, but also the petty aspirations, of the world conspired to put him on the cross.

But if it's important for Luke that Jesus and Herod meet at last, it is still more important that the true Lord of the world meets the representative of the political lord of the world. Luke's readers know that Jesus hasn't in fact forbidden people to give tribute to Caesar, but it was a plausible charge for one who, by speaking of his exaltation as the **son of man** (22.69), showed that he saw himself as the rightful and royal representative of Israel. If he was the king of the Jews, and would be elevated as king over all earthly powers, then Caesar too would be pushed down from his throne. This, as Luke implied at the start of his story (2.1; 3.1), was what the **kingdom of God** was all about.

This double meeting of Jesus with Herod and with Caesar's representative foreshadows the confrontations in Acts. There, Jesus is first heralded as king of the Jews, ending with the death of (a different) Herod (Acts 1—12), and is then announced as 'another king' (Acts 17.7), that is, a rival to Caesar, with the **gospel** finally reaching Rome itself (Acts 13—28). Jesus can be announced publicly as king of the world not least because, in this scene, he remains largely silent; that is part of the paradox of the gospel. His sovereign gentleness, and his refusal to yell and bluster as others would have done, already spoke volumes long before his prayer on the cross (23.34).

And – another Lukan touch – there is a wonderful irony to the new-found friendship of the Jewish king and the **Gentile** ruler. Luke's whole book has spoken of the gospel reaching out into the lands beyond, beyond official Judaism, beyond the racial and geographical boundaries of Israel, beyond prejudice and blindness, bringing together Jew and Gentile, young and old, the hated Samaritan, the tax-collector. Now, even without believing in Jesus, Herod and Pilate are reconciled. It is as though, with Jesus on the way to the cross, reconciliation cannot help breaking out all over the place.

There is, of course, no real comparison between the shady deal struck between the petty princeling and the scheming governor, and the rich fellowship in the gospel enjoyed by Jewish and Gentile believers. But Luke is alert, and wants us to be too, for every sign that the world is becoming a new place through Jesus and his crucifixion. If even Herod and Pilate can become friends through this, he says to both his church and ours, think how you too could be reconciled with anyone at all, once you both come under the shadow of the cross.

LUKE 23.13-26

Pilate Pressured by the Crowds

[13]So Pilate called the chief priests, the rulers and the people.

[14]'You brought this man before me', he said to them, 'on the grounds that he was leading the people astray. Look here, then: I examined him in your presence and I found no evidence in him of the charges you're bringing against him. [15]Nor did Herod; he sent him back to me. Look: there is no sign that he's done anything to deserve death. [16]So I'm going to flog him and let him go.'

[18]'Take him away!' they shouted out all together. 'Release Barabbas for us!' [19](Barabbas had been thrown into prison because of an uprising that had taken place in the city, and for murder.) [20]Pilate spoke to them again, with the intention of letting Jesus go, [21]but they shouted back, 'Crucify him! Crucify him!'

[22]'Why?' he said for the third time. 'What's he done wrong? I can't find anything he's done that deserves death, so I'm going to beat him and let him go.'

[23]But they went on shouting out at the tops of their voices, demanding that he be crucified; and eventually their shouts won the day. [24]Pilate gave his verdict that their request should be granted. [25]He released the man they asked for, the one who'd been thrown into prison because of rebellion and murder, and gave Jesus over to their demands.

[26]As they led him away, they grabbed a man from Cyrene called Simon, who was coming in to the city from the countryside, and they forced him to carry the cross-beam behind Jesus.

Shakespeare peopled his plays, as Charles Dickens did his novels, with fascinating minor characters. Each has his or her own tale to tell; none is a mere cardboard figure. Even the bear in *A Winter's Tale* is important.

Among the Evangelists, Luke has the most interesting cast of minor characters, and two of them come into focus here: Barabbas, and Simon of Cyrene. Together they help Luke tell us not only what happened to Jesus, but why it happened and what it means for us. We need to think into their own life stories, to see the tragic day unfold from their perspective, and to learn from them both.

Barabbas was not a common criminal. Luke informs us that he had been thrown into prison for his part in a violent rebellion that had taken place in Jerusalem. This is all we know about this particular rebellion, since the non-Christian historian Josephus doesn't mention another uprising at this time; we can assume that such events were a regular occurrence, and that in the ancient world (as, alas, in the modern) the Middle East would be a place where political and social frustration would regularly spill over into violence, sometimes focused on particular targets, sometimes mindless and born of the apparent hopelessness of the cause. It was, of course, because of such events that both the Romans and the chief **priests** were nervous of popular or **messianic** movements, not least at the time of major festivals. We know about Barabbas, but we must assume that he was only one of many rebel leaders in the period. He escaped crucifixion that Passover time, but the cross claimed many, perhaps dozens or even hundreds, even when no major disturbance had taken place.

Luke describes the event in such a way that we can hardly miss the point. Barabbas is guilty of some of the crimes of which Jesus, though innocent, is charged: stirring up the people, leading a rebellion. We don't know whether he saw himself, or whether his followers saw him, as a possible 'king of the Jews', but that is not unlikely. One of them is to die, and it turns out to be Jesus. Luke does not explain, as Mark and Matthew do, the custom whereby Pilate used to release one prisoner for the crowds to celebrate the holiday (some manuscripts add an extra verse, verse 17, to give this explanation, but this almost certainly wasn't originally in Luke), but it is clear that things come down to a choice. Either Barabbas or Jesus must die; either the one who stands for violent revolution, which Jesus has opposed from the beginning, or the one who has offered and urged the way of peace. Jesus ends up dying the death appropriate for the violent rebel. He predicted that he would be 'reckoned with the lawless' (22.37), and it has happened all too soon.

Luke's readers are by now used to seeing Jesus in company with tax-collectors and sinners. We have been told, from many angles and with many **parables**, that this was the appropriate and necessary focus of his ministry, embodying the outstretched love of God to all in need, going in search of lost sheep wherever they might be found. We were not, perhaps, quite prepared for it to end like this. It is one thing for Jesus to go in to eat with a man who is a sinner (19.7). It is a considerable step beyond that for him to go off and die the death of the violent rebel.

But this is in fact the climax and focus of the whole **gospel**. This is the point for which Luke has been preparing us all along. All sinners, all rebels, all the human race are invited to see themselves in the figure of Barabbas; and, as we do so, we discover in this story that Jesus comes to take our place, under condemnation for sins and wickednesses great and small. In the strange justice of God, which overrules the unjust 'justice' of Rome and every human system, God's mercy reaches out where human mercy could not, not only sharing, but in this case substituting for, the sinner's fate.

It is because of this that the call goes out, once we realize what Jesus is doing, for each of us to take up our own cross and follow him. This is of course where the call to Simon comes in. He had come on pilgrimage to Jerusalem from one of the Jewish communities in North Africa (the shores of the eastern Mediterranean were covered with Greek and Roman settlements, and in most there was a sizeable Jewish community), and found himself a pilgrim in a very different sense. Criminals on their way to execution normally carried the cross-piece of their own cross, as part of the shame and torture of the whole experience.

Luke does not explain why Jesus was unable to carry it for himself, but it takes little imagination to fill in the blank. The previous twenty-four hours had exhausted him, and he could barely stagger through the streets to the western gate. On several occasions in the gospel Jesus has urged his followers to take up their cross and follow him. Here at last someone is doing so, and even more: carrying Jesus' own cross, Simon becomes the model for all those who, in devotion, holiness and service, tread behind Jesus on the road of humility, pain and even death.

Though Barabbas and Simon are the key to this passage, we should once more notice the crowds, and sorrowfully identify with them. The mixture of disappointment at a failed messianic movement, and fear of what might now happen if the Romans or the chief priests regarded them as supportive of its leader, drove the mob to make what all history has regarded as the wrong choice. At the same time, Luke was well aware of God's overruling of this, too, for the purposes of salvation. God turns even human wrath and mistakes to serve his plans.

And, as we reflect on the role of the small parts within Luke's large drama, we should remind ourselves that our own parts, small though they may seem, may also contribute substantially to the work of the gospel as it goes forwards. Neither Barabbas nor Simon dreamed, that day, that their names would be known, and their stories told around the world, two thousand years hence. How much more, when we follow this Jesus and carry his cross, can we be sure that God will use our small labours and sufferings within his larger work.

LUKE 23.27–43

The Crucifixion

²⁷A great crowd of the people followed Jesus, including women who were mourning and wailing for him. ²⁸Jesus turned and spoke to them.

'Daughters of Jerusalem,' he said, 'don't cry for me. Cry for yourselves instead! Cry for your children! ²⁹Listen: the time is coming when you will say, "A blessing on the barren! A blessing on wombs that never bore children, and breasts that never nursed them!" ³⁰At that time people will start to say to the mountains, "Fall on us", and to the hills, "Cover us"! ³¹Yes: if this is what they do with the green tree, what will happen to the dry one?'

³²Two other criminals were taken away with him to be executed. ³³When they came to the place called The Skull, they crucified him there, with the criminals, one on his right and one on his left.

³⁴'Father,' said Jesus, 'forgive them! They don't know what they're doing!'

They divided his clothes, casting lots for them.
[35]The people stood around watching. The rulers hurled abuse at him. 'He rescued others,' they said, 'let him try rescuing himself, if he really is the Messiah, God's chosen one!'
[36]The soldiers added their taunts, coming up and offering him cheap wine.
[37]'If you're the king of the Jews,' they said, 'rescue yourself!'
[38]The charge was written above him: 'This is the King of the Jews.'
[39]One of the bad characters who was hanging there began to insult him. 'Aren't you the Messiah?' he said. 'Rescue yourself – and us, too!'
[40]But the other one told him off. 'Don't you fear God?' he said. 'You're sharing the same fate that he is! [41]In our case it's fair enough; we're getting exactly what we asked for. But this fellow hasn't done anything out of order.
[42]'Jesus,' he went on, 'remember me when you finally become king.'
[43]'I'm telling you the truth,' replied Jesus, 'you'll be with me in paradise, this very day.'

My first day at the lumber camp was probably the hardest. I was issued with thick leather gloves, and sent off to the first shed, where the planks arrived after the huge trees had been sliced up. The boards came out sideways on a huge conveyor belt, and had to be man-handled, in their different sizes, on to the trucks that took them to the next stage of the process. Up till this point, they were heavy and wet, partly because they were freshly cut and partly because they had arrived at the camp by being floated down the river. This conveyor system was known as the 'green chain'; this is where the 'green' lumber arrived and was dealt with.

The next stage was to dry the planks, which was done in a huge drying shed, after which they were cut again and sent to the 'dry chain', where they were sorted for shipping. That's where I ended up working for most of the time. By now the wood was about half the weight; all the moisture had been dried out of the planks, and they were easier to handle and ready for use.

The contrast between 'green' and 'dry' wood supplied Jesus with one of his darkest sayings. But if we find our way to the heart of it we will learn a lot about what he, and Luke as well, thought the cross was all about. 'If this is what they do with the green tree,' he said, 'what will happen to the dry one?' (verse 31).

Jesus wasn't a rebel leader; he wasn't 'dry wood', timber ready for burning. On the contrary, he was 'green wood': his mission was about peace and **repentance**, about God's reconciling **kingdom** for Israel and the nations. But, he is saying, if they are even doing this to him, what will they do when Jerusalem is filled with young hotheads, firebrands eager to do anything they can to create violence and mayhem? If the Romans crucify the prince of peace, what will they do to genuine warlords?

Jesus, we must realize, knows that he is dying the death of the brigand, the holy revolutionary. That is part of the point. He is bearing in himself the fate he had predicted so often for the warlike nation; the woes he had pronounced on Jerusalem and its inhabitants (e.g. 13.1–5) were coming true in him. The One was bearing the sins of the many. But if the many refuse, even now, to turn and follow him, to repent of their violence, then the fate in store for them will make his crucifixion seem mild by comparison. The judgment that Rome will mete out on them will be so severe that people will beg the earth to open and swallow them up, as the prophets had warned (Hosea 10.8).

This explains the rest of the passage about the women, including its terrifying upside-down 'beatitude'. Much earlier in the **gospel** Jesus had invoked God's blessing on the poor, the meek, the hungry, the mourners. Now he tells the women that they will soon invoke that same blessing on those who didn't have children, who would normally be deeply ashamed of the fact (compare 1.25). These mothers will see their own sons grow up to revolt against Rome, and will watch them suffer the fate that Rome always inflicted on rebels. Jesus combines the clear statement of his own intention, to suffer Israel's fate on her behalf, with the clear warning, echoing the warnings throughout the gospel, for those who do not follow him.

Luke makes the same point in a different way by contrasting the two who were crucified on either side of Jesus. The one taunts, but the other expresses Luke's view of the whole scene. Jesus, once again, is dying the death appropriate for the rebel, the brigand, the criminal; he is bearing the sins of the many, innocent though he himself is.

At the heart of Luke's picture of the cross is the mocking of Jesus as king of the Jews, which draws into a single stark sketch the meaning expressed by the various characters and the small incidents elsewhere in the narrative. Jesus has stood on its head the meaning of kingship, the meaning of the kingdom itself. He has celebrated with the wrong people, offered peace and hope to the wrong people, and warned the wrong people of God's coming judgment. Now he is hailed as king at last, but in mockery. Here comes his royal cupbearer, only it's a Roman soldier offering him the sour wine that poor people drank. Here is his royal placard, announcing his kingship to the world, but it is in fact the criminal charge which explains his cruel death.

His true royalty, though, shines out in his prayer and his promise, both recorded only in Luke. Unlike traditional martyrs, who died with a curse against their torturers, Jesus prays for their forgiveness. Like a king on his way to enthronement, Jesus promises a place of honour and bliss to one who requests it. ('Paradise' in Jewish thought wasn't necessarily the final resting place, but the place of rest and refreshment before the gift of new life in the **resurrection**.) The prayer shows that the promise is not to be taken as meaning that the only hope is in a life after death, vital though that of course is. Forgiveness brings the life of **heaven** to earth, God's future into the present.

LUKE 23.44–56

The Death and Burial of Jesus

⁴⁴By the time of the sixth hour, darkness came over all the land. ⁴⁵The sunlight vanished until the ninth hour. The veil of the Temple was ripped down the middle. ⁴⁶Then Jesus shouted out at the top of his voice, 'Here's my spirit, father! You can take care of it now!' And with that he died.

⁴⁷The centurion saw what happened, and praised God.

'This fellow', he said, 'really was in the right.'

⁴⁸All the crowds who had come together for the spectacle saw what happened, and they went away beating their breasts. ⁴⁹Those who knew Jesus, including the women who had followed him from Galilee, remained at a distance and watched the scene.

⁵⁰Now there was a man named Joseph, a member of the council. He was a good and righteous man, ⁵¹and had not given his consent to the court's verdict or actions. He was from Arimathea, a town in Judaea, and he was longing for God's kingdom. ⁵²He approached Pilate and asked for Jesus' body. ⁵³He took it down, wrapped it in a shroud, and put it in a tomb hollowed out of the rock, where no one had ever been laid. ⁵⁴It was the day of Preparation, and the sabbath was beginning.

⁵⁵The women who had followed Jesus, the ones who had come with him from Galilee, saw the tomb and how the body was laid. ⁵⁶Then they went back to prepare spices and ointments. On the sabbath they rested, as the commandment specified.

It really happened. It wasn't a mistake. We didn't get it wrong. It's true. You can rely on it. This is the main emphasis of Luke's account of Jesus' death and burial.

He began his book by telling 'Theophilus' that he could rely on these facts, and now that the most vital one is before us he presents his witnesses one by one. The centurion saw what happened, and made his comment. The crowds standing by saw what happened, and went home shocked and sad. Jesus' followers, not least the women, were standing at some distance, but they too saw what had happened. Then the burial: again, the women saw what happened, and how the body was laid out. Evidence. Eyewitnesses. This is what Luke promised, and this is what he's now giving us.

But it's not just the fact of Jesus' death and burial that Luke is interested in at this point. He is equally clear that Jesus died an innocent, righteous man. In Mark's **gospel**, the centurion in charge of the execution squad declares that Jesus really was God's son. In Luke, his comment is equally positive but slanted in a different direction: he really was innocent, he was in the right, he was a victim not a villain, he didn't deserve to die. Just in case anyone in Luke's audience, perhaps an educated Roman, might comment that if Roman justice executed Jesus then there must have been some reason, Luke presents his Roman witness to make it clear, as he will do in Acts in relation to Paul, that Jesus was not guilty, that he had done nothing worthy of death. This was not, of course, the first Roman centurion to look with **faith** at Jesus (see 7.2–10); Luke, naturally, wants his likely audience to identify with men like this, Romans with their feet on the ground, not people to be taken in by some religious trickster.

The third thing he is anxious to get across in this passage is that the people associated with Jesus' burial were, like the minor characters Elisabeth and Zechariah at the start of the gospel, good and law-abiding Jews. Joseph is a member of the council, though Luke of course insists that he had not agreed with the verdict they had reached on Jesus. The women, eager as they are to anoint Jesus' body, didn't have time to do it on the Friday night, because the **sabbath** began at sunset and they were rightly going to observe it. It would be Sunday morning before they could return, and Luke has made sure that we know they will go to the right tomb.

He has also explained enough about the burial for first-century readers to understand another important part of the story. Jewish burial customs varied considerably, but in this case the burial was to be in two stages. First, the body would be laid on a ledge in a cave, in this case a man-made one (though many natural caves were used for the same purpose). It would be wrapped up, with spices and ointments to cover the smell of rotting flesh. The expense this would incur was necessary because the tomb would be used again, perhaps several times, in the coming months before decay was complete; other bodies would be placed on other ledges. When all the flesh had rotted away, the remaining bones would be reverently collected and placed in a small ossuary, a bone-box. Unlike modern Western burials, therefore (and of course quite unlike cremations), an initial burial of this sort marked a stage on the road of saying a farewell, not the end of that road. Luke doesn't tell us, but he assumes we know, that tombs like this were shut with a large rolling stone across the door (see 24.2).

Hence the importance of knowing which tomb it was. Hence, too, the importance of our being told that it was a new tomb which had never been used before. Jesus' body was the only one in it. There was no chance of a mistake, as there might have been had there been three or four bodies, at different stages of decomposition, on various shelves in a dark cave.

So Luke's story of Jesus' death and burial is already looking forward, quite naturally, to the main purpose of the gospel: to announce to the watching **Gentile** world the most basic facts about Jesus. It is vital that we know that the one who died and was buried (and, in the next chapter, rose again) was the one who did and said the things described earlier in the gospel. But it is more vital still that we know that the one who announced God's **kingdom**, and lived out its reality, with its solemn warnings and its lavish celebrations, was then crucified, dead and buried. He takes with him into the tomb the hopes and fears of Israel and the world, and as far as Luke is concerned they belong to him still.

If Jesus had simply been a great prophet, his violent death would not have presented his followers with a theological problem. Many prophets died cruel deaths, and were venerated as martyrs. But Jesus' followers believed he was not just a prophet, but the **Messiah**; and nobody expected the Messiah to die at the hands of the pagans. He was supposed to defeat them, not to succumb to their violence. The crucifixion might have made Jesus a great martyr, or sealed his career as a great prophet, but by itself it meant that he could not have been God's anointed, the Messiah.

So if Jesus had remained in the tomb, he would have been regarded by everybody, including his own followers, as a false Messiah, and the court would have been right to decide that he was leading the people astray. In addition, if Jerusalem remained unjudged, still standing for centuries to come, he would have been seen as a false prophet, for all his noble death. But already in this story there are signs of what is to come. In the midst of the darkness, the darkness which is both spiritual (22.53) and actual, the **Temple** veil is torn in two, symbolizing the judgment that will come on the city, the system and the Temple itself that has rejected Jesus and his kingdom-message. Out of the darkness comes Jesus' cry of resignation, entrusting his **spirit** to his Father. And then, before any suggestion of Easter, the centurion speaks for all who, Luke hopes, will come to see in this crucifixion not just another messy death but the hope of the world: this man really was innocent.

Here the narrative pauses, poised and ready for the extraordinary things that will happen next.

LUKE 24.1-12

The Resurrection

¹The women went to the tomb in the very early morning of the first day of the week, carrying the spices they had prepared. ²They found the stone rolled away from the tomb, ³and when they went in they didn't find the body of the Lord Jesus.

⁴As they were at a loss what to make of it all, suddenly two men in shining clothes stood beside them. ⁵The women were terrified, and bowed their faces towards the ground.

But the men said to them, 'Why look for the living with the dead? ⁶He isn't here – he's been raised! Don't you remember? While you were still in Galilee he told you that ⁷the son of man must be handed over into the hands of sinners, and be crucified, and rise again on the third day.'

⁸And they remembered his words.

⁹They went back, away from the tomb, and told all this to the eleven and all the others. ¹⁰It was Mary Magdalene, Joanna, and Mary the mother of James, and the others with them. They said this to the apostles; ¹¹and this message seemed to them just stupid, useless talk, and they didn't believe them.

¹²Peter, though, got up and ran to the tomb. He stooped down and saw only the grave-clothes. He went back home, perplexed at what had happened.

Many years ago, a colleague of mine in Oxford wrote a series of articles in a university magazine, discussing various changes that were being proposed to the way the university and the colleges were run. He warned of what would happen if certain things were done, and if certain other things were not done. His advice went largely unheeded, and in later years he looked back with the unsatisfying satisfaction of seeing his warnings come true. 'If I ever write an autobiography,' he once told me, 'I shall call it *I Told You So.*'

It sometimes seems impossible for people to believe what they are being told. Even in a society that prides itself on thinking clearly and rationally, there are fashions in ideas just as in clothing, and often certain thoughts are so out of style as to be almost literally unthinkable. Even if people say things over and over again, if fashion dictates that we should think something else we will simply ignore them, or remain unable to understand them. We can't, as we say, 'hear' them; that is, we hear the sound the words make, but they don't go any further than our eardrums.

Jesus had spoken of his own **resurrection** at various stages, from 9.22 onwards. Two of his greatest stories had ended with a strong reference to rising from the dead (15.24, 32; 16.31). But nobody had 'heard' what he was saying. They were puzzled, and understandably so; 'resurrection', in that world, was what God would do in the end for all the righteous dead, giving new embodiment to everyone from Abraham, Isaac and Jacob down to the most recent righteous martyrs. Though people could speak of a prophet like Elijah or **John the Baptist** returning from the dead, what they probably meant by that was that someone would come who seemed to embody the same **spirit**, the same fiery prophecy. 'The resurrection' itself would be a large-scale event. After Israel's great and final suffering, all God's people would be given new **life**, new bodies.

We shouldn't be surprised, then, at how surprised they were on the first Easter morning. It wasn't just a lack of **faith** that had stopped them understanding what Jesus had said in Galilee about his rising again. It was simply that nobody had ever dreamed that one single living person would be killed stone dead and then raised to a new sort of bodily life the other side of the grave, while the rest of the world carried on as before.

The women, obviously, weren't expecting it. They weren't going to the tomb saying to themselves, 'Well, we've got the spices in case he's still dead, but let's hope he's alive again.' They knew well enough that dead people remained dead. The eleven (the Twelve without Judas; Luke doesn't reveal his fate until the start of Acts) certainly weren't expecting it. If Luke had been making this story up a generation or more after the event, as people sometimes suggest, not only would he not have had women going first to the tomb (women were not regarded as credible witnesses in the ancient world, as this story itself bears out); he would have had the **apostles** believe the story at once, ready to be models of faith and to lead the young church into God's future. Not so: it seemed to them a silly fantasy, exactly the sort of thing (they will have thought) that you'd expect from a few women crazy with grief and lack of sleep.

Nor does Luke attempt to describe, any more than the other **gospels** do, the moment when Jesus actually arose. This part of the story is a masterpiece of suspense. The whole chapter is another example of his great artistry, with the long middle story (the two on the road to Emmaus, 24.13–35) flanked on either side by the stories of the women and the eleven. These opening verses raise the question: something very odd has happened, but what? The middle story only gives us the answer step by step, because Luke is concerned that we understand what it is we're going to hear. Only then can we, the readers, meet the risen Jesus face to face and know who he is and what's going on.

The opening mood of Easter morning, then, is one of surprise, astonishment, fear and confusion. Yes, Jesus did say something like this would occur; he told us so all right. But we still don't know what's going on, what it all means, what will happen next. There is no sense here – as, alas, one sometimes finds in churches around Easter time – that throughout the story of the passion, Jesus himself was regarding the coming events as an unpleasant task which would soon be over, and that we can follow the story through for ourselves in the same way. Easter is always a surprise, whether we meet it in celebrating the feast itself, or in the sudden surges of God's grace overturning tragedy in our own lives or in the world.

No doubt our own resurrection will be as much of a surprise, in its own way, as that of Jesus. From the beginning, the gospel is **good news** not least because it dares to tell us things we didn't expect, weren't inclined to believe, and couldn't understand. Did we expect the gospel would be something obvious, something we could have dreamed up for ourselves?

LUKE 24.13–27

On the Road to Emmaus

[13]That very day, two of them were going to a village called Emmaus, which lay about seven miles from Jerusalem. [14]They were discussing with each other all the various things that had taken place. [15]As they were discussing, and arguing with each other, Jesus himself approached and walked with them. [16]Their eyes, though, were prevented from recognizing him.

[17]'You're obviously having a very important discussion on your walk,' he said; 'what's it all about?'

They stood still, a picture of gloom. [18]Then one of them, Cleopas by name, answered him.

'You must be the only person around Jerusalem,' he said, 'who doesn't know what's been going on there these last few days.'

[19]'What things?' he asked.

'To do with Jesus of Nazareth,' they said to him. 'He was a prophet. He acted with power and he spoke with power, before God and all the people. [20]Our chief priests and rulers handed him over to be condemned to death, and they crucified him. [21]But we were hoping that he was going to redeem Israel!

'And now, what with all this, it's the third day since it happened. [22]But some women from our group have astonished us. They went to his tomb very early this morning, [23]and didn't find his body. They came back saying they'd seen a vision of angels, who said he was alive. [24]Some of the folk with us went to the tomb and found it just as the women had said, but they didn't see *him*.'

²⁵'You are so senseless!' he said to them. 'So slow in your hearts to believe all the things the prophets said to you! Don't you see? ²⁶This is what *had* to happen: the Messiah had to suffer, and then come into his glory!'
²⁷So he began with Moses, and with all the prophets, and explained to them the things about himself throughout the whole Bible.

If the story of the prodigal son has a claim to be the finest story Jesus ever told, the tale of the two on the road to Emmaus must have an equal claim to be the finest scene Luke ever sketched. It's a shame to break it in half, as we've done (the story continues to verse 35); but it would be even more of a pity to squash it all together into one short comment, when it is as rich in its detail as it is in its outline.

At the level of drama it has everything. Sorrow, suspense, puzzlement, gradual dawning of light; then, in the second half, unexpected actions, astonished recognition, a flurry of excitement and activity. It is both a wonderful, unique, spellbinding tale, and also a model (and Luke surely knew this) for a great deal of what being a Christian, from that day to this, is all about. The slow, sad dismay at the failure of human hopes; the turning to someone who might or might not help; the discovery that in scripture, all unexpected, there lay keys which might unlock the central mysteries and enable us to find the truth; the sudden realization of Jesus himself, present with us, warming our hearts with his truth, showing us himself as bread is broken. This describes the experience of innumerable Christians, and indeed goes quite a long way to explaining what it is about Christianity that grasps us and holds us in the face of so much that is wrong with the world, with the church and with ourselves.

The story as a whole is often used, and rightly so, as a focus for meditation, not least when people find themselves in difficulties. Bring your problem, your agony, on the road to Emmaus with Cleopas and his companion; be prepared to share it in prayer with the stranger who approaches; and learn to listen for his voice, explaining, leading forwards, warming your heart by applying scripture to what's going on. Learn to live inside this story, and you will find it inexhaustible.

The couple on the road may well have been husband and wife, Cleopas and Mary (see John 19.25; 'Clopas' there is probably the same person as 'Cleopas' here). Though we cannot be sure of this, many couples have found the story a wonderful focus for bringing their lives, their problems and their questions before Jesus.

Even before we start looking for deeper meanings within the story, the surface meaning itself is powerful enough. Cleopas must have thought at first that the stranger might have been a spy; it must have

218

taken a certain amount of courage – though perhaps by then he was beyond caring – to reveal that the two of them were part of Jesus' following. In any case, the story he tells is simple, profound and poignant. They had regarded Jesus as a prophet, and more than a prophet. God's power had been present with him in his **miracles** and his teaching, and they couldn't doubt that this was the man of God's choice. He was the one who would redeem Israel. Clearly, for them, this referred (as Luke has been saying all along) to the new **Exodus**: just as Israel had been 'redeemed' from slavery in Egypt at the first Passover, so they had hoped that now Israel would be 'redeemed', that God would purchase her freedom. They hoped that Israel would be liberated once for all from pagan domination, free to serve God in peace and holiness.

That's why the crucifixion was so devastating. It wasn't just that Jesus had been the bearer of their hopes and he was now dead and gone. It was sharper than that: if Jesus had been the one to redeem Israel, he should have been *defeating* the pagans, not dying at their hands! Cleopas's puzzled statement only needs the slightest twist to turn it into a joyful statement of early Christian **faith**: 'They crucified him – but we had hoped he would redeem Israel' would shortly become, 'They crucified him – and that was how he *did* redeem Israel.' And it was, of course, the **resurrection** that made the difference.

But before they could begin to understand what had just happened they had to be prepared. They, like everybody else in Israel, had been reading the Bible through the wrong end of the telescope. They had been seeing it as the long story of how God would redeem Israel *from* suffering, but it was instead the story of how God would redeem Israel *through* suffering; through, in particular, the suffering which would be taken on himself by Israel's representative, the **Messiah**. When Luke says that Jesus interpreted to them all the things about himself, throughout the Bible, he doesn't mean that Jesus collected a few, or even a few dozen, isolated texts, verses chosen at random. He means that the whole *story*, from Genesis to Chronicles (the last book of the Hebrew Bible; the prophets came earlier), pointed forwards to a fulfilment which could only be found when God's anointed took Israel's suffering, and hence the world's suffering, on to himself, died under its weight, and rose again as the beginning of God's new creation, God's new people. This is what had to happen; and now it just had.

It wasn't simply, then, that they couldn't recognize him. This is a very strange feature of the resurrection stories, in Matthew (28.17) and John (20.14; 21.4, 12) as well as here. There was nothing in the Jewish resurrection hope to indicate that this would happen, but it seems that Jesus' body, emerging from the tomb, had been transformed. It was the same, yet different – a mystery which we shall perhaps never unravel until we ourselves share the same risen life. But the fact that they couldn't recognize Jesus at first seems to have gone with the fact that they couldn't recognize the events that had just happened as the story of God's redemption. Perhaps Luke is saying that we can only now know Jesus, can only recognize him in any sense, when we learn to see him within the true story of God, Israel and the world.

For that we need to learn how to read the scriptures; and for that we need, as our teacher, the risen Lord himself. This passage forms one of the most powerful encouragements to pray for his presence, and sense of guidance, whenever we study the Bible, individually, in pairs or in larger groups. We need to be prepared for him to rebuke our foolish and faithless readings, and to listen for his fresh interpretation. Only with him at our side will our hearts burn within us (verse 32), and lead us to the point where we see him face to face.

LUKE 24.28–35

Jesus Revealed at Emmaus

[28]They drew near to the village where they were heading. Jesus gave the impression that he was going further, [29]but they urged him strongly not to.

'Stay with us', they said. 'It's nearly evening; the day is almost gone.' And he went in to stay with them.

[30]As he was sitting at table with them he took the bread and gave thanks. He broke it and gave it to them. [31]Then the eyes of both of them were opened, and they recognized him; and he vanished from their sight.

[32]Then they said to each other, 'Don't you remember how our hearts were burning inside us, as he talked to us on the road, as he opened up the Bible for us?'

[33]And they got up then and there and went back to Jerusalem. There they found the eleven gathered together, and the people with them. [34]They were saying, 'The Lord really has been raised! He's appeared to Simon!' [35]Then they told what had happened on the road, and how he was known to them in the breaking of the bread.

Think of the first meal in the Bible. The moment is heavy with significance. 'The woman took some of the fruit, and ate it; she gave it to her husband, and he ate it; then the eyes of them both were opened, and they knew that they were naked' (Genesis 3.6–7). The tale was told, over and over, as the beginning of the woes that had come upon the human race. Death itself was traced to that moment of rebellion. The whole creation was subjected to decay, futility and sorrow.

Now Luke, echoing that story, describes the first meal of the new creation. 'He took the bread and gave thanks. He broke it and gave it to them. Then the eyes of both of them were opened, and they recognized him' (verses 30–31). The couple at Emmaus – probably Cleopas and Mary, husband and wife – discover that the long curse has been broken. Death itself has been defeated. God's new creation, brimming with life and joy and new possibility, has burst in upon the world of decay and sorrow.

Jesus himself, risen from the dead, is the beginning and the sign of this new world. He isn't just alive again in the same way that Jairus's daughter, or the widow's son at Nain, were. They, poor things, would have to face death again in due course. He has, it seems, gone through death and out the other side into a new world, a world of new and deathless creation, still physical only somehow transformed. We shall look at this in more detail when we read the next, and last, section of the gospel.

Luke has, of course, told the story in such a way as to help us live in it ourselves. We too are invited to listen to the exposition of the Bible, to have our hearts burning within us as fresh truth comes out of the old pages and sets us on fire. In this and the following passage Luke emphasizes what the church all too easily forgets: that the careful study of the Bible is meant to bring together head and heart, understanding and excited application. This will happen as we learn to think through the story of God and the world, of Israel and Jesus, not in the way our various cultures try to make us think, but in the way that God himself has sketched out. Only when we see the Old Testament as reaching its natural climax in Jesus will we have understood it. Equally, we will only understand Jesus himself when we see him as the one to whom scripture points, not in isolated prooftexts but in the entire flow of the story. And, when we grasp this, we, like Cleopas and Mary, will find our hearts burning within us.

So, too, we are invited to know Jesus in the breaking of the bread. The way Luke has described the simple mealtime takes our minds back to the upper room, and to many other meals that Jesus had shared with his followers. Cleopas and Mary, not being members of the Twelve, were not present at the Last Supper, but what Jesus did then was (apart from the special words) typical, most likely, of the way he had always broken bread with them. But Luke also intends that his readers should see this simple meal pointing forwards, to the breaking of bread which quickly became the central symbolic action of Jesus' people. Though Jesus was no longer physically present, they were to discover him living with and in them through this meal (Acts 2.42). Scripture and sacrament, **word** and meal, are joined tightly together, here as elsewhere.

Take scripture away, and the sacrament becomes a piece of magic. Take the sacrament away, and scripture becomes an intellectual or emotional exercise, detached from real life. Put them together, and you have the centre of Christian living as Luke understood it.

There is one more sign of Luke's artistry to be discovered here. He has told this story as part of his framework for the entire gospel. In 2.41–52 we read how Mary and Joseph went a day's journey away from Jerusalem, and then, realizing Jesus wasn't with them, looked for him for three days before discovering him in the **Temple** with the learned teachers. 'Didn't you know', he said to the frantic Mary, 'that I would have to be involved with my father's work?' Now here we have a different couple, likewise at the end of three days' agony of mental and spiritual searching. 'Didn't you know', says Jesus to them, in effect, 'that I would have to be doing my Father's work?' The whole gospel story is framed between these very human scenes. Luke has invited us to accompany him on a journey of **faith**, faith that will take us through anxiety and sorrow to meet the Jesus who has accomplished his Father's work, and longs to share the secret of it – and the gift of his own presence – with us, his followers.

Luke has therefore described for us, as he said he would, the new **Exodus** that Jesus would accomplish at Jerusalem (9.31). The real slave-master, keeping the human race in bondage, is death itself. Earthly tyrants borrow power from death to boost their rule; that's why crucifixion was such a symbol of Roman authority. Victory over death robs the powers of their main threat. Sin, which means humans rebelling against God and so conspiring with death to deface God's good creation, is likewise defeated. Jesus has led God's new people out of slavery, and now invites them to accompany him on the new journey to the promised land. The road to Emmaus is just the beginning. Hearing Jesus' voice in scripture, knowing him in the breaking of bread, is the way. Welcome to God's new world.

LUKE 24.36–53

Jesus' Promise and Ascension

[36] As they were saying this, Jesus himself stood in the midst of them, and said, 'Peace be with you.' [37] They were terrified and alarmed, and thought they were seeing a ghost.

[38] 'Why are you so disturbed?' he said. 'Why do these questionings come up in your hearts? [39] Look at my hands and feet; it really is me, myself. Touch me and see! Ghosts don't have flesh and bones like you can see I have.'

[40] With these words, he showed them his hands and feet.

⁴¹While they were still in disbelief and amazement from sheer joy, he said to them, 'Have you got something here to eat?' ⁴²They gave him a piece of baked fish, ⁴³which he took and ate in front of them. ⁴⁴Then he said to them, 'This is what I was explaining to you when I was still with you. Everything written about me in the law of Moses, and in the prophets and the Psalms, had to be fulfilled.' ⁴⁵Then he opened their minds to understand the Bible.

⁴⁶'This is what is written', he said. 'The Messiah must suffer and rise from the dead on the third day, ⁴⁷and in his name repentance, for the forgiveness of sins, must be announced to all the nations, beginning from Jerusalem. ⁴⁸You are the witnesses for all this. ⁴⁹Now, look: I'm sending upon you what my father has promised. But stay in the city until you are clothed with power from on high.'

⁵⁰Then he took them out as far as Bethany, and lifted up his hands and blessed them. ⁵¹As he was blessing them, he was separated from them and carried into heaven.

⁵²They worshipped him, and went back to Jerusalem with great joy. ⁵³They spent all their time in the Temple, praising God.

Luke's closing scene, for all its joy and excitement, brings into focus for us the real problem of what happened at Easter. What sort of a body did Jesus have? How could it at the same time be solid and real, with flesh and bones, able to eat baked fish, and to demonstrate that it wasn't a ghost – and also to appear and disappear apparently at will, and at the end to be carried into **heaven**? Just what sort of a body are we talking about?

That, I think, is the hardest thing for us to grasp about the **resurrection**. It takes St Paul a long chapter to thrash it out (1 Corinthians 15), and many misunderstand it even then. People often think that 'resurrection' simply means 'life after death' or 'going to heaven', but in the Jewish world of the first century it meant a new *embodied* life in God's new world; a life *after* 'life after death', if you like. But the new body which will be given at the end is not identical to the previous one. In an act of new creation parallel only to the original creation itself, God will make a new type of material, no longer subject to death, out of the old one. In Jesus' case, of course, this happened right away, without his original body decaying, so that the new body was actually the transformation of the old one. For the rest of us, whose bodies will decay, and whose bones may well be burnt, it will take a complete act of new creation.

The new body – and this is the point – will belong in *both* the dimensions of God's world, in both heaven and earth. (At the end of the book of Revelation, heaven and earth will finally be joined together into one, so there won't be any shuttling to and fro; the two dimensions will be

223

fused together at last.) At the moment our bodies are earthly only; Jesus' new body is at home in both earth and heaven. If our mental pictures of 'heaven' need adjusting to allow for this startling possibility, so be it. Only this explains the otherwise very puzzling stories, here and in John's similar account. Of course the resurrection, and the ascension, stretch our minds and imaginations further than we normally like. We who live, even as Christians, with our thinking conditioned by the world of sin and death, find it a huge struggle to adjust to God's new world. That is part of the challenge of the gospel.

But if our minds are still reeling from trying to take all this in – and it seems, not surprisingly, as though that's how the **disciples** were too – then what Jesus has to say in his last days with them is very practical, and points the way to the whole mission of the church. People often ask me, 'What, after all, is the point of Jesus dying and rising again? It's no doubt very nice for him to be alive again, but what does it have to do with the rest of us?' The answer is here, in a few sentences which will take a lifetime, and in fact all the history of the church, to work out. The church is to be rooted in scripture and active in mission. '**Repentance**, for the forgiveness of sins, must be announced to all the nations.' The Bible always envisaged that when God finally acted to fulfil all the promises made to Abraham, Moses and the prophets, then the whole world would be brought into the embrace of God's saving and healing love. That is what must now happen.

'Repentance' and 'forgiveness of sins' are not, therefore, simply a matter for the individual, though they certainly are that. At the heart of being a Christian is the personal turning away from sin, and celebrating God's forgiveness, which is after all at the heart of the Lord's Prayer itself. But these two words go much wider as well. They are the agenda which can change the world.

Today's world is full of disputes, large and small, only a few of which get into the newspapers. Nations, ethnic groups, political factions, tribes and economic alliances struggle for supremacy. Each can tell stories of the atrocities committed by their opponents. Each one claims that they therefore have the right to the moral high ground, and must be allowed redress, revenge, satisfaction. But, as anyone who has studied the complicated history of the Middle East, Rwanda or Northern Ireland will know, it is simply impossible to give an account of the conflict in which one side is responsible for all the evil and the other side is a completely innocent victim. The only way forward is the one we all find the hardest at every level: repentance and forgiveness. The resolute application of the **gospel**, under the Lordship of the risen Jesus, is the only way forward towards the creation of new hope and possibilities. The extraordinary work of the Truth and Reconciliation Commission in South Africa, under the leadership of Archbishop Desmond Tutu, showed the way in the last years of the twentieth century. He offers a wonderful example: who will follow?

Jesus promised his followers that they would be equipped with power from God to engage in their new tasks; the book of Acts is the story of what began to happen as a result. But Luke's gospel ends, as it began, in the **Temple** at Jerusalem. Worship of the living God, now revealed in Jesus of Nazareth, is at the heart of Luke's vision of the Christian life.

GLOSSARY

the accuser, *see* the satan

age to come, *see* present age

apostle, disciple, the Twelve

'Apostle' means 'one who is sent'. It could be used of an ambassador or official delegate. In the New Testament it is sometimes used specifically of Jesus' inner circle of twelve; but Paul sees not only himself but several others outside the Twelve as 'apostles', the criterion being whether the person had personally seen the risen Jesus. Jesus' own choice of twelve close associates symbolized his plan to renew God's people, Israel (who traditionally thought of themselves as having twelve tribes); after the death of Judas Iscariot (Matthew 27.5; Acts 1.18), Matthias was chosen by lot to take his place, preserving the symbolic meaning. During Jesus' lifetime they, and many other followers, were seen as his 'disciples', which means 'pupils' or 'apprentices'.

baptism

Literally, 'plunging' people into water. From within a wider Jewish tradition of ritual washings and bathings, **John the Baptist** undertook a vocation of baptizing people in the Jordan, not as one ritual among others but as a unique moment of repentance, preparing them for the coming of the **kingdom of God**. Jesus himself was baptized by John, identifying himself with this renewal movement and developing it in his own way. His followers in turn baptized others. After his **resurrection**, and the sending of the **holy spirit**, baptism became the normal sign and means of entry into the community of Jesus' people. As early as Paul it was aligned both with the **Exodus** from Egypt (1 Corinthians 10.2) and with Jesus' death and resurrection (Romans 6.2–11).

circumcision

The cutting off of the foreskin. Male circumcision was a major mark of identity for Jews, following its initial commandment to Abraham (Genesis 17), reinforced by Joshua (Joshua 5.2–9). Other peoples, e.g. the Egyptians, also circumcised male children. A line of thought from Deuteronomy (e.g. 30.6), through Jeremiah (e.g. 31.33), to the **Dead Sea Scrolls** and the New Testament (e.g. Romans 2.29) speaks of 'circumcision of the heart' as God's real desire, by which one may become inwardly what the male Jew is outwardly, that is, marked out as part of God's people. At periods of Jewish assimilation into the surrounding culture, some Jews tried to remove the marks of circumcision (e.g. 1 Maccabees 1.11–15).

Christ, *see* **Messiah**

covenant

At the heart of Jewish belief is the conviction that the one God, YHWH, who had made the whole world, had called Abraham and his family to belong to him in a special way. The promises God made to Abraham and his family, and the requirements that were laid on them as a result, came to be seen in terms either of the agreement that a king would make with a subject people, or of the marriage bond between husband and wife. One regular way of describing this relationship was 'covenant', which can thus include both promise and **law**. The covenant was renewed at Mount Sinai with the giving of the **Torah**; in Deuteronomy before the entry to the promised land; and, in a more focused way, with David (e.g. Psalm 89). Jeremiah 31 promised that after the punishment of **exile** God would make a 'new covenant' with his people, forgiving them and binding them to him more intimately. Jesus believed that this was coming true through his **kingdom**-proclamation and his death and **resurrection**. The early Christians developed these ideas in various ways, believing that in Jesus the promises had at last been fulfilled.

David's son, *see* **son of David**

Dead Sea Scrolls

A collection of texts, some in remarkably good repair, some extremely fragmentary, found in the late 1940s around Qumran (near the north-east corner of the Dead Sea), and virtually all now edited, translated and in the public domain. They formed all or part of the library of a strict monastic group, most likely Essenes, founded in the mid-second century BC and lasting until the Jewish – Roman war of AD 66–70. The scrolls include the earliest existing manuscripts of the Hebrew and Aramaic scriptures, and several other important documents of community regulations, scriptural exegesis, hymns, wisdom writings, and other literature. They shed a flood of light on one small segment within the Judaism of Jesus' day, helping us to understand how some Jews at least were thinking, praying and reading scripture. Despite attempts to prove the contrary, they make no reference to **John the Baptist**, Jesus, Paul, James or early Christianity in general.

demons, *see* **the satan**

disciple, *see* **apostle**

Essenes, *see* **Dead Sea Scrolls**

exile

Deuteronomy (29—30) warned that if Israel disobeyed YHWH, he would send his people into exile, but that if they then repented he would bring them back. When the Babylonians sacked Jerusalem and took the people into exile, prophets such as Jeremiah interpreted this as the fulfilment of this prophecy, and made further promises about how long exile would last (70 years, according to Jeremiah 25.12; 29.10). Sure enough, exiles began to return in the late sixth century BC (Ezra 1.1). However, the post-exilic period was largely a disappointment, since the people were still enslaved to foreigners (Nehemiah 9.36); and at the height of persecution by the Syrians Daniel 9.2, 24 spoke of the 'real' exile lasting not for 70 years but for 70 *weeks* of years, i.e. 490 years. Longing for the real 'return from exile', when the prophecies of Isaiah, Jeremiah, etc. would be fulfilled, and redemption from pagan oppression accomplished, continued to characterize many Jewish movements, and was a major theme in Jesus' proclamation and his summons to **repentance**.

Exodus

The Exodus from Egypt took place, according to the book of that name, under the leadership of Moses, after long years in which the Israelites had been enslaved there. (According to Genesis 15.13f., this was itself part of God's covenanted promise to Abraham.) It demonstrated, to them and to Pharaoh, King of Egypt, that Israel was God's special child (Exodus 4.22). They then wandered through the Sinai wilderness for 40 years, led by God in a pillar of cloud and fire; early on in this time they were given the **Torah** on Mount Sinai itself. Finally, after the death of Moses and under the leadership of Joshua, they crossed the Jordan and entered, and eventually conquered, the promised land of Canaan. This event, commemorated annually in Passover and other Jewish festivals, gave the Israelites not only a powerful memory of what had made them a people, but also a particular shape and content to their faith in YHWH as not only creator but also redeemer; and in subsequent enslavements, particularly the **exile**, they looked for a further redemption which would be, in effect, a new Exodus. Probably no other past event so dominated the imagination of first-century Jews; among them the early Christians, following the lead of Jesus himself, continually referred back to the Exodus to give meaning and shape to their own critical events, most particularly Jesus' death and **resurrection**.

faith

Faith in the New Testament covers a wide area of human trust and trustworthiness, merging into love at one end of the scale and loyalty at the other. Within Jewish and Christian thinking faith in God also includes *belief*, accepting certain things as true about God, and what he has done in the world (e.g. bringing Israel out of Egypt; raising Jesus from the dead). For Jesus, 'faith' often seems to mean 'recognizing that God is decisively at work to bring the **kingdom** through

Jesus'. For Paul, 'faith' is both the specific belief that Jesus is Lord and that God raised him from the dead (Romans 10.9) and the response of grateful human love to sovereign divine love (Galatians 2.20). This faith is, for Paul, the solitary badge of membership in God's people in Christ, marking them out in a way that **Torah**, and the works it prescribes, can never do.

Gentiles

The Jews divided the world into Jews and non-Jews. The Hebrew word for non-Jews, *goyim*, carries overtones both of family identity (i.e. not of Jewish ancestry) and of worship (i.e. of idols, not of the one true God YHWH). Though many Jews established good relations with Gentiles, not least in the Jewish Diaspora (the dispersion of Jews away from Palestine), officially there were taboos against contact such as intermarriage. In the New Testament the Greek word *ethne*, 'nations', carries the same meanings as *goyim*. Part of Paul's overmastering agenda was to insist that Gentiles who believed in Jesus had full rights in the Christian community alongside believing Jews, without having to become **circumcised**.

Gehenna, hell

Gehenna is, literally, the valley of Hinnom, on the south-west slopes of Jerusalem. From ancient times it was used as a garbage dump, smouldering with a continual fire. Already by the time of Jesus some Jews used it as an image for the place of punishment after death. Jesus' own usage blends the two meanings in his warnings both to Jerusalem itself (unless it repents, the whole city will become a smouldering heap of garbage) and to people in general (to beware of God's final judgment).

good news, gospel, message, word

The idea of 'good news', for which an older English word is 'gospel', had two principal meanings for first-century Jews. First, with roots in Isaiah, it meant the news of YHWH's long-awaited victory over evil and rescue of his people. Second, it was used in the Roman world for the accession, or birthday, of the Emperor. Since for Jesus and Paul the announcement of God's inbreaking **kingdom** was both the fulfilment of prophecy and a challenge to the world's present rulers, 'gospel' became an important shorthand for both the message of Jesus himself and the apostolic message about him. Paul saw this message as itself the vehicle of God's saving power (Romans 1.16; 1 Thessalonians 2.13).

The four canonical 'gospels' tell the story of Jesus in such a way as to bring out both these aspects (unlike some other so-called 'gospels' circulated in the second and subsequent centuries, which tended both to cut off the scriptural and Jewish roots of Jesus' achievement and to inculcate a private spirituality rather than confrontation with the world's rulers). Since in Isaiah this creative, life-giving good news was seen as God's own powerful word (40.8; 55.11), the early Christians could use 'word' or 'message' as another shorthand for the basic Christian proclamation.

gospel, *see* **good news**

heaven

Heaven is God's dimension of the created order (Genesis 1.1; Psalm 115.16; Matthew 6.9), whereas 'earth' is the world of space, time and matter that we know. 'Heaven' thus sometimes stands, reverentially, for 'God' (as in Matthew's regular '**kingdom of heaven**'). Normally hidden from human sight, heaven is occasionally revealed or unveiled so that people can see God's dimension of ordinary life (e.g. 2 Kings 6.17; Revelation 1, 4—5). Heaven in the New Testament is thus not usually seen as the place where God's people go after death; at the end, the New Jerusalem descends *from* heaven *to* earth, joining the two dimensions for ever. 'Entering the kingdom of heaven' does not mean 'going to heaven after death', but belonging in the present to the people who steer their earthly course by the standards and purposes of heaven (cf. the Lord's Prayer: 'on earth as in heaven', Matthew 6.10), and who are assured of membership in the **age to come.**

hell, *see* **Gehenna**

Herodians

Herod the Great ruled Judaea from 37 to 4 BC; after his death his territory was divided between his sons Archelaus, Herod Antipas (the Herod of the **gospels**), and Philip. The Herodians supported the claims of Antipas to be the true king of the Jews. Though the **Pharisees** would normally oppose such a claim, they could make common cause with the Herodians when facing a common threat (e.g. Jesus, Mark 3.6).

high priest, *see* **priests**

holy spirit

In Genesis 1.2, the spirit is God's presence and power *within* creation, without God being identified with creation. The same spirit entered people, notably the prophets, enabling them to speak and act for God. At his **baptism** by **John the Baptist**, Jesus was specially equipped with the spirit, resulting in his remarkable public career (Acts 10.38). After his **resurrection**, his followers were themselves filled (Acts 2) by the same spirit, now identified as Jesus' own spirit: the creator God was acting afresh, remaking the world and them too. The spirit enabled them to live out a holiness which the **Torah** could not, producing 'fruit' in their lives, giving them 'gifts' with which to serve God, the world and the church, and assuring them of future **resurrection** (Romans 8; Galatians 4—5; 1 Corinthians 12—14). From very early in Christianity (e.g. Galatians 4.1-7), the spirit became part of the new revolutionary definition of God himself: 'the one who sends the son and the spirit of the son'.

John (the Baptist)

Jesus' cousin on his mother's side, born a few months before Jesus; his father was a **priest**. He acted as a prophet, baptizing in the Jordan – dramatically re-enacting the **Exodus** from Egypt – to prepare people, by **repentance**, for God's coming judgment. He may have had some contact with the **Essenes**, though his eventual public message was different from theirs. Jesus' own vocation was decisively confirmed at his **baptism** by John. As part of John's message of the **kingdom**, he outspokenly criticized Herod Antipas for marrying his brother's wife. Herod had him imprisoned, and then beheaded him at his wife's request (Mark 6.14–29). Groups of John's disciples continued a separate existence, without merging into Christianity, for some time afterwards (e.g. Acts 19.1–7).

justification

God's declaration, from his position as judge of all the world, that someone is in the right, despite universal sin. This declaration will be made on the last day on the basis of an entire life (Romans 2.1–16), but is brought forward into the present on the basis of Jesus' achievement, because sin has been dealt with through his cross (Romans 3.21—4.25); the means of this present justification is simply **faith**. This means, particularly, that Jews and **Gentiles** alike are full members of the family promised by God to Abraham (Galatians 3; Romans 4).

kingdom of God, kingdom of heaven

Best understood as the king*ship*, or sovereign and saving rule, of Israel's God YHWH, as celebrated in several psalms (e.g. 99.1) and prophecies (e.g. Daniel 6.26f.). Because YHWH was the creator God, when he finally became king in the way he intended this would involve setting the world to rights, and particularly rescuing Israel from its enemies. 'Kingdom of God' and various equivalents (e.g. 'No king but God!') became revolutionary slogans around the time of Jesus. Jesus' own announcement of God's kingdom redefined these expectations around his own very different plan and vocation. His invitation to people to 'enter' the kingdom was a way of summoning them to allegiance to himself and his programme, seen as the start of God's long-awaited saving reign. For Jesus, the kingdom was coming not in a single move, but in stages, of which his own public career was one, his death and resurrection another, and a still future consummation another. Note that 'kingdom of **heaven**' is Matthew's preferred form for the same phrase, following a regular Jewish practice of saying 'heaven' rather than 'God'. It does not refer to a place ('heaven'), but to the fact of God's becoming king in and through Jesus and his achievement. Paul speaks of Jesus, as **Messiah**, already in possession of his kingdom, waiting to hand it over finally to the Father (1 Corinthians 15.23–8; cf. Ephesians 5.5).

law, *see* Torah

lawyers, legal experts, *see* Pharisees

leper, leprosy

In a world without modern medicine, tight medical controls were needed to prevent the spread of contagious diseases. Several such conditions, mostly severe skin problems, were referred to as 'leprosy', and two long biblical chapters (Leviticus 13—14) are devoted to diagnosis and prevention of it. Sufferers had to live away from towns and shout 'unclean' to warn others not to approach them (13.45). If they were healed, this had to be certified by a **priest** (14.2–32).

life, soul, spirit

Ancient people held many different views about what made human beings the special creatures they are. Some, including many Jews, believed that to be complete, humans needed bodies as well as inner selves. Others, including many influenced by the philosophy of Plato (fourth century BC), believed that the important part of a human was the 'soul' (Gk: *psyche*), which at death would be happily freed from its bodily prison. Confusingly for us, the same word *psyche* is often used in the New Testament within a Jewish framework where it clearly means 'life' or 'true self', without implying a body/soul dualism that devalues the body. Human inwardness of experience and understanding can also be referred to as 'spirit'. *See also* **holy spirit; resurrection.**

message, *see* good news

Messiah, messianic, Christ

The Hebrew word means literally 'anointed one', hence in theory either a prophet, **priest** or king. In Greek this translates as *Christos*; 'Christ' in early Christianity was a title, and only gradually became an alternative proper name for Jesus. In practice 'Messiah' is mostly restricted to the notion, which took various forms in ancient Judaism, of the coming king who would be David's true heir, through whom YHWH would rescue Israel from pagan enemies. There was no single template of expectations. Scriptural stories and promises contributed to different ideals and movements, often focused on (a) decisive military defeat of Israel's enemies and (b) rebuilding or cleansing the **Temple**. The **Dead Sea Scrolls** speak of two 'Messiahs', one a priest and the other a king. The universal early Christian belief that Jesus was Messiah is only explicable, granted his crucifixion by the Romans (which would have been seen as a clear sign that he was not the Messiah), by their belief that God had raised him from the dead, so vindicating the implicit messianic claims of his earlier ministry.

miracles

Like some of the old prophets, notably Elijah and Elisha, Jesus performed many deeds of remarkable power, particularly healings. The **gospels** refer to these as 'deeds of power', 'signs', 'marvels', or 'paradoxes'. Our word 'miracle' tends to imply that God, normally 'outside' the closed system of the world, sometimes 'intervenes'; miracles have then frequently been denied by sceptics as a matter of principle. However, in the Bible God is always present, however strangely, and 'deeds of power' are seen as *special* acts of a *present* God rather than as *intrusive* acts of an *absent* one. Jesus' own 'mighty works' are seen particularly, following prophecy, as evidence of his messiahship (e.g. Matthew 11.2–6).

Mishnah

The main codification of Jewish law (**Torah**) by the **rabbis**, produced in about AD 200, reducing to writing the 'oral Torah' which in Jesus' day ran parallel to the 'written Torah'. The Mishnah is itself the basis of the much larger collections of traditions in the two Talmuds (roughly AD 400).

parables

From the Old Testament onwards, prophets and other teachers used various storytelling devices as vehicles for their challenge to Israel (e.g. 2 Samuel 12.1–7). Sometimes these appeared as visions with interpretations (e.g. Daniel 7). Similar techniques were used by the **rabbis**. Jesus made his own creative adaptation of these traditions, in order to break open the world-view of his contemporaries and to invite them to share his vision of God's **kingdom** instead. His stories portrayed this as something that was *happening*, not just a timeless truth, and enabled his hearers to step inside the story and make it their own. As with some Old Testament visions, some of Jesus' parables have their own interpretations (e.g. the sower, Mark 4); others are thinly disguised retellings of the prophetic story of Israel (e.g. the wicked tenants, Mark 12).

parousia

Literally, it means 'presence', as opposed to 'absence', and sometimes used by Paul with this sense (e.g. Philippians 2.12). It was already used in the Roman world for the ceremonial arrival of, for example, the Emperor at a subject city or colony. Although the ascended Lord is not 'absent' from the church, when he 'appears' (Colossians 3.4; 1 John 3.2) in his 'second coming' this will be, in effect, an 'arrival' like that of the Emperor, and Paul uses it thus in 1 Corinthians 15.23; 1 Thessalonians 2.19; etc. In the **gospels** it is found only in Matthew 24 (verses 3, 27, 39).

Pharisees, lawyers, legal experts, rabbis

The Pharisees were an unofficial but powerful Jewish pressure group through most of the first centuries BC and AD. Largely lay-led, though including some **priests**, their aim was to purify Israel through intensified observance of the Jewish law (**Torah**), developing their own traditions about the precise meaning and application of scripture, their own patterns of prayer and other devotion, and their own calculations of the national hope. Though not all legal experts were Pharisees, most Pharisees were thus legal experts.

They effected a democratization of Israel's life, since for them the study and practice of Torah was equivalent to worshipping in the **Temple** – though they were adamant in pressing their own rules for the Temple liturgy on an unwilling (and often **Sadducean**) priesthood. This enabled them to survive AD 70 and, merging into the early rabbinic movement, to develop new ways forward. Politically they stood up for ancestral traditions, and were at the forefront of various movements of revolt against both pagan overlordship and compromised Jewish leaders. By Jesus' day there were two distinct schools, the stricter one of Shammai, more inclined towards armed revolt, and the more lenient one of Hillel, ready to live and let live.

Jesus' debates with the Pharisees are at least as much a matter of agenda and policy (Jesus strongly opposed their separatist nationalism) as about details of theology and piety. Saul of Tarsus was a fervent right-wing Pharisee, presumably a Shammaite, until his conversion.

After the disastrous war of AD 66–70, these schools of Hillel and Shammai continued bitter debate on appropriate policy. Following the further disaster of AD 135 (the failed Bar-Kochba revolt against Rome) their traditions were carried on by the rabbis who, though looking to the earlier Pharisees for inspiration, developed a Torah-piety in which personal holiness and purity took the place of political agendas.

present age, age to come, the life of God's coming age

By the time of Jesus many Jewish thinkers divided history into two periods: 'the present age' and 'the age to come' – the latter being the time when YHWH would at last act decisively to judge evil, to rescue Israel, and to create a new world of justice and peace. The early Christians believed that, though the full blessings of the coming age lay still in the future, it had already begun with Jesus, particularly with his death and **resurrection**, and that by **faith** and **baptism** they were able to enter it already. For this reason, the customary translation 'eternal life' is rendered here as 'the life of God's coming age'.

priests, high priest

Aaron, the older brother of Moses, was appointed Israel's first high priest (Exodus 28—29), and in theory his descendants were Israel's priests thereafter. Other members of his tribe (Levi) were 'Levites', performing other liturgical duties but not sacrificing. Priests lived among the people all around the country, having a local teaching role (Leviticus 10.11; Malachi 2.7), and going to Jerusalem by rotation to perform the **Temple** liturgy (e.g. Luke 2.8).

David appointed Zadok (whose Aaronic ancestry is sometimes questioned) as high priest, and his family remained thereafter the senior priests in Jerusalem, probably the ancestors of the **Sadducees**. One explanation of the origins of the Qumran **Essenes** is that they were a dissident group who believed themselves to be the rightful chief priests.

Qumran, *see* Dead Sea Scrolls

rabbis, *see* Pharisees

repentance

Literally, this means 'turning back'. It is widely used in Old Testament and subsequent Jewish literature to indicate both a personal turning away from sin and Israel's corporate turning away from idolatry and back to YHWH. Through both meanings, it is linked to the idea of 'return from exile'; if Israel is to 'return' in all senses, it must 'return' to YHWH. This is at the heart of the summons of both John the Baptist and Jesus. In Paul's writings it is mostly used for Gentiles turning away from idols to serve the true God; also for sinning Christians who need to return to Jesus.

resurrection

In most biblical thought, human bodies matter and are not merely disposable prisons for the soul. When ancient Israelites wrestled with the goodness and justice of YHWH, the creator, they ultimately came to insist that he must raise the dead (Isaiah 26.19; Daniel 12.2–3) – a suggestion firmly resisted by classical pagan thought. The longed-for return from exile was also spoken of in terms of YHWH raising dry bones to new life (Ezekiel 37.1–14). These ideas were developed in the second-Temple period, not least at times of martyrdom (e.g. 2 Maccabees 7). Resurrection was not just 'life after death', but a newly embodied life after 'life after death'; those at present dead were either 'asleep', or seen as 'souls', 'angels' or 'spirits', awaiting new embodiment.

The early Christian belief that Jesus had been raised from the dead was not that he had 'gone to heaven', or that he had been 'exalted', or was 'divine'; they believed all those as well, but each could have been expressed without mention of resurrection. Only the bodily resurrection of Jesus explains the rise of the early church, particularly its belief in Jesus' messiahship (which his crucifixion would have called into question). The early Christians believed that they themselves would be raised to a new, transformed bodily life at the time of the Lord's return or parousia (e.g. Philippians 3.20f.).

sabbath

The Jewish sabbath, the seventh day of the week, was a regular reminder both of creation (Genesis 2.3; Exodus 20.8–11) and of the Exodus (Deuteronomy 5.15). Along with circumcision and the food laws, it was one of the badges of Jewish identity within the pagan world of late antiquity, and a considerable body of Jewish law and custom grew up around its observance.

sacrifice

Like all ancient people, the Israelites offered animal and vegetable sacrifices to their God. Unlike others, they possessed a highly detailed written code (mostly in Leviticus) for what to offer and how to offer it; this in turn was developed in the Mishnah (c. AD 200). The Old Testament specifies that sacrifices can only be offered in the Jerusalem Temple; after this was destroyed in AD 70, sacrifices ceased, and Judaism developed further the idea, already present in some teachings, of prayer, fasting and almsgiving as alternative forms of sacrifice. The early Christians used the language of sacrifice in connection with such things as holiness, evangelism and the eucharist.

Sadducees

By Jesus' day, the Sadducees were the aristocracy of Judaism, possibly tracing their origins to the family of Zadok, David's **high priest**. Based in Jerusalem, and including most of the leading priestly families, they had their own traditions and attempted to resist the pressure of the **Pharisees** to conform to theirs. They claimed to rely only on the Pentateuch (the first five books of the Old Testament), and denied any doctrine of a future life, particularly of the **resurrection** and other ideas associated with it, presumably because of the encouragement such beliefs gave to revolutionary movements. No writings from the Sadducees have survived, unless the apocryphal book of Ben-Sirach (Ecclesiasticus) comes from them. The Sadducees themselves did not survive the destruction of Jerusalem and the **Temple** in AD 70.

the satan, the accuser, demons

The Bible is never very precise about the identity of the figure known as 'the satan'. The Hebrew word means 'the accuser', and at times the satan seems to be a member of YHWH's heavenly council, with special responsibility as director of prosecutions (1 Chronicles 21.1; Job 1—2; Zechariah 3.1f.). However, it becomes identified variously with the serpent of the garden of Eden (Genesis 3.1–15) and with the rebellious daystar cast out of **heaven** (Isaiah 14.12–15), and was seen by many Jews as the quasi-personal source of evil standing behind both human wickedness and large-scale injustice, and sometimes operating through semi-independent 'demons'. By Jesus' time various words were used to denote this figure, including Beelzebul/b (lit. 'Lord of the flies') and simply 'the evil one'; Jesus warned his followers against the deceits this figure could perpetrate. His opponents accused him of being in league with the satan, but the early Christians believed that Jesus in fact defeated it both in his own struggles with temptation (Matthew 4; Luke 4), his exorcisms of demons, and his death (1 Corinthians 2.8; Colossians 2.15). Final victory over this ultimate enemy is thus assured (Revelation 20), though the struggle can still be fierce for Christians (Ephesians 6.10–20).

scribes

In a world where many could not write, or not very well, a trained class of writers ('scribes') performed the important function of drawing up contracts for business, marriage, etc. Many scribes would thus be legal experts, and quite possibly **Pharisees**, though being a scribe was compatible with various political and religious standpoints. The work of Christian scribes was of vital importance in copying early Christian writings, particularly the stories about Jesus.

son of David, David's son

An alternative, and infrequently used, title for **Messiah**. The messianic promises of the Old Testament often focus specifically on David's son, for example 2 Samuel 7.12–16; Psalm 89.19–37. Joseph, Mary's husband, is called 'son of David' by the angel in Matthew 1.20.

son of God

Originally a title for Israel (Exodus 4.22) and the Davidic king (Psalm 2.7); also used of ancient angelic figures (Genesis 6.2). By the New Testament period it was already used as a **messianic** title, for example, in the **Dead Sea Scrolls**. There, and when used of Jesus in the **gospels** (e.g. Matthew 16.16), it means, or reinforces, 'Messiah', without the later significance of 'divine'. However, already in Paul the transition to the fuller meaning (one who was already equal with God and was sent by him to become human and to become Messiah) is apparent, without loss of the meaning 'Messiah' itself (e.g. Galatians 4.4).

son of man

In Hebrew or Aramaic, this simply means 'mortal', or 'human being'; in later Judaism, it is sometimes used to mean 'I' or 'someone like me'. In the New Testament the phrase is frequently linked to Daniel 7.13, where 'one like a son of man' is brought on the clouds of **heaven** to 'the Ancient of Days', being vindicated after a period of suffering, and is given kingly power. Though Daniel 7 itself interprets this as code for 'the people of the saints of the Most High', by the first century some Jews understood it as a **messianic** promise. Jesus developed this in his own way in certain key sayings which are best understood as promises that God would vindicate him, and judge those who had opposed him, after his own suffering (e.g. Mark 14.62). Jesus was thus able to use the phrase as a cryptic self-designation, hinting at his coming suffering, his vindication, and his God-given authority.

soul, *see* life

spirit, *see* life, holy spirit

Temple

The Temple in Jerusalem was planned by David (*c.* 1000 BC) and built by his son Solomon as the central sanctuary for all Israel. After reforms under Hezekiah and Josiah in the seventh century BC, it was destroyed by Babylon in 587 BC. Rebuilding by the returned **exiles** began in 538 BC, and was completed in 516, initiating the 'second Temple period'. Judas Maccabaeus cleansed it in 164 BC after its desecration by Antiochus Epiphanes (167). Herod the Great began to rebuild and beautify it in 19 BC; the work was completed in AD 63. The Temple was destroyed by the Romans in AD 70. Many Jews believed it should and would be rebuilt; some still do. The Temple was not only the place of **sacrifice**; it was believed to be the unique dwelling of YHWH on earth, the place where **heaven** and earth met.

Torah, Jewish law

'Torah', narrowly conceived, consists of the first five books of the Old Testament, the 'five books of Moses' or 'Pentateuch'. (These contain much law, but also much narrative.) It can also be used for the whole Old Testament scriptures, though strictly these are the 'law, prophets and writings'. In a broader sense, it refers to the whole developing corpus of Jewish legal tradition, written and oral; the oral Torah was initially codified in the **Mishnah** around AD 200, with wider developments found in the two Talmuds, of Babylon and Jerusalem, codified around AD 400. Many Jews in the time of Jesus and Paul regarded the Torah as being so strongly God-given as to be almost itself, in some sense, divine; some (e.g. Ecclesiasticus 24) identified it with the figure of 'Wisdom'. Doing what Torah said was not seen as a means of earning God's favour, but rather of expressing gratitude, and as a key badge of Jewish identity.

the Twelve, *see* apostle

word, *see* good news

YHWH

The ancient Israelite name for God, from at least the time of the **Exodus** (Exodus 6.2f.). It may originally have been pronounced 'Yahweh', but by the time of Jesus it was considered too holy to speak out loud, except for the **high priest** once a year in the Holy of Holies in the **Temple**. Instead, when reading scripture, pious Jews would say *Adonai*, 'Lord', marking this usage by adding the vowels of *Adonai* to the consonants of YHWH, eventually producing the hybrid 'Jehovah'. The word YHWH is formed from the verb 'to be', combining 'I am who I am', 'I will be who I will be', and perhaps 'I am because I am', emphasizing YHWH's sovereign creative power.

STUDY GUIDE

Introducing the Study

Luke for Everyone is one in a series of commentaries written by N. T. Wright, noted Pauline and New Testament scholar, who intended these to be guides for readers ready to delve deeper into the scriptures. Suitable for group or individual study, Wright provides his own translation of the Lucan gospel. Wright notes that 'this particular volume opens up one of the most brilliant writings in early Christianity. Luke tells us that he had a chance to stand back from the extraordinary events that had been going on, to talk to the people involved, to read some earlier writings and to make his own quite full version so that readers could know the truth about the things written about Jesus. Luke was an educated and cultured man, the first historian to write about Jesus' (page xiv).

The commentary includes Wright's translation of the biblical text divided into small sections, accompanied by insights into its context and in-depth explanation of each segment. Notice that Wright provides a glossary for key words at the end of the volume. Your personal preparation for each session might include studying the selected texts in different translations as well as praying for guidance in understanding and relating those scriptures to your own life. Listen for the spirit's encouragement to you as you encounter the scripture, and recall Wright's reminder to us in the introduction: 'On the very first occasion when someone stood up in public to tell people about Jesus, he made it very clear: this message is for everyone'.

If Using the Guide for Individual Study

In addition to your copy of *Luke for Everyone*, you may wish to read Wright's translations alongside other translations, which you can find online or perhaps in a local library. Did you study a language in school? Consider finding a copy of the New Testament in that language; the additional insights coming from the unfamiliarity of that language can be spiritually revealing. Completing the questions for each text in writing (never mind complete sentences, and bullet points get full marks) and completing the suggested activities as if a good friend was by your side will enrich your experience.

If Using the Guide as a Group Member

- Be prepared by reading the scriptures before the sessions.
- Be on time for each session.
- Be encouraging to everyone.
- Be willing to contribute to group discussions.
- Be prayerful that great things will come from this study.

If Serving Others by Facilitating a Group

God bless you! This guide was prepared with you in mind, in the hope and prayer that spiritual blessings are abundant for you as well as those you lead. Every group is unique, so take this guide as a starting place, adapting and using the resources provided. Written for four one-hour sessions, you could adapt the length of your study to meet your needs. The session divisions for this study are arbitrary, chosen to cover roughly one-fourth of the gospel per session. You may wish to spend more time on some of the scriptures than others, so feel free to take as much time as you need, but certainly do cover the entire gospel. Since the final session covers so many important events in the gospel, consider adding an additional session or adding additional time to the final session. You may need to choose from among the questions in the 'Exploring the Scriptures' activity in the suggested format.

Suggested Session Format

Opening Prayer (1 minute)
Group Opening (5 minutes)
Exploring the Scriptures (30 minutes)
Applying the Scriptures (15 minutes)
Sharing 'Oh Wow' Moments (5 minutes)
Closing Prayer (1 minute)
Ticket Out the Door (3 minutes)

Readings for Each Session

Session 1—Luke 1.1—7.10
Session 2—Luke 7.11—12.12
Session 3—Luke 12.13—17.19
Session 4—17.20—24.53

Helpful Hints for Facilitators

- Set up the room where you will meet early. Create expectations for learning by changing the usual appearance of the room. (Be sure to get permission before making any changes!)
- Ask others to lead a part of the session.
- Allow time for reflection. Silence may improve the quality of group responses.
- Involve as many persons as possible. Extend conversations by replying, 'Yes, and . . .'
- Engage the group to reset the room to its original condition, building a sense of purpose for the group.
- Pray for the members individually and as a group. The message of these letters will change hearts and lives as well as churches.

SESSION 1: LUKE 1.1—7.10
JESUS' BIRTH TO EARLY MINISTRY IN GALILEE
(PAGES 1–61)

Opening Prayer (1 minute)

God of infinite, dazzling light, overwhelm our blindness to your word and your works in Christ Jesus our Lord. Pierce our hearts with your love, and open our eyes to the truth of the gospel, we pray. Amen.

Group Opening (5 minutes)

The gospel of Luke is one of the synoptic gospels, along with Matthew and Mark, meaning that these three share common sources and stories about Jesus along with a parallel understanding of his life and ministry. John's gospel has a different flavor but the same essential message; it is likely that it was written in a different context. Luke's gospel contains about 35 percent of the material in Mark, used in such a way that Luke's dependence on Mark is incontrovertible. Mark, Matthew and Luke share another trove of stories told by Jesus and about Jesus known as the 'Source', commonly abbreviated as Q among scholars. The Q material composes more than 20 percent of the material in Luke. Somewhere between one-third and 40 percent of Luke comes from his own, unique sources. In two places, 6.20—8.3 and 9.51—18.14, Luke uses sources only found in his gospel. When considering the gospel and the Acts of the Apostles, Luke wrote about one quarter of the New Testament.

Exploring the Scriptures (30 minutes)

1. Unlike the other gospels, Luke opens with a statement of his intentions and sources in telling the story of Jesus. From the time of the ancient Greeks until today, authors of serious works of history, philosophy and religion have begun their works in the same manner. Luke intends to draw up an 'orderly' account, probably intended to signal to us that he will organize and reorder some of the material covered in the other gospels. He does not claim to be an eyewitness of the ministry of Jesus; rather, he states that he has used eyewitness accounts as well as those of 'stewards of the word'. Who did Wright describe as the stewards? Who was Theophilus?

2. For that matter, who is the author of this gospel? Ask for a volunteer to read the three references Wright mentions. When do you think this gospel was written? Why did Luke write this gospel?

3. As you read, try keeping track of the number of times someone is said to be afraid or an angel needs to tell someone not to be afraid. Keep track also of all the celebrations mentioned in Luke.

4. In the Bible, only two couples are presented as being of great age and as not having children. Luke, with characteristic skill, recalls Abram and Sarah, the first couple, by introducing us to the second, Zechariah and Elizabeth. What did Zechariah learn about his son? What do we learn about Zechariah and Elizabeth? What role does their story play in this gospel, both with reference to earlier stories in Israel's history as well as in the story of the strange things to happen to Mary and Joseph?

5. What is the political or royal meaning Luke gives to the birth of Jesus?

6. Ask a volunteer to read the song of Hannah in 1 Samuel 2, and then read the Magnificat in Luke 1.46–55, which is called a canticle, a biblical song. (Other persons sing canticles in Luke as well.)

7. What do we learn about the mission of John from Zechariah's prophecy (Luke 1.68–79)?

8. What point is Luke making in the second chapter, according to Wright?

9. Simeon and Anna foreshadow the role that Jesus will play in the redemption of Israel. What sort of story do they tell about Jesus, and what prophecy is made about Mary?

10. Luke wants to make sure his readers understand the purpose Jesus had in relation to the Jewish law. What are some of the ways he leads readers to make that connection in chapters 1 and 2?

11. John came with a 'baptism of repentance for the forgiveness of sins' (Luke 3.3). What were his other teachings about Jesus?

12. In 3.21, when Jesus was baptized by John, Luke says, 'he was pray-ing'. Note that at nearly every major event in Jesus' life, Luke states that Jesus was praying.

13. What is the message Luke wants for his readers to understand about Jesus in the temptation event?

14. In Luke 4.14–30, Jesus returns to Nazareth and teaches in the syna-gogue, reading from Isaiah 61 and stating clearly that he was the fulfillment of that prophecy, which so enraged the people listening that they seized him and intended to throw him off the mountain. Why did Jesus choose that passage to read, and what was so dis-ruptive about his teaching afterward? According to Wright, what hint appears in verse 22?

15. In chapter five, Luke arranges the calling of Peter and the fisher-men to follow him, the healing of a leper, the healing of a para-lyzed man and a table discussion with Pharisees into a narrative of Jesus' power and authority as well as teachings about the type of kingdom that Jesus is bringing. Jesus demonstrates that this new kingdom is so powerfully attractive that even down-to-earth working men like fishermen will abandon their livelihood to follow Jesus. How does Wright describe the messages in each of these scenes?

16. Luke 6.12–49 contains his record of the teaching of Jesus, which is comparable to Matthew's Sermon on the Mount, but in this instance it is delivered on a large level plain filled with followers. He first named his chosen apostles, choosing twelve to serve him and the people he attracted. There were twelve tribes of Israel, and now there are twelve apostles; clearly Jesus is claiming to be the leader of a new kind of Jewish kingdom. His teaching still rever-berates in our world, so how does Wright summarize the message Jesus taught in that setting (page 55)?

17. In 6.39–49 Jesus describes a series of four word pictures and gives a warning to those who listened that the purpose of Jesus' teach-ings was to produce a new kind of follower, someone prepared to change her life as well as to encourage others to make the same sort of commitment. What does Wright say about the meanings of those word pictures?

18. What is the central teaching of the story of the centurion's servant? What about the centurion's behaviour astonishes and delights Jesus?

Applying the Scriptures (15 minutes)

The purpose of this section of the study is to gather the threads discov-ered in the study and to weave them into a deeper understanding of the message of the gospel of Luke. As time permits, use the suggested activities to extend what you have learned.

1. In these first chapters of Luke's gospel, 'Hunting for Jesus' could be a plausible subtitle. Which persons or groups searched for Jesus? How did they know when they found him? What happened to them because they found him? What lessons can you draw from these biblical characters?

2. As a part of the events in Nazareth, when Jesus returned to that synagogue to teach, people rose in opposition to him and his teaching and would have thrown him off a mountain. Writing about this event, Wright asserts, 'Unless they could see that this was their time for their God to be gracious, unless they abandoned their futile dreams of a military victory over their national enemies, they would suffer defeat themselves at every level – military, political and theological' (page 36). What implications did this truth have on the Jewish leaders of the time? What implications could it have for our world?

3. On page 20, Wright says of following Jesus, 'In becoming your story, it will become your vocation'. After reading the quote in context, what did he mean, and how did that meaning change the lives of the first followers of Jesus? How did it change your life?

Sharing 'Oh Wow' Moments (5 minutes)

In these brief moments, members of the group can share moments of realization or reproof they experienced during this study: The kingdom that Jesus preached and lived was all about a glorious, uproarious, absurd generosity. Think of the best thing you can do for the worst person, and go ahead and do it.

Closing Prayer (1 minute)

O blessed Jesus Christ, send us forth in your calming peace, inspiring us to be uproarious messengers of your gospel of good news to a world dying to hear it. Amen.

Ticket Out the Door (3 minutes)

On a slip of paper, write down one thing you understood well from today's study and one thing you would like to know more about, and give your slip of paper to the facilitator as you leave.

SESSION 2: LUKE 7.11—12.12
JESUS TEACHES HIS FOLLOWERS
(PAGES 61–112)

Opening Prayer (1 minute)

Great Teacher, enlighten our hearts with your teaching in your word. Focus our efforts so that we may learn with all our heart, soul, mind and strength. Amen.

Group Opening (5 minutes)

Examine the feedback you received at the end of the first session, and choose several for response, using them to remind the group about the themes and points of emphasis in Luke's gospel.

Exploring the Scriptures (30 minutes)

1. In 7.18–35, Luke tells of the disciples of John the Baptist visiting Jesus as he heals, and Jesus cleanses lepers and raises the dead. Afterward, they return to John and Jesus clarifies the place of John in the ministry of Jesus, the one who comes before the Messiah and prepares his way. Wright says that John must have wondered what sort of Messiah Jesus would be, since Jesus kept defying expectations cherished by Jews of the Messiah of a great political and military leader. The common people celebrated Jesus; Pharisees and the rich criticized Jesus. Luke's point seems to be that the kingdom brought by Jesus would differ greatly from the hopes of the rich and powerful.
2. The next two scenes portray Jesus discussing the interaction between two contrasting types of people via a real-life situation and a parable about sowing seeds. The vastly different circumstances between the two stories highlight Luke's writing skills, but one essential question is raised – where are you in these stories, in your relationship with Jesus?
3. Luke 8.19–21 is puzzling to read. The mother and brothers of Jesus come to see him, and Jesus is rather rude to them, seemingly excluding them from the company of his followers. How does Wright use references to Mark and John to give context to the scene? What does Wright mean when he says, 'The choice of faith is absolute' (page 73)?
4. The healing of the man possessed by demons has a moment of revelation in its ending. What was that revelation, and how does Wright explain it?

5. How does Wright connect Luke 8.40–56 to the major themes of Luke's gospel? Does Wright make a convincing case that the writer of the gospel was a physician?

6. Once again in Luke 9.18–45 we see the brilliance of Luke as a story-teller at work; in this instance, he connects the sending out of the twelve disciples, the feeding of the great crowd, and the transfiguration with the recurrent portrayal of Jesus as a man serious about prayer, which is his way of maintaining his extraordinary relationship with God.

7. Luke's retelling of the transfiguration is one of those times when the story itself is overwhelming in its emotional impact, and yet Luke intends the reader to mine a deeper meaning from it. As Jesus was talking to Moses and Elijah, Luke interjects that they 'were speaking of his departure' (page 85). How does Wright reveal the nature of that conversation, and what deeper meaning did it have for Jesus?

8. In Wright's estimation, what was at stake in the story of the Good Samaritan?

9. The story of Mary, Martha and Jesus is another uniquely Lucan contribution to the gospel message. In what ways was this story radical, and how does Wright connect it to the story of the Good Samaritan?

10. What characterization does Wright use to describe the Lord's Prayer? In what ways is the prayer Jesus taught appropriate to your journey?

11. Is the parable attached to the Lord's Prayer about getting what you ask for? Does it mean that you must badger God to get something you want or that God's answer to prayer is dependent on your earnestness? According to Wright, what teaching is central to this parable?

12. Explain the following quote from the author with reference to the story of Jesus and Beelzebul: 'When the word of God is at work, what is required is not applause but obedience' (page 103).

13. 'Who are the Pharisees in today's society?' Wright asks (pages 107–9), granting that the traditional, easy answer is religious leaders and teachers. How does Wright react to this answer? How would you answer this question?

14. What attitude commonly experienced in Christianity today is the target of Jesus' warnings in Luke 12.1–12?

Applying the Scriptures (15 minutes)

The purpose of this section of the study is to gather the threads discovered in the study and to weave them into a deeper understanding of the message of the gospel of Luke. Use the suggested activities as time permits to extend what you have learned.

1. In Luke 12.11–12, at the end of a passage in which Jesus speaks to large crowds, teaching and admonishing them, he instructs the people on how to behave when they are brought to account before religious or political authorities: 'When they bring you before synagogues, rulers and authorities, don't worry about how to give an answer or what to say. The holy spirit will teach you what to say at that very moment'. Recount for the group how you felt and what you did in that moment.

2. Discuss the question Wright proposes on page 109, consolidate group answers and report to the large group your insights into this question: 'Where does the gospel of Jesus confront not just alternative religious or would-be Christian views today, but the strongly held agendas that exist in the wider world?'

3. 'People today still judge Jesus by their expectations', Wright states on page 66. In your experience, how has this been true? Discuss in a small group before leading the larger group in a discussion of this question.

Sharing 'Oh Wow' Moments (5 minutes)

In these brief moments, members of the group can share moments of realization or reproof they experienced during this study.

Closing Prayer (1 minute)

Spirit of the living and guiding God, plant the memories of our hearing and learning today deep into our hearts and minds, so that we may continue to benefit from today in the years to come. Amen.

Ticket Out the Door (3 minutes)

The theme of this session might be 'Jesus reveals unexpected ways in which he is the Messiah'.

Respond to this statement on a slip of paper by telling one way in which Jesus acts unexpectedly.

SESSION 3: LUKE 12.13—17.19
JESUS TEACHES ON THE WAY TO JERUSALEM
(PAGES 112–54)

Opening Prayer (1 minute)

We are all on the road to somewhere, Lord. Make our journeys meaningful and our destinations pleasing to you, we ask in Jesus' name. Amen.

Group Opening (5 minutes)

Ask group members to share their responses to last session's Ticket Out the Door

Exploring the Scriptures (30 minutes)

1. In Luke 13.5, Jesus continues a conversation about Jews in Galilee who had been killed by Herod. Commenting on that verse, what does Wright assert that Jesus has made clear?
2. As Jesus was teaching in the synagogue one sabbath, he encountered a woman crippled by disease for eighteen years. He stretched out his hand and healed the woman, igniting a dispute with the president of the synagogue. Jesus responded by telling a parable of a donkey which needed water. What does Wright say was the larger meaning of this parable?
3. Luke relates a story of Jesus teaching as he made his way to Jerusalem and being questioned about why only a few would be saved. (The question was likely based on the assumption that only Jews would be saved.) To try and understand the scene of judgment, begin by answering these questions in your own mind: Who was the householder? Which people would be denied salvation? Who were the people in verse 29? What was the meaning of this teaching according to Wright?
4. Pharisees approach Jesus in Luke 13.31 to tell him that Herod wanted to kill him. This is the most ominous response yet from the Pharisees, and their motivation is unclear. How would you interpret the response of Jesus to their warning?
5. What three levels of meaning does Wright find in the parable of the great banquet? What is the lesson here for today's Christians and churches?
6. Among the most sobering questions any aspiring young teacher must ask themselves is whether they are willing to die protecting their students. This is not an abstract question as the roll of teachers who die in the line of duty continues to grow. Jesus' statement in 14.26 should be interpreted in that context: Would you place yourself in harm's way, with dire effect to your own family, to do your duty to your students?
7. The parables of the lost sheep and lost coin relate to the theme of celebration in Luke. Why were the Pharisees, scribes and others so upset with Jesus? (Hint: They were the 'ninety-nine people' who didn't need repentance!)
8. Wright divides the parable of the prodigal son into two episodes and subtitles the first 'The Father and the Younger Son'. What other

title does Wright suggest for this part of the parable? Does the image suggested have any particular message for you? Share your thoughts with a neighbour.

9. In the second half of the parable, who does the elder son represent? As described in the parable, how do the actions of the older son relate to those of the Pharisees and religious leaders?

10. How does Wright explain the actions of the shrewd manager in reducing the amounts owed to the master? In what ways does this parable relate to Israel? What advice does Jesus give to those who are about to be excluded from the kingdom to come?

11. Luke moves beyond parables in his recounting of the teachings of Jesus about wealth and its uses in Luke 16.10–18. What, according to Wright, is the key to understanding this passage? What does Wright say was the general attitude in the Jewish law towards wealth in contrast to the teachings of Jesus? How is the concept of a trust related to the Christian use of earthly wealth?

12. What new note does the parable of the rich man and Lazarus bring to the old folk story about reversal of fortunes after death for the rich and the poor?

13. At the end of his commentary about this parable, Wright compares verse 31 to 'a great crashing chord on an organ' (page 150). What are the different 'notes' in that chord, and to what do they speak?

14. The primary lesson in Luke 17.1–10 is the need for humility in word and attitude. How is humility related to the warning about the 'little ones'? Taking the question a step further, when the subject is a brother or sister, how should we treat someone who sins against us? What role does humility have in forgiveness?

15. Don't miss Wright's commentary on the verse concerning the apostle's request for greater faith: 'It's not great faith that you need; it is faith in a great God' (page 152). How does an attitude of humility regulate our relationship to God?

16. Luke 17.11–19 is about faith, healing and gratitude. What other element is present which is consistent with the teaching of Jesus as he traveled to Jerusalem? How does the instruction to 'get up!' relate to that teaching?

Applying the Scriptures (15 minutes)

The purpose of this section of the study is to gather the threads discovered in the study and to weave them into a deeper understanding of the message of the gospel of Luke. Use the suggested activities as time permits to extend what you have learned.

1. On a memorable sabbath, Jesus healed a woman bent double for eighteen years. He faced a hailstorm of criticism from the synagogue president, but the people were overjoyed. In pointing out the hypocrisy of those who found fault, Jesus pointed out that the law would allow an animal to be untied and led to drink, and wasn't this woman more important than an animal? Wright notes that the woman represented Judaism under the law, crippled by legalism and rigid application of the law. Jesus followed with the story of the mustard seed and the 'dough-starter' a woman hid in her flour until the entire flour supply was leavened. What was the lesson connecting the healing, the mustard seed and the lumps of leaven? Have you ever seen small acts lead to great victories in your own life? Share your experience with the group and perhaps with the large group.

2. However we identify them, church rolls are filled with 'elder brothers' who have been offended by something or someone in the past and now are inactive Christians. As Wright asks, 'How can we celebrate the party of God's love in such a way as to welcome not only the younger brothers who have come back from the dead, but also the older brothers who thought there was nothing wrong with them?' (page 143). Discuss this problem, propose the responses generated in your group, and be prepared to present your findings to the larger group.

3. Commenting on the encounter between Jesus and a Pharisee, the author writes, 'Pride, notoriously, is the great cloud which blots out the sun of God's generosity; if I reckon that I deserve to be favoured by God, not only do I declare that I don't need his grace, mercy and love, but I imply that those who don't deserve it shouldn't have it' (pages 130–31). Similarly, when explicating the 'forgive seventy times seven' statement from Jesus, Wright states that we are called on to show to others the forgiveness that God has shown us. 'That, after all, is the real source of humility. If in doubt, meditate on God's grace' (page 151). Make a list of all the virtues arising from knowing the mercy of God. Prepare to present your list as well as examples of how that process has worked in the lives of your group members.

Sharing 'Oh Wow' Moments (5 minutes)

In these brief moments, members of the group can share moments of realization or reproof they experienced during this study.

Closing Prayer (1 minute)

Let the words of our mouths and the meditations of our hearts be acceptable in thy sight, O Lord, we pray. Amen.

Ticket Out the Door (3 minutes)

Write on a slip of paper one thing you would like to learn about in our study of the last week of Jesus' life, and give it to your facilitator as you leave.

SESSION 4: LUKE 17.20—24.53
JESUS THE SAVIOUR

(PAGES 154-225)

This session will cover the entry into Jerusalem, the events of Jesus' last week, the Upper Room, Jesus' trial, crucifixion and resurrection. You may wish to have a longer than usual session or even create two sessions from this material. If so, you might wish to cover 17.20—21.38 in the first session and finish the gospel in the second.

Opening Prayer (1 minute)

Saviour Jesus, your deep love for us transcends all boundaries we can imagine. Grant us a 'holy imagination' so that the truth of your love can become reality in our minds and hearts. Transform us with the power of your loving spirit, we pray in Jesus' name. Amen.

Group Opening (5 minutes)

React to as many of the tickets from the last session as time allows.

Exploring the Scriptures (30 minutes)

1. Many interpreters assign Luke 17.20–37 to the genre of apocalyptic (end times) literature and think that the message of Jesus in this passage is about the rapture. In reference to Daniel 7, Jesus equates the fourth, and most dangerous, army to come not as the Roman army but rather with Israel itself, which was focused on the Temple and its hierarchy and included the Pharisees and their love of the law. This dramatic twist of thinking means that the one taken is the one in danger and that the destruction of Jerusalem in AD 70 is the fulfillment of this scripture.

2. Why does Wright translate 17.21 as 'God's kingdom is within your grasp'?
3. Luke 18.1–14 is a continuation of the previous passage, pointing to a time when the followers of Jesus will be justified by their faith and the religious leadership of Judaism will be judged guilty of not heeding the message of Jesus. How are the two scenes connected in this passage, and what is their deeper meaning?
4. The story of Jesus healing a blind beggar on the road to Jerusalem reveals anew the storytelling skill of Luke. The twelve disciples continue to follow Jesus but do not understand his message while a blind beggar realizes the power of Jesus, asking for his sight to be renewed. In the end, the beggar can see but the twelve disciples continue in their blindness!
5. The last parable told by Jesus before his entry to Jerusalem was about a king returning to his kingdom and investigating the behaviour of his servant, a situation so aligned with Jesus' entry to Jerusalem that surely even the disciples could not miss its import. According to Wright, what was the message of this passage to its hearers?
6. Wright's commentary on the triumphal entry is masterful, culminating in a series of questions each person needs to answer: Do we follow hoping Jesus will fulfil some of our needs and desires, or are we ready to follow him into 'trouble, controversy, trial and death' (page 171)?
7. How does Wright connect prophecy with the cleansing of the Temple, and what was the meaning of that prophecy?
8. When the entourage of Temple leadership asked Jesus about authority, was his reply a clever answer? What deeper authority did Jesus claim?
9. In the telling of the parable of the tenants (pages 175–76), Jesus takes off the boxing gloves. He even quotes Psalm 118.22, the same psalm that others used to praise him the day before. None of the message was subtle, and the rulers of the synagogue knew Jesus was condemning them. What was their initial response, and what did they do finally in response?
10. On page 181, the author describes four challenges to Jesus that occurred between his entry into Jerusalem and his arrest. Make a list of those challenges.
11. What does the reader of Luke gain from the picture of Jesus which emerges from those challenges? What does the reader learn about the resurrection?
12. Luke 20.41–21.4 is about measuring wealth, human worth, human pride, human greed and the humility of the truly great in God's

kingdom. How does Wright explain God's expectations on this subject?

13. In Luke's telling of the Lord's Supper, what did Jesus expect the apostles to learn or understand? What meanings or information did Luke intend to convey through the manner in which he told the story?

14. In his commentary on Luke 22.24–38, Wright draws attention to three principles and promises located in this scene. What are they, and how do they clarify what will happen next to Jesus and the apostles?

15. How does Wright explain Jesus' agony in the garden of Gethsemane?

16. Neither Pilate nor Herod was ready to pronounce Jesus guilty of the crimes he was accused of by the chief priests. How does Wright explain that fact? Why does he call Jesus' silence a paradox of the gospel?

17. How were Barabbas and Simon key to understanding the trial of Jesus?

18. What does Wright say is at the heart of Luke's picture of the cross? Where did Jesus' true royalty shine out while he was on the cross, according to Wright?

19. In Wright's understanding, what was Luke anxious to highlight in his account of the death of Jesus?

20. What can we learn of first-century Jewish burial customs from reading Luke? Why was it important that the tomb had never been used before?

21. What does Wright suggest as reasons that the apostles and close followers did not expect Jesus to be resurrected?

22. In what ways does Wright say the Emmaus road story parallels the experience of many Christians?

23. Who might have been the other traveling companion of Cleopas?

24. Does Luke 24.31 and its commentary change your mind about the traveling companion of Cleopas?

25. How might the Jewish followers of Jesus have misunderstood the message of Jesus and his messiahship, according to Wright?

26. Earlier in the book, Wright made a connection between the three days Joseph and Mary spent searching for Jesus before finding him in the Temple and the Emmaus road story. How does Wright extend that connection in this commentary (page 222)?

27. What does Wright say about the nature of the post-resurrection body? Does his explanation shed new light on this issue for you?

Applying the Scriptures (15 minutes)

The purpose of this section of the study is to gather the threads discovered in the study and to weave them into a deeper understanding of the message of the gospel of Luke. Use the suggested activities as time permits to extend what you have learned. Additional group activities are provided in the case that more than one session is used in this study.

1. Write your own commentary for the Zacchaeus story in Luke 19.1–10. This story is well-known, giving you a chance to exercise your 'holy imagination' to bring the story to life. If you are so inclined, you might write your commentary from a different point of view, say that of a child present at that scene or even that of Zacchaeus himself. Copy and distribute your commentary or read it to the larger group.

2. Read and react to this paragraph taken from the parable of the tenants:

   If this was what happened when Jesus came to Jerusalem, what should we expect today when his followers go to the places of power and injustice? What sort of reaction will the gospel receive when it is announced in places where people use religion – including Christianity – as a means of reinforcing their own security instead of shining God's light into the world? It may well mean rejection and violence; the history of Christian martyrdom, not least in the last century, bears stark witness to that. (pages 177–78)

   As a thought experiment, imagine going with a group to protest on some issue which is important to you and which is central to Luke's gospel. Where would you go? To whom would you protest? Would you get the permits necessary for a lawful protest, or would civil disobedience be more effective? Would you use a speaker, chants, songs or silence? How would you choose what words to use?

3. Following Jesus' command, how would you give to God what belongs to him? Decide what you would give, how you would give, where you would give it and to whom you would give it, and then write a letter to a local newspaper explaining your action. Do you have a blog, even one that is unrelated to this question? As an act of faith, publish your response on your blog, podcast or other appropriate social media location. Please, however, remember the grace and mercy shown to you and respond in the spirit of humility.

4. In commenting on Peter's denial of Jesus, the author leads us to consider what we might have done in Peter's shoes and concludes that Peter's actions and ours might be the same. He also remarks

in a number of places that Luke is not writing a theological treatise but skillfully recounting the life and ministry of Jesus, so when we come to the torture of Jesus by the Roman soldiers, he simply points to the biblical record and concludes: 'As Luke leads our eyes to the foot of the cross, he means us to feel not just sorrow and pity, but shame' (page 204). In our modern Western societies, shame is a four-letter word. Misused, as it has too often been in the past, shame can cripple a person's development into maturity and mis-shape a growing faith. Wright believes that shame is an appropriate response in this context. Discuss this question in a small group in preparation for leading a large group discussion of this topic.

5. In most ways, Luke displays the greatest range of emotional intel-ligence of all the gospels. Name an emotion and you will likely find an appropriate example in Luke's gospel. Fear, sorrow, joy, confusion, anger, jealousy, pride, humility and thoughtfulness are all found there. Writing of the resurrection morning, Wright discovers surprise: 'Easter is always a surprise, whether we meet it in celebrating the feast itself or in our sudden surges of God's grace overturning tragedy in our own lives or in the world' (page 217). How have you been surprised by Easter? Volunteer to share your surprising Easter experiences with the whole group.

Sharing 'Oh Wow' Moments (5 minutes)

In these brief moments, members of the group can share moments of realization or reproof they experienced during this study.

Closing Prayer (1 minute)

Love so amazing, so divine, demands my soul, my life, my all. Amen.

Ticket Out the Door (3 minutes, for use if continuing with a fifth session)

Respond to this question on a slip of paper before leaving it with your facilitator: *What event in the post-resurrection appearances of Jesus means the most to you?*